SHADOWS OF WAR

VIOLENCE, POWER, AND INTERNATIONAL PROFITEERING IN THE TWENTY-FIRST CENTURY

CAROLYN NORDSTROM

UNIVERSITY OF CALIFORNIA PRESS
BERKELEY LOS ANGELES LONDON

University of California Press
Berkeley and Los Angeles, California

University of California Press, Ltd.
London, England

Library of Congress Cataloging-in-Publication Data

Nordstrom, Carolyn, 1953–.
Shadows of war : violence, power, and international profiteering in the twenty-first century / Carolyn Nordstrom.
p. cm. — (California series in public anthropology; 10)
Includes bibliographical references and index.
ISBN 0-520-23977-6 (cloth)
1. War and society. 2. War — Economic aspects. 3. Informal sector (Economics) I. Title. II. Series.

HM554.N67 2004
303.6'6 — dc22 2003060803

Manufactured in the United States of America
13 12 11 10 09 08 07 06 05
10 9 8 7 6 5 4

The paper used in this publication meets the minimum requirements of ANSI/NISO Z39.48–1992 (R 1997) (*Permanence of Paper*).

PRAISE FOR CAROLYN NORDSTROM'S *SHADOWS OF WAR*

"Neither a prurient journalist nor a reflective diarist, Nordstrom is a compassionate scholar who simply and doggedly uses ethnography to follow the question. Nordstom's approach takes her from the spectacular violence of armed conflict—the flames and mobs and murder—to the even more destructive but hidden structural violence—the 'shadows' that few seek to understand. This is engaged, urgent scholarship at its best."

—Paul Farmer, M.D., author of *Pathologies of Power*

SHADOWS OF WAR

CALIFORNIA SERIES IN PUBLIC ANTHROPOLOGY

The California Series in Public Anthropology emphasizes the anthropologist's role as an engaged intellectual. It continues anthropology's commitment to being an ethnographic witness, to describing, in human terms, how life is lived beyond the borders of many readers' experiences. But it also adds a commitment, through ethnography, to reframing the terms of public debate—transforming received, accepted understandings of social issues with new insights, new framings.

1. *Twice Dead: Organ Transplants and the Reinvention of Death,* by Margaret Lock
2. *Birthing the Nation: Strategies of Palestinian Women in Israel,* by Rhoda Ann Kanaaneh (with a Foreword by Hannan Ashrawi)
3. *Annihilating Difference: The Anthropology of Genocide,* edited by Alexander Laban Hinton (with a Foreword by Kenneth Roth)
4. *Pathologies of Power: Structural Violence and the Assault on Health and Human Rights,* by Paul Farmer (with a Foreword by Amartya Sen)
5. *Buddha is Hiding: Refugees, Citizenship, and the New America,* by Aihwa Ong
6. *Chechnya: The Making of a War-Torn Society,* by Valery Tishkov
7. *Total Confinement: Madness and Reason in the Maximum Security Prison,* by Lorna A. Rhodes
8. *Paradise in Ashes: A Guatemalan Journey of Courage, Terror, and Hope,* by Beatriz Manz
9. *Laughter Out of Place: Race, Class, Violence, and Sexuality in a Rio Shantytown,* by Donna M. Goldstein
10. *Shadows of War: Violence, Power, and International Profiteering in the Twenty-First Century,* by Carolyn Nordstrom

For Patricia Churchill
who told me when I was five
that I could go anywhere I wanted.
The Vagabond's House . . .

CONTENTS

WELCOME

ACKNOWLEDGMENTS

In 1996 when I was traveling in Southern Africa for a year and a half, I began a novel about a young war orphan. The first page opened by saying that the story was true, but the only way to tell a true war story was in fiction. The novel allowed me to write down what academia had few solutions for: writing real stories of real people without getting them, or me, into danger. In the intervening years, academia has become more open to writing that requires special sensitivities and responsibilities, and I have become more practiced in telling a war story without giving the proverbial "name, rank, and serial number."

My acknowledgments are thus more important, and more difficult, as I cannot directly thank in print most of those who made this book possible. This book is about warzones and illicit economies: my fieldwork is populated with the hopeful and the hopeless, torture victims and torturers, rogues and thieves, smugglers and heroes, the terrified and the powerful. Most do not want their names in print. These people sat down and opened their homes and their lives to me, shared their ideas and their food, and trusted me with their stories. This book chronicles many of them, sans names.

Many went out of their way to tell me their stories. The autobiography of a man called Peace in this book is a good example. Peace came up to me one day on the road and asked me for a camera. I first met Peace when he was a youth on the streets, but did not know him well. Now he was a full-grown man who looked as hard as the streets on which he slept. I hesitated a moment, wondering if I should go to the "markets" (as the book shows, the "unavailable" in a warzone is always available in some market, however far from any definitions of legal it may be) to get a camera for Peace. I decided that no matter what he did with the camera — from selling it to taking pictures — it was a story. Peace was waiting for me at the break of dawn the morning after I gave him a camera. He had spent the entire night walking the streets of the city taking pictures. He handed me the camera and said, "I want people to understand the suffering of those of us who live in war and on the streets — the real suffering." At risk to himself, he had taken pictures of police beating street youth, kids smoking crack, prostitutes serving the powerful, gaunt hungry preteens rummaging for a scrap of food in dumpsters — the stories of night. On his own initiative, he had interviewed many of these people and written up their biographies to accompany the photos. Why would a man who most see as a dangerous street thief do this? Perhaps because he cares. The most important thing I have learned from my research is that even the worst violence cannot extinguish the spark of humanity in most people. As powerful as Peace's story is for me, for his own protection I have deleted all references in his autobiography that can identify him. It is Peace, and all the people like him in this book, that I most want to thank.

There are some I can name. This research would not have been possible without a year-and-a-half grant from the John T. and Catherine C. MacArthur Foundation. I want to thank them for extending a grant to research that broke with the traditional, a grant that allowed me to cross conceptual, political, and continental borders in following the flows of people and goods that populate this book.

I am also grateful to the United States Institute of Peace: my work on extra-legal economies first began several years ago with a year-and-a-half grant from USIP that allowed me to do comparative ethnographic work on warzones in several countries. The Institute for International Studies at the University of California, Berkeley, provided me with an institutional home during this research.

The University of Notre Dame supported this research with both grants and generous sabbatical time; my colleagues kept the proverbial candle burning in the window for me. University Eduardo Mondlane in Mozambique and the University of Witswatersrand in South Africa extended institutional and collegial support. I want to thank Debi LeBeau for the amazing road trips, Ana LaForte for her good advice, Joel Chiziane for his insights into war, Marissa Moreman and Leandro Lopes for their unwavering help and companionship, Alexander Aboagye for his assistance in understanding non-formal economies, Casimira Benge and Lidia Borba for their warm assistance in Angola, Crystal Prentice for being an excellent research assistant, and Katia Airola, Alex Laskaris, Mary Pat Selvaggio, Carole Swayne, Justin Wylie, and Sonja and John McKenna and all the people at The Cottages, for opening their homes and stories to me. Equally important, my sincerest thanks go to the pilots who ferried me endless miles in Africa and to the people at AfricaCare, Concern, Médecins Sans Frontières, Save the Children, Christian Children's Fund, UNICEF, International Committee of the Red Cross, InterOcean, Halo Trust, and the UN, who welcomed me into their homes, their jobs, and their parties in some pretty war-torn locales. These are the people who let me sleep on their office floors in out-of-the-way locales, who graciously share their last potatoes with me, and who take me out into their field sites — where they work, often at considerable risk to themselves, far from the praising light of CNN cameras and official recorders. The epilogue is dedicated to them. And my warmest thanks to Leela, who disappeared into war one day, but taught me how to fight back.

Finally, I'd like to thank the people who made this book possible: Naomi Schneider and Rob Borofsky: may their dreams for a vibrant new anthropology come true. And may all authors have such a good time at meals with their editors.

Photo credits: All the photos in the book are mine — they are a testimony to anthropology at its best and rawest: taken with street-market cameras in conditions where cameras are seldom welcome, and developed on the road in local conditions. They are stories in themselves.

PART ONE

INTRODUCTIONS

Wars and illicit economies make strange bedfellows. War's shadows cast widely; and in the areas of poor illumination lives and fortunes are forged and lost. As nations grow and crumble under the banners of progress and the weight of violence, each citizen tells or paints or dances or bleeds his or her story of survival. The sum total of these stories tells us the nature of war and the prospects for peace. Few reach the light of international recognition, most are lost in the shadows.

Ethnography is a discipline sophisticated in its simplicity: it travels with the anthropologist to the front lines and across lights and shadows to collect these stories; to illuminate strange bedfellows, and, if one were to put it bluntly, to care.

This book is dedicated to collecting stories of war, peace, and illicit economies across people's lives, and across zones of war and peace in different countries and on different continents. Neither the stories nor the ethnographies of the twenty-first century are bound to single locales: what patterns ripple across cultural landscapes, sovereign borders, and theoretical domains? As an arms merchant steps on an airplane to fly from one warzone to another, he or she hears a gunshot, a victim falls, a story unfolds. As the merchant steps off the plane a continent away, he or she notices another gunshot. What patterns of politics, of economics, and of personal heroism and tragedy define our world in the intersections of power, profit, survival, and humanity—in the shot of a gun? What experiences from the front lines of wars and the back lines of profiteering bring these understandings to life?

死亡的危
DENGER
OF
DEATH

CHAPTER 1

PROLOGUE

> These people say that war is a crocodile which is always hungry. It has dishonest eyes and a thrashing tail. It creeps up quietly while you wash at the river, while you pound your corn, while you rock your old mother in her time of dying.
>
> It is with you always, war, waiting to explode your life and throw you down beside a river to die. War wants death, always; war wants to quiet your mother's songs. War wants your sorrow.[1]

War is one of those impossible words: it refers to war as a soldier in Sudan lives it, as a child in Sri Lanka experiences it, as a torture victim in Argentina's dirty war felt it, as a Greek in Troy died it. A mere three letters covers a sweep of hundreds of thousands of events across several millennia. How do we understand so vast a phenomenon while retaining the vibrancy of the lives that constitute it?

There is an image of war that has stuck in my mind for nearly two decades. It seems to point toward some deep understanding, something that stands just outside of conscious grasp, or maybe beyond intellectual thought to a more profound conception of . . . what? Not just war, but something that tugs at the heart of what it means to be human. And in the curious combination that links devastating disasters with the profoundly mundane, this image involves a watermelon amid some of the worst violence marking recent decades. A Sri Lankan acquaintance and I had traveled to the July 1983 Kataragama religious festival in southeastern Sri Lanka. She is a middle-aged woman from the capital city of Colombo, a mother with a ready laugh and a maternal charm that holds a bit of impishness. We had shared a room, and I remember her unpacking her travel bag the first day; she had a towel, food, and other useful items I had not thought to pack. She laughingly lectured me: "Carry what you will need."

The 1983 riots in which thousands were killed in seven days broke out the last night of the festival.[2] No one knew the violence was about to erupt as they said goodbye to one another and began their journeys home. Almost no one: curiously, the last two evenings of the festival several of the homeless "mentally ill" people spoke at length and with great emotion about the impending violence. One directed his agitated monologue at me, perhaps because I was a foreigner. As a large crowd gathered around us, he launched into an aggressive explanation of the cataclysmic violence that was soon to erupt, the blood that would stain the streets and homes of the country, the screams of pain and anger he could hear, and the ways in which the responsibility for this violence went all the way to my country in cycles of global inequality. The audience around us sought to brush off his belligerent words with a reference to his madness, but a troubling clarity in his speech unsettled all of us.

Just before my traveling companion and I left Kataragama, she found a large watermelon, and bought it to take home to her family. She tried to give me a hug as we parted company to travel to our respective homes and broke out laughing as she juggled her suitcase in one hand and the watermelon in the other.

The bus she took to Colombo arrived at a city overtaken by flames and overrun by mobs. The next time I saw her, she told me of that night:

> We left the Kataragama festival that is meant to put the world together and arrived home to find the world being taken apart. We arrived to a nightmare worse than any the mind could conceive in dream. As we took the bus out of Kataragama, night began to fall, and we were lulled to sleep by the rocking of the bus, the camaraderie of sharing food, and warm memories of the festival. Sometime after midnight as we began to near Colombo, we opened our eyes to a world gone mad. Entire blocks of buildings were in flames, and people broke out of these buildings aflame themselves. Buses and cars burned in the roads, some with the occupants locked inside. Crowds of people ran in the streets, some shouting and beating people, overturning cars and setting them on fire, attacking homes and businesses . . . others running for safety and for their lives. Nothing made sense. As buses were being stopped, passengers being hauled out and killed, and the vehicles firebombed, our bus driver stopped suddenly and turned all of us passengers out onto the street, and drove away. It was nowhere near the bus terminal, and none of us knew where we were.

This fact startles me to this day: I grew up in this city, I know it as home; I know its streets and alleys, its shops and landmarks. I know my way around by a lifetime of knowledge—the pretty wall Mr. Wickramasingham built on this corner, the funny shaped tree in the open field by Mrs. Dharmaratna's shop, the temple my friend took her child to when he fell ill, the movie theatre painted bright blue. But that night, I didn't know where I was, or how to get home. I didn't recognize the city I spent my whole life in. Even that isn't really true: it tore such a cruel wound because I recognized it and I didn't, all at once. Amid the familiar was such horror. Those pretty walls and funny trees, the shops and temples, were in flames or destroyed, the dead and wounded lay there now, and mobs seemed to appear from empty space, overpower all reason, and disappear again, only to be replaced by another just down the road. The police did nothing, or maybe they did too much.

I had all my belongings from my trip with me, my handbag, my wrap, my suitcase, and that large watermelon. I just set my feet moving and tried to find my way home. Every street I turned down seemed as unfamiliar as the last. The horror never stopped. Fires, mobs, beatings, murder. I was exhausted, and my mind could not grasp what it saw. Nothing was clear: not who was killing whom, nor why. Not where it might be safe nor how to get there. Not how to respond nor whom to turn to, and no way of finding out.

I walked for hours. I grew painfully tired, and the things I was carrying seemed to weigh more and more. At some point, I stopped and set my handbag down on the sidewalk and left it there. It just seemed too much to carry. A while later I took my wrap and wiped the sweat and soot off my face, and left the wrap there on someone's fence as I picked up my suitcase and that watermelon and trudged off again in search of my home. Somehow in my mind I thought I'd go back and collect my handbag the next day—I really thought it would just be sitting there where I left it. That's how hard it is to think realistically when everything around you is unrealistic. I left all my identification, my money, everything sitting there on the road while I carried off that heavy unwieldy watermelon with me. Sometime later, it might have been hours or days to my mind, the suitcase became unbearably heavy, and I set that down too and left it. But I never let go of that watermelon. To this day, I can't explain it. But I carried that watermelon all night long through all the chaos and horror, and finally arrived home clutching that darned thing, having left everything else on the road.

You know, my handbag had all my necessities in it: my identification, my money and bank cards, my glasses and licenses. My suitcase had my favorite saris, my daily necessities and medicines, and presents and blessed religious relics for my family. I have always been considered the organized and responsible one of the family. And yet I left all these beside the road and carried home a heavy watermelon through some of the worst rioting imaginable. I will always wonder at that, at the will I had to get home, to keep walking through hell, and to carry a watermelon. How it is we all survive the unbearable.

This is the image that sticks with me: what made my friend drop her bags, with their familial associations and useful documents, in fatigue and terror, but hold on to a watermelon? "Carry what you need," she had said in Kataragama. In the seven days of the rioting, I watched thousands of people act and react to the events at hand, each in his or her own unique way; and hundreds of these people's responses made a strong impression on me. Each story, each behavior I observed during the riots, was a piece of the puzzle, a call to follow the question. But what was the puzzle, what was the question? Perhaps this watermelon is why I study war.

. . .

I doubt she would want me to use her real name. I was speaking with her half a world away, and nearly two decades after the Sri Lankan riots. But she would understand the story of the watermelon: she lives in a warzone where one-third of the entire population has been forced to flee their homes, and one-twelfth of the population have lost their lives to war in the last ten years. She had made time in a very busy day to sit and talk with me about the impact of the war on daily life. As the conversation came to an end, I thanked her for her time and asked her if there was anything I could do for her, to reciprocate her kindness.

> Yes, *she said*, there is. We have tens of thousands of internally displaced people in this area who have lost everything to the war. They do any kind of work to try to make enough to buy food and keep their families alive. This often falls on the women's shoulders: do you know, in most of the camps for the displaced here, the majority of households are headed by a woman? Women and girls scrape together just enough to get some food or goods to sell to make some money to feed their families.
>
> And then you see the police and the military, taking what little these girls and women have. They feel entitled. You see it all the time: a woman will be walking down the street with goods to sell, and the police or the soldiers will just go up and take it.
>
> They have the power, she has nothing now. And she may not make it without that bit to sell—how is she to survive?
>
> What can you do for me? Tell this story. Write about it. Tell the truth of war and what happens to people like these women who stand on the thin line of survival.

For the people standing on that thin line of survival between living and becoming a casualty of war, the impact of these actions is of existential proportions. They may even be cataclysmic. But for most people in the world, these brushes with life, death, and profiteering are largely invisible. They are invisible because militarily, much of war violates human sensibilities; because logistically, the front lines are difficult to document with neutrality; because economically, fortunes are made and lost in less than ethical ways; because politically, power covers its tracks.

The story doesn't end with the women giving up their goods to the police and military. This is just ground zero of the front-line intersections of war and invisible economies that ultimately extend worldwide. Just as these troops demand payment from poor women, so must they pay up the ladder, compensating their commanding officers. And their commanding officers are able to demand far greater goods in their own sphere of work: at the highest levels of power, they may control national concessions over valuable resources, as well as the companies that work the concessions, transport the goods, and oversee the profits. This might be called corruption if it stopped at the national level, but these systems of profit are international. In the shadows, beyond public scrutiny, commanders may partner with international wildcatters who move consumer items, from weapons to cigarettes, into a warzone while moving valuable resources, from diamonds to timber, out to the cosmopolitan centers of the world in less than legal ways.[3] More visibly, they may partner with international state-sponsored vendors to procure expensive weapons and goods — exports that peacetime countries are eager to sell for their own profits, but which rarely match the actual needs of the purchasing country and its war.

Systems of partnership, alliance, coercion, dependency, and outright violation variously mark these transactions, from the poor woman who gives up her only food to the foot soldier all the way to the vast global flows of weapons or resources for hard currency. It is in these intersections that power in its most fundamental sense is forged. In the midst of vast political systems in which riots and wars scar human landscapes and mold global economies, a woman discards her handbags and clutches a watermelon in trying to get home in a city besieged by mobs. This, in total, is the body of war and the hope for peace.

How do we understand, not abstract text-bound definitions of war's violence, but what it lives like, experiences like, tastes, feels, looks, and moves like? Many of the truths of war disappear in unsung deeds and unrecorded acts.[4] "The war tells us: nothing is what it seems. But the war also says: I am the reality, I am the ground under your feet, the certainty that lies beneath all uncertainties."[5] What place do we give to the profound good that beats in the hearts of so many I meet on the front lines that "conventional wisdom" tells us are populated with Hobbesian brutes? At the broadest level these inquiries merge into the question: "What is war?" Or perhaps more accurately, "Why would humans engage in one of the most profoundly unpleasant activities imaginable—one capable of extinguishing humans themselves?"

I soon found that there are no theories of war or—depending on what you are willing to accept as a "theory"—far too many of them. Ask a scholar for an explanation of war, and he or she will most likely snicker at your naiveté in expecting that something so large and poorly defined could even be explained. Ask a nonspecialist, however, and you will get any of a dozen explanations, each proffered with utter confidence: it is because of our innate aggressiveness . . . or because of innate male aggressiveness . . . or because of imperialism and greed . . . or overpopulation and a shortage of resources . . . or it is simply a manifestation of unknowable evil . . . Our understanding of war, it occurred to me, is about as confused and uninformed as theories of disease were roughly 200 years ago.[6]

These questions have led me along a continually unfolding set of inquiries, across several continents, and through two decades of research. After the 1983 Sri Lankan riots I began to study riot phenomena; as the war in Sri Lanka escalated, I went on to research paramilitary, military, and guerrilla warfare. Each inquiry prompted further questions. What happens to women, female guerrillas, children, and healers treating not only war wounds but also entire societies bleeding from assaults on their core institutions and values? How do civilians live their lives on the front lines? Who are the true brokers of war? Of peace? After conducting research in Sri Lanka for a decade, I began comparative work in Southern Africa in 1988, focusing on Mozambique at the height of its war. When Mozambique moved from one of the most destructive wars of the time to a successfully brokered peace, my research explored the "good," as well as the violence, that exists on the front lines and ultimately makes peace possible. In 1996 I began work in Angola, a country in many ways similar to Mozambique, but itself unable to maintain a peace accord until 2002. Violence is defined both by local realities and histories and by internationally forged norms of militarization: a large and well-developed set of networks stretch across the globe and into the most remote battlefield localities to provide everything required by militaries, from weapons to training manuals, food, medicines, tools, and state-of-the-art computers. If war is powerfully shaped by the intersections of individual acts, national histories, and transnational cultures of militarization and economic gain, so too are the more profound questions that attach to studies of war: What is power? Violence? In/humanity? Resolution?

These observations set in motion a new set of research issues: much of this trade passes across boundaries of il/legality. In doing the research for this book, I found these "extra-state" exchange systems — what I here call "shadow" networks — are fundamental to war, and in a profound irony, are central to processes of development, for good or bad. Simultaneously, my research showed that their centrality in world economic and power systems is accompanied by an almost inverse proportion of information on them. As this book will explore, a startlingly large portion of the entire global economy passes through the shadows: 90 percent of Angola's economy; 50 percent of Kenya's, Italy's, and Peru's economies; 40 to 60 percent of Russia's economy; and between 10 and 30 percent of the United States economy enters into extra-state transactions.[7] But a comparable percentage of research and publication does not take place on the non-legal. This of course prompts the question, "Why?"

The repercussions of leaving extra-state realities in the analytical shadows are extensive. Today, trillions of dollars and millions of people circulate around the globe outside of formal legal reckoning. This set of economic and personnel flows ranges from the mundane (the trade in cigarettes and pirated software), through the illicit (gems and timber), to the dangerous (weapons and illegal narcotics).

The trillions generated in these extra-legal financial empires must be laundered to legitimacy, and thus enter global financial markets in uncharted ways. The relative freedom from controls found in warzones and the financial powerhouses found in the cosmopolitan centers of the world combine in ways that tend to merge war and global profiteering.

Complex production, transport, distribution, and consumption systems have emerged to move goods and services through the shadows. Sophisticated banking systems exist to transfer unregulated monies. Highly developed regulatory mechanisms are in place to oversee extra-state trade — from lawyers to conflict resolution specialists. The profits have a substantial impact on the economies of all of the world's countries. And much of this remains invisible to formal state-based accounting systems and theories. We can't, with any accuracy, tell what impact hundreds of billions of dollars worth of illicit weapons gains has on European stock markets; how laundered drug proceeds affect the financial viability of smaller states; how market manipulation of unregulated goods affects interest rates and currency valuations internationally.

Nor, without studying the shadows, can we predict crises such as the

Asian market crash in the late 1990s or the September 11, 2001, attack on the USA. The shadows permeate these realms. Extra-state economies are central to the world's power grids.

We have grown used to a world where formal texts on military and economic matters deal only tangentially, if at all, with the extra-state. But this is a dangerous habit: what professional discipline can condone understanding only a part of the scope of its field of inquiry? The consequences of this practice are visible in myriad ways, which the chapters of this book will explore. An example suffices here: the United States intelligence services have taken considerable criticism for not predicting and averting the September 11 attack. But much of what undergirded the assaults took place along shadow channels. The intelligence services, for all their purported interest in the invisible world, function in an epistemological universe that still relies heavily on the classical economic, political, and military texts — texts that take their definitions from the realm of the formal and the state based. If a more developed knowledge of extra-state and extra-legal networks existed, the impending attack — and the activities of those who orchestrated it — would have been more visible. Solutions are predicated on knowing the whole of the problem, not merely the classically visible parts.

. . .

This book follows a very straightforward organizational format: war, extra-state realities, and (the problems of) peace — beginning to end. Each chapter is devoted to a stage along this continuum: the beginnings of political violence; the heights of war and the experiences of violence; the nature of power; the shadowy il/legalities that sustain war; the move toward peace; the impediments to resolution; and the reemergence of shadow powers as a central influence in in/stability, peace, and development on a global scale.

It may be that in the past we could understand a locale solely by focusing our gaze on it. Perhaps not. But today, clearly, locales are not islands surrounded by the vast and churning waters of fluid geographical space. Today humans feel the tug and pull of societal waves generated in regions far afield; they share the currents, even the riptides, that move across vast global stretches. For example, my experiences in Sri Lanka took on greater meaning when I began to do research in Mozambique. When I saw the same cast of characters selling arms, profiteering, and brokering peace in Mozambique as I had in Sri Lanka, I realized that these international players were not necessarily ideologically linked to the causes defining either South Asia or Southern Africa, nor were they necessarily drawn into a national drama for a specific set of reasons unique to this "locale." They were international players. In following the networks brokering war and peace across all distinctions of legal and illegal, I realized that these represent anthropological flows that span the globe both physically and epistemologically — at once dependent on locales and local cultural knowledges but also linking across them.

What, then, is ethnography?

The answer is not the same for everyone. But for me, and for this particular research, ethnography *must be able to follow the question.* It must be able to capture not only the site, but also the smell, feel, taste, and motion of a locale, of a people that share a common space and intertwined lives. It must be able to grasp at least a fleeting glimpse of the dreams that people carry with them and that carry people to distant places of world and mind; of the creative imaginary through which people give substance to their thoughts and lives. And quite pragmatically, it must be able to delve into why a soldier pulls the trigger against one human and not another; to illuminate how people suffer the ravages of violence and grieving and still craft humanitarian resistance; to chart the realities of how weapons are traded for diamonds and power, and the lives of those who trade them.

Today, such questions can't be encompassed by studying a single site.[8] The gun that fires the bullet in Mozambique was made in the USA, or Bulgaria, or Brazil, or China. It was traded through a vast network of agents, "advisors," and alliances — all of whom have a say in how the weapon should be used: who can legitimately be killed (and who cannot, starting with the arms vendors), and how this is all to be justified. Perhaps the weapon was smuggled through the legal world into the shadows, entering another global set of alliances. The soldier who aims the gun aims along years of training, not only on how to kill, but how to draw divisions, hatred, fears, and justifications — a mix of cultural and military lore that has been fed by everything from local grievances through foreign military advisors to global media and music.[9] All of this intersects to shape the lives of everyone involved in war, from the elite decision makers to the youth-soldiers fighting on shifting and hazy front lines.

. . .

"We just got a dead Irish Protestant mercenary, you want to see his body?" the fifteen-year-old said as he propped his AK-47 against a tree trunk, sat down next to me, and asked for a cigarette. It was at the height of the war in Mozambique, itself a long way from Europe and the conflicts in Northern Ireland. The boy and I sat in a bombed-out town in the middle of Mozambique, many hundreds of kilometers from the country's capital and cosmopolitan centers. We were, as traditional scholarship would say, in a profoundly "local" setting. "No thanks," I replied, "but how do you know he's a Protestant from Northern Ireland?"

"We looked at his identity papers," the boy said, looking at me as if I were a half-wit. The boy was thin, and dressed only in a pair of tattered shorts and a T-shirt. His gun was strung on an old piece of cloth. He had been press-ganged into joining the military, and had never left his home village region until he walked out as a "soldier" about the time he hit puberty. The boy settled in the sun, and began to talk:

> You know, these white guys are often a whole lot meaner than we are. I mean, we fight and we kill and all, but it's like these white guys think killing is the answer to everything. We have so many white guys, so many foreigners, around; training us, getting mad at us, fighting us, making money from us. Some are OK, I got sent to this training camp far away, and there were some who were friendly, tried to make sure we got enough to eat, and worked to teach us. People from all over. Got a whole lot of strange ideas, stuff that sometimes' useful, but a lot of times just didn't make a lot of sense, like it was a lot of trouble to do things that way, and dangerous too. I think fighting like that gives them weird ideas about fighting. Bruce Lee, *he laughs*, now that's who they should send out to train us. That's where it's at. But who knows, it's all beyond trying to guess. Truth is, I don't think a lot of these guys care if we win or lose. We all see them moving on the mines, doing "business." Someone's making a whole lot in this war, and I can tell you, it sure isn't me.

If I were going to understand this war, and this youth's experiences in it, what story would I best follow? I could follow his movements; those of his compatriots and the foreigners he interacted with; the media and movies that shaped his ideas; the war merchants and profiteers from around the world that passed through his life, his country, and its war; the various cultures of militarization that move from warzone to warzone around the world; the vast international systems of economic gain that shape political violence. This "local" youth-soldier was far from "local." The Mozambican war was deeply internationalized. Where does war begin and end?

Ethnography must be able to bring a people and a place to life in the eyes and hearts of those who have not been there. But it must also be able to follow not a place, but "place-less-ness," the flows of a good, an idea, an international military culture, a shadow; of the way these place-less realities intersect and are shaped by associations with other places and other place-less forces. And, as this book will explore in discussing shadow powers, ethnography must be able to illuminate not only a non-place, but also the invisible — that which is rendered non-visible for reasons of power and profit. Power circulates in the corridors of institutions *and* in the shadows. I will in fact argue that ethnography is an excellent way to study the invisibilities of power — invisibility that is in part constructed by convincing people not to study the shadows, convincing them that the place-less is impossible to situate in study, that it is "out of site." Ethnography gives substance and site to all human endeavor, merely by caring about the day to day of human existence.

In a study such as this, some things must remain in the shadows, unseen. And this in turn requires new considerations of what constitutes ethnography. Anthropology developed as a discipline rooted in fieldwork, and as such it named names and mapped places. In the localized settings in which anthropologists worked, every quote was enmeshed in a web of social relations such that everyone knew who spoke, to whom, and why. It was this "factuality" that lent anthropology an aura of objectivity; and alternatively, the respect of the subject.

But war and the shadows change this equation. Local knowledge is crucial to understanding, yet quoting local informants can mean a death sentence for them. When it comes to massacres, human rights violations, massive corruption, and global profiteering, even situating one's quotes and data in a "locatable" place and person can be dangerous. Academic responsibility here rests in protecting one's sources, not in revealing them.

Traditional scholarship might say that leaving out the names and the places behind the quotes waters down the impact of the research. Having struggled with this question for years now, I have come to disagree. Part of the reason so many aspects of war and extra-state behavior are "invisible" to formal accounting is precisely the problems and dangers of the research: people elect not to publish at all in lieu of endangering their work by asking, and then repeating, the "unspeakable." Perhaps even more important than "naming names and mapping places" at this stage of research into the intersections of war, peace, and shadows is understanding how these systems of human interaction unfold across people's lives and global transactions. The systems of knowledge and action that undergird these realities resonate around the world. Exposing the name of the poor peasant who saw his family murdered will not shed light on the circumstances surrounding that murder — it will merely endanger his life; and exposing the name of the general who is profiteering from war will not illuminate the international networks of extra-legal economies and power — it will merely endanger my ability to return to this field site.

This is not to leave a study hanging in mid-air. The field data presented in my work is all firsthand. In lieu of naming specific names, it sheds light on roles found from one conflict to the next; it maps the flux and flow of violence, shadow powers, and peace-building along connected sites to larger transnational patterns. The quotes throughout this work are from people who populate the immediacy of these realities. In protecting these people and their larger stories, I have given considerable thought as to how to present each story: in some cases I situate it in a locale; in others a region, and in those most sensitive I leave the story sans-locale altogether. When asked to provide more concrete and situated data — the names and places of traditional scholarship — I must respond that endangering those with whom we work endangers the very integrity of our discipline. Weaving together these layers and levels is the best way I know at present to explore, and begin to expose, the visible and invisible realities that attend to war, peace, and shadow powers that are shaping the course of the twenty-first century.

. . .

I'll never know why my friend in Sri Lanka left her handbag, wrap, and suitcase in the roadway, yet carried a watermelon as she struggled to get home through the rioting. She says she doubts she will ever figure it out herself. But we speculated about this for months:

> You know, *she said*, it seems illogical to leave what I might most need in the midst of a life-threatening night. But, when you think of it, it seems illogical to kill people for an identity: are you Tamil, Sinhalese, Hindu, Muslim, Buddhist? It seems illogical to target people on their jobs and associations, voter registration designations, and location of their homes. My handbag was filled with such "identity": my registrations and designations, licenses and addresses. It just occurred to me: these are like licenses to kill. Leaving my glasses, my keys? Perhaps I just didn't want to see what was going on; and what are keys but an illusion of safety shattered by mobs who just break windows and enter houses? What did I care that night if I broke my window to get into my home? If I had to break in, that would be wonderful, it would mean my house had not been attacked. My suitcase? It was heavy, and when your life is on the line, all those pretty saris and comfortable shoes don't mean a whole lot. But I think it was more: all around me people were loot-

ing the goods of the maimed and the murdered, of the burning shops and the deserted houses. What have we humans become, I believe I worried that night, that we will feast on the dead for a television or a trinket? When did we begin to value goods above good? My suitcase, filled with my goods, became heavy in more ways than one. I left those behind. I left behind the presents I bought for my family. Somehow I think they seemed to embody the religious strife that was tearing my country to shreds that night. But that watermelon. It was heavy, and unwieldy, and I can't imagine what I looked like, an old mother struggling down burning streets covered in dirt and ash carrying a large watermelon in her arms. But it was something pure of violence; a present for my family that cost no one their life; something that seemed to represent sanity and succor in a world gone mad. A watermelon carries its own seeds for the future. Perhaps that is what I was trying to do.

FRONT-LINE MARKET: BEER AND BISCUITS AMIDST THE RUINS.

CHAPTER 2

A CONVERSATION IN A BAR AT THE FRONT

I had gotten a ride on an unexpected cargo flight to a province on a distant Mozambican battlefront. It was 1990, and the war was so serious at this time people were calling the country the killing fields of Africa. I had been trying to get to this location for weeks. It was a land of contradictions. It was considered a backwater by African standards: the place where people were sent when they really messed up either by breaking the law or running afoul of the government. Yet it had a strong frontier ethos and a set of vibrant cultures. The province had little governmental support, and perhaps because of this, strong cross-border extra-state linkages with larger regional networks. Given the unpredictabilities of the war, and the frequent attacks on trade routes, combined with the government's lack of interest in the region, you never knew if the markets would have three potatoes to feed an entire town, or be brimming with unusual items from a recent successful cross-border run. The only item in town that was in abundance — given its centrality to survival — was information.

Just arrived, I was walking down the street when a woman called across the street to me, "Are you the anthropologist or the public health person?" Long since past wondering how people got information that to me seemed inaccessible, I replied, "the anthropologist." "Well," she said, "I'm the town's only surgeon, but more importantly, a shipment of beer from the next country over has just arrived in town. Let's go." "Go where?" I asked. "For a beer. We haven't seen beer here in ages. Everyone will be going. We can talk there." She and I converged on the local bar — a simple cane and wood construction with a few plastic tables and benches, along with an assortment of the town's denizens. Over warm flat beer — some of the worst I have ever tasted — stories flowed around the table.

Doctor: What a week! I've been operating day and night. War's heated up this week. Carolyn, I'll run you by the hospital soon enough, but it's rough: virtually no electricity in town, and we often can't get enough fuel for the generator. No running water. Almost no medicines; this month, no surgical sutures: I've been sewing people up with my own stock of sewing thread. Don't know what I'll do when that runs out.

Journalist: Yeah, the war has been bad these days. I just got back from a week-long trip up north with some of the soldiers. Christ, we walked forever. Not enough food, too much sickness . . . But these guys are OK. They told stories from their home villages, and about what they would do when the war ended. One of the guys stepped on a land mine and blew his foot pretty badly. We carried him back to town—it took days, seemed to take forever, him trying to be strong and then screaming when he couldn't take it anymore.

Doctor: What a case he was. By the time you all got him to me, he was days past wounded. You had that great bloody bandage on his foot. He's wide awake when he arrives, I don't have even a little anesthetic to put him out with. So I unwrap this bandage, and he and I both look at what's left of his foot and leg, and it's crawling with maggots. He takes one look at this leg of his, and without uttering a word, tries to crawl backward away from it, like it's not his, like he can get away from it. You could see it in his face: he knew his body, it didn't look like this, this horrible thing at the end of his leg must belong to someone, something, else. But as he backs up on the operating table, his leg follows him, and he keeps trying to get away from it. It was pretty awful: I had to pick the maggots out one by one with tweezers. Took hours. But I got him patched up, and he's going to be OK. Well, as OK as you can be after having parts of your body blown off.

Journalist: I have a good story from the trip. Way up north, up by the border, there's this region where the people live pretty much by themselves. A world away. But it's a great place. And it has managed this peace in the middle of the war. Seems the chief holds all the power there—never mind the government or the rebels. He's a decent kind of guy, cares about his community. And he has power. He's done ceremonies to protect his entire region—protect it from war and soldiers, from their violence. Troops don't enter, they don't kidnap people, they don't come and harass the women. Place is nice to get to—you can feel it when you arrive, people don't have that hunted, that haunted, look in their eyes. No one doubts this chief has powers—but his canniness in cross-border trade is a nice piece of the story. A whole little economy up there. But the place was attacked recently. No one could figure out why, after such a long time of peace and protection.

Then the story comes out—seems the chief is having love problems. You know, the protective ceremonies only work if the chief upholds key moral values. He can't abuse anyone in the community, he can't break sexual restrictions, he can't overindulge in pleasures and laziness, he can't take what is not his. So he's distraught over this love affair, and he loses his perspective. Mopes, drinks too much, tries to have sex when he shouldn't. Generally makes a mess of it all. A chief isn't supposed to be reduced to this by a woman. He's supposed to be in complete control, in charge . . . If he can't control his love life, how can he take care of the entire populace under his protection? So anyway, the community begins to get nervous, and with good reason. One night, the place is overrun with rebel soldiers. They shoot the place up, kill some people, loot the towns, kidnap people to porter what they have looted. The soldiers stay in the area, and come by daily demanding food, medicines, livestock, clothing, money, goods, women, whatever takes their fancy.

The townspeople are frantic, and decide to go to their chief and tell him that the reason they have been attacked is clear: would he please clean up his female troubles and act like a chief again? The chief took their words to heart. He sorted out his woman problems, and then began to perform the protective ceremonies to rid his region of war and the soldiers occupying them. The townspeople say the troops just left. Perhaps they did. But I suspect the chief regained his will to fight, and with this, the townspeople rallied too. I suspect too the chief began to call on his cross-border alliances, and on the neighboring regions. The soldiers probably saw resistance and fighting coming, and decided to leave before they found themselves ambushed one day. But perhaps not. Perhaps it's as the townspeople say, that the chief solved his love problems and his protective ceremonies regained their full force. Whatever the explanation, the region has returned to a calm and peaceful footing in a country of war.

Merchant: Of course it was his protective powers. That and his connections . . . How do you think we get this beer?

NGO staffperson: Shit!

[Everyone follows the NGO staffperson's glance and sees that a group of air force officers have entered the bar.]

Doctor: *[leaning over and whispering to me]* He was in a reeducation camp and still fears anything in uniform.

NGO staffperson: *[overhearing]* What, like everyone doesn't know my story? OK, OK, so I was in a reeducation camp. *[Turning to me]* My father was with the colonial police . . .

Merchant: Secret police.

NGO staffperson: . . . and when the country gained independence, some of us found ourselves on the outside, without much means. I didn't do anything wrong, I just made the opportunities I could, but it wasn't patriotic enough. Especially given my family's history. So I was sent to a "reeducation" camp. What a joke that word is, reeducation. More like concentration camps.

Merchant: Opportunities, huh? You better be careful now, you and your opportunities . . . Those little rocks of opportunity [gems] you keep moving will land you back in the shit if you get caught.

NGO staffperson: What nonsense are you talking? Anyway, those officers are pure danger. Your life is worth nothing if they look your way. They control this country, and they will do whatever it takes to keep it that way. There are rules, unwritten rules, things you do and don't do, you just know it. You just do it, or your life is dust.

CN: In my experience, air force officers all over the world have this "right stuff" attitude: professional, but with that touch of wild—that military pilot pride in being beholden to no one. Do people really have to fear them that much?

NGO staffperson: If you don't believe it, you are a fool. You understand nothing if you don't understand this.

[Everyone falls silent for a moment, but I can't tell if it's in agreement or in discomfort with the topic.]

Doctor: Well, I do know one thing. They shouldn't let the security guys get drunk and carry their weapons at the same

> time. Every time a shipment of booze hits town and the soldiers party, it seems some guy shoots off his gun. Military decided the guy that guards my place needed an assault rifle, and gave him one this month. I woke up the other night and heard gunfire coming from the next neighborhood over, where the guard lives. I just put my feet in my shoes and pulled on my surgicals and walked over to the hospital to wait for the casualties to come it: I knew my guard had his nose in the drink and then pulled out his gun. What a crazy war.

The conversation continued for hours. It wound through the common conversation topics that marked these war years: the casualties these people had suffered in their families and communities, the ever-present search for food, medicines, and essentials; the stories of hope and humor that keep them going. If the war was about soldiers stepping on land mines, gem smuggling, and the fear of getting caught on the wrong side, it was also about conversations in bars and quiet acts of individual heroism. Every one of the people at the table that day, with the exception of the NGO staffperson who had his salary and also smuggled gems, made a pittance of a salary, one they couldn't easily sustain their families on. And all of them devoted most of their days, year in and year out, to helping their communities during the war as best they could. All had skills that could have taken them to safer and richer locales, but they lived in a town where war had taken away the basic comforts of life, and they worked in difficult and sometimes life-threatening situations. They do not stay and help for financial gain, or power, or prestige. They live and work in these conditions because they believe in their communities. This, too, is the face of war.

TITUS THE MAGICIAN, AT THE TIME OF THE 1983 RIOTS IN SRI LANKA.
"I AM," TITUS SAID, "ALL POLITICS AND FREE OF ALL POLITICS."

CHAPTER 3

MAKING THINGS ~~INVISIBLE~~

The Mozambican soldier leaned back again the tree trunk, lit a cigarette, and opened a warm beer smuggled in from Malawi. It was 1990, the war in Mozambique was at its height, and we were talking in an embattled zone in the center of the country.

> Shape-shifters; people who walk among us we can't see—people say only we Africans practice such things. But don't believe it, there are plenty of shape-shifters in your country, throughout the world. The Europeans say this is witchcraft, but what nonsense. It is power, pure and simple.
>
> You know, some call me hero, and I've been recognized for my bravery in battles. But I suppose some call me a scoundrel. Yeah, I do some deals, I do some "business." But you know how this is possible? While I'm out here in the middle of the shooting, the big guys are doing even bigger business. Look at the South African Defense Force walking in talking war and walking out clutching bags of gems. And those guys who fly in those cargo planes from all over the world trading out everything from guns to laptops in the name of supporting us, or them, or someone. Yeah, I do some deals, but it's possible only because the world has set up a bazaar at my campsite. Now tell me these people aren't shape-shifters: these guys travel around from all over the world, working the night. And they say only Africans believe in this ability to turn invisible.

WARS AND INVISIBILITIES

There are layers and layers of invisibility surrounding war, and surrounding the extra-legal. How are these complex relationships of truth, untruth, and silencing produced — and perhaps more importantly, why?

The soldier quoted above may be right; webs of invisibility permeate many aspects of war economies and transnational profits. But the lives of the people populating the front lines, from the impoverished to the powerful, are equally subject to erasure — deleted because the truths of war little match the myths that sustain war. Before returning to the soldier's story of front-line "business," this section will explore the political acts of erasure, of "editing out" significant aspects of violence. To begin, I return to the 1983 riots in Sri Lanka.

"The world's gone crazy," my friend said, visibly shaken. It was one of the first conversations I had after the rioting began, and I remember well this man's words as they painted a strong image of the riots. It was only over days that I realized everyone had a different experience, a different set of images, defining the violence and devastation.

> I was trying to get across the street on Galle Road, the violence, you know, it was everywhere. These kids, they were young teenagers, they started beating this old lady right in front of me. She fell down and they kept on kicking her, shouting some goddamned thing or another, none of it made any sense. But they thought it did. It was ugly, them beating her like that, like they had this right. All over town, it's just crazy like this.

For him, the violence of the youth and the helplessness of the old woman stood out. We all carried different images of shock. I have several. I think the first for me was finding a bullock cart set aflame in the middle of Galle Road south of Colombo city. All over the major thoroughfares, buses and cars had been stopped, and the drivers and passengers were either hauled out and variously let loose, beaten, or killed, or they were forced to remain inside and burn as the vehicle was set aflame. These were scenes beyond horror. But somehow that burned bullock cart — a poor man's simple wooden cart, the goods he was taking to market blazing, the man dead, and the bullock struggling to free itself from the ropes that tied it to certain death — symbolized the extremes of violence to me.

The second strong image for me was watching the mob coalesce that killed seven Tamils in the Colombo train station. The rioters were the denizens of downtown: men in sarongs; youths in trousers; women in skirts, saris, or traditional wraps; bureaucrats in office clothes; some white-haired elders. I remember being surprised at how quickly the mob formed, and with how little verbal communication. The mob was fueled by a nebulous rallying cry that "terrorists were entering into the city by train" and that "everyone's life was in danger unless they were stopped."

I noticed the eclectic nature of the mob, that they came from all walks of life, and that they emerged to join the group from stores and shops and sites along the road — but I didn't find this unusual until in the months following the riots the violence was attributed to "organized men with voter lists systematically attacking Tamils."

> A neighbor of mine, a teenage male, saw a different riot. He came over to my house in agitated excitement:
>
> "We got one," he said.
>
> "One what?" I asked.
>
> "A Tamil. A guy from our school. Me and my friends, about five of us, and this guy, we were walking along the road toward home talking. When we got to this place with a bunch of trees and no houses, we started shouting at him about how Tamils are ruining our country, about how they want to take over, that they want to see the Sinhalese finished. We began to beat him up. Then one of the lads stabbed him with this knife he had. And we pulled him into the bushes and trees and left him there."
>
> "But he was a school friend," I said, feeling sick, "a boy you know had nothing to do with politics or violence; you know he's no threat."
>
> "Yeah, but he's Tamil, and now there's one less to try and take over Sri Lanka."

In the days and months that followed the riots, I was taken aback at how inaccurate the reports were on what had taken place. The youth, the women, the elders, the children disappeared from accounts, to be replaced by various explanations that focused on adult men. The government harped on the "unseen hand"; the intellectuals focused on "men in trousers with voter lists identifying Tamils versus Sinhalese households"; those critical of the role of the government decried the participation of troops and government officials' "private armies of hired thugs." None of these explanations is wrong (with the exception of the "unseen hand"), but they are partial at best. "The Sinhalese rioted against the Tamils," headlines shouted. The impression given was that all Sinhalese participated. My experiences paint a far different picture.

In avoiding several mobs in Colombo city one day, I had walked quite a distance from where I was staying. The brutal groups had passed for the moment, a few firemen were battling blazes, and I was trying to wend my way home when I saw a three-wheeler drive by and signal that he was open for business. It reminded me of a Fellini movie. Grateful for the ride, I jumped in the cab and asked the man why on earth he was out plying his trade amid the burning husks of cars that had lost in their encounters with politics gone bad.

> "Aren't you scared?" I asked.
> "Naw," he said. "Life is risky business always, and besides, my kids got to eat. What do the bigwigs think, that we poor folk got money put aside for riot days? I don't work, my family doesn't eat."

When he dropped me off, I asked him how much money I owed him, wondering about hazard pay in riots. He waved his hand, saying he didn't want any money. I reminded him about feeding his kids.

> "I got out here," he waved at the burned-out buildings and broken cityscape, "and found a whole lot of people worse off than me. People who have lost everything, who maybe don't even have family members to find food for anymore. I decided to do what I could to help."

I looked at the man: by every stereotype a rough-looking "street tough," the kind of face the media uses to represent aggressive thugs; the kind of clothes that signal a man not overly concerned with fastidiousness. "The Sinhalese are rioting against the Tamils," proclaimed the radios. Not all of them, not even most of them, I thought. I had to reach over and put some money in the man's shirt pocket as he drove off.

The 1983 communal violence in Sri Lanka stands as a graphic example not only of the way many of the front-line actors and actions are deleted from formal narratives and "official accounts," but also of the way daily realities of life under extreme violence are erased in "accepted" war stories. About five days into the rioting, I was walking along a major street in Colombo and stopped at a corner to rest and to try and grapple with what I was seeing. In a short space of time, I was in several conversations, which I repeat here. These, to me, represent a real core of people's experiences of violence—multiplied across all the street corners in all the towns in Sri Lanka.

A long line of people stretched down the block, all queued up at a shop door that was closed and barred. Most of them were women. They ran the gamut of ages and backgrounds, but virtually all seemed to share the same expression: a powerful combination of fear, exhaustion, pain, resignation, yet some will to carry on. "What is it?" I asked.

> We heard this shop might open today, and that it still has some food left. We've all been scouring the city, looking for food. There's just nothing around. A lot of shops have been burned out. Not a stick of food left. Many more have been gutted by looting. People have been looting shops down to the last grain of rice. The shop owners whose shops have not been hit yet have locked and barred them, not daring to open for fear of another mob attack or a band of looters. The markets are bare. Who in their right mind would take goods to sell in the market today?

> No one is eating, our children are hungry, we can't see a solution. It's not just the shops; the warehouses have been burned, storage containers broken into and emptied. No flights are coming in with food to the airport, the trucks that haven't been burned out are parked and hidden, no one is driving supplies to town, and even if they were, crops have been burned out and gardens stripped bare.

As we were talking, a man with a bloody leg stumbled in the street. Several of us went over to assist him. He began to wipe tears from his face: "My child is sick, so sick, I have to find a pharmacy that is open, that still has medicines to fill this prescription for my child. Nothing is open, nothing is available, no one is working."

One of the women from the line commiserated:

> It's not just the food. There are no medicines to be found. The pharmacies are all burned up or looted out or shut and barred. My little girl has been wounded. We took her to the hospital, but no one was available—hardly any medical staff were there, and those that were had hundreds vying for their attention. There were no supplies at the hospital, anyway. We went to another hospital south of town, and it was filled to bursting with people seeking refuge. There was no medical attention, but hundreds of people who had been attacked, who had lost their homes, or who had been threatened with death gathered there in some hope of finding safety. So we returned home again, and my husband is out now walking all over town trying to find anyone that is selling medicines, while I look for food.

At this point a youth came up and stopped at the street corner, and, standing in one place, began a repetitive series of actions: lifting one foot, starting to walk, sagging down, stopping, reaching up, and repeating the gestures again.

> Poor child, *one of the women said.* I've seen him before. He lost his family in the attacks. He somehow escaped and got away with his life, but it broke his mind. We see him wandering the streets day and night, just like this now; unaware of the violence around him. If you try and talk to him, he just says, "I can't find my home."

Before I was caught in these riots, media and literary accounts had taught me to think of communal violence as consisting only of "rioters" and "victims," and of riots as being explosive one-day events. These accounts did not convey the fact that there is no escaping the riots—for anyone. It never occurred to me before this time that riots involved looking for nonexistent food and medicines long since burned and looted; that people "of the rioters' side" risked their lives to protect people "on the other side"; that young children were caught in the violence, standing with eyes open too wide, wondering what to do and what was happening to their world — and that all these experiences were as much the meat of political violence as the rioters attacking the victims.

There are some 15 million people in Sri Lanka, and there were 15 million stories of political violence, all equally central. Most were never heard. Some were actively silenced. The reporting on the riots in Sri Lanka improved little over time, and the stereotypes continued: rioters (adult males) and victims (variously, terrorists or entire innocent families identified as mass casualties, generally nameless) — "the Sinhalese rioting against the Tamils." Worse, attitudes and policies were formed on this misinformation that tended to foment ongoing cycles of violence. I first thought that the erroneous views commonly propagated were a result of a lack of information: how many impartial researchers conduct viable research in the midst of a firefight? During the time I was in the midst of this communal violence that took thousands of lives, few people were taking notes and most people were taking sides. Many "official" political versions of the riots were based on vested interests. Most researchers who wrote on the violence did so by flying in and conducting interviews after the aggression had abated and relative order was restored. It is a cliché to note that people involved in aggression clean up their stories of violence after the fact. Few admit they firebombed a neighbor's house or stabbed an unarmed person. The victims themselves often hide the truth for fear of retaliation.

It was this difficulty of studying violence firsthand that I initially assumed underlay the misinformation that I saw published on the events I had witnessed. I further assumed that the policies based on this erroneous information — policies doomed to fail because they were based on fictions and not facts — would change to embrace more accurate information should it become available. But the first time I publicly presented my research on the political violence I had seen, I began to form another view. People from the audience stood up, incensed, to challenge my data. "How can you say that priests were involved in violence?" For others, I was being offensive by saying some youths participated in the violence, or that trusted members of the community harmed children. "Women don't join mobs, they are only assaulted by them!" And for still others I violated sensibilities by saying troops condoned, even assisted, massacres of civilians. The list of offenses went on. It did not matter that I had witnessed these events personally, talked to the people involved. *The offense was speaking of these things.*

Most people spoke, not from a position of knowledge, but from positions of privilege and passion. Militaries didn't want to be tainted with the accusations of killing civilians. The religious didn't want to face the fact that some priests fomented communal aggression. Professionals far removed from the political conflicts didn't want to believe that others like them, perhaps they themselves at some future time, could target the innocent and become pawns in ugly political power struggles. For many, the sheer barbarity of the violence was unsettling, and needed to be bracketed in comfortable myths. People did not want to hear stories like that of my young neighbor, who along with his schoolmates killed another schoolmate because he was Tamil. Senseless violence is generally associated with rioting: Freud's mob theory of the eternal child—humans reduced to their lowest common denominator, willing to do anything, however irrational, for a father-like figure—is widely accepted in general society. The problem with the story of my neighbor is that reasonable, economically comfortable, schooled people are not supposed to give in to these primal emotions: it is the poor and uneducated, the marginal, and the criminal who are blamed for irrational violence. It is the poor three-wheeler driver street tough who is supposed to fuel the flames of mob violence, not the nice schoolboy or the respected doctor.

Amid all this, another set of dirty secrets was kept. Under cover of the "truth" shouted from media headlines that "the Sinhalese were rioting against the Tamils," businesspeople burned out competitors' stores, neighbors set fire to the house of a person against whom they held a grudge, and countless thousands of people looted goods anywhere they found the chance. These were acts of acquisition and antipathy that had little, if anything, to do with ethnicity. Old scores were revisited and settled, and considerable fortunes were lost and made under cover of rioting.

By the time everyone had their say, I began to understand the images of war conveyed in the media and literature. They were variously devoid of priests and women, children and rogue troops, low-class altruists and high-class profiteers. Political violence is corralled as the province of rational militaries and mostly rational soldiers controlling the dangerous elements and explosive fissures inherent in human society. A comfortable picture, but a mythological one. As the chapters of this book will illustrate, this same pattern of deleting significant aspects of political violence from public accounts occurs from riots to full-scale wars, from Asia through Europe and the Americas to Africa. Most of the people I meet at the epicenters of wars, and most of the events I see take place, are never represented in public accounts of political violence. Serious and representative stories of front-line realities do circulate in the media and literature worldwide. But in all too many, the central actors and the central victims fall out of the telling.

Why is so much invested in erasing the truths of war?

I have no simple answers. On the one hand, I am forced to ask whether we, the general public, simply don't want to know the full extent of the suffering in people's lives. In writing on the war in Yugoslavia, Mattijs van de Port asks: "Isn't it utter nonsense to suppose that you may bridge the gap between the world of the academy and war?"[1] He then challenges the academy's most cherished claim to the pursuit of knowledge in noting that he is forced to wonder whether we truly

> *want* to understand how "the beast in man" is mysteriously connected with the urges and motives that derive from social reality, whether such research does not run up against strongest inhibitions in its path. Are we prepared to give up our neat picture of the world? (I am only too aware of my own reluctance to do so.) Do we really want an academic text that is disturbing? (I have read very few myself).[2]

This is a question van de Port returns to time and again in his ethnography of war in former Yugoslavia, deciding, in the course of his explorations, that "experiences obtained in the terrible reality of the war, in which these confrontations with the most brutal violations of the integrity of the human body — violations of what is perhaps the ultimate story we have to tell about ourselves: the story that says that we are more than just skin, bones, blood and brains — seem to bring about an utter alienation."[3]

This is a theme taken up as well by Arthur Redding in *Raids on Human Consciousness: Writing, Anarchism, and Violence:* "Violence bespeaks a perpetually elusive, abstract, yet paradoxically germane horror, a shifting gravitational field tugging at the tides of our collective dread."[4] And he concludes that "violence will always be situated as extratextual."[5]

This certainly fits my observation in discussing the riots in Sri Lanka: the offense rests not in the realities of violence, but in *speaking* of them. In fact, violence is often rendered as "unspeakable." But *why* should we be trained to believe that the horrors of war are too horrible to speak, indeed to contemplate — that hearing the story we tell ourselves about ourselves, in Geertzian terms, is too awful to tell? Why do we omit the telling and in so doing allow the acts behind the telling to continue?

What is it that we are not supposed to know? Several considerations come to mind:

In the wars of the world today most casualties are civilian. This fact has become fairly obvious in recent years, though it has become no less palatable, and perhaps for this reason it is often overpowered by the myth that war equals soldier equals male. Despite the fact that some 90 percent of all casualties today are civilians, that more children die in war than soldiers, and that the front lines run through average citizens' homes and livelihoods, texts on war, museums, military novels, art, and statues all help reinforce the idea and the ideal that war is about male soldiering.

People who are harmed and killed in war often die unnecessarily gruesome deaths, often at the hands of those in uniforms. This plays hell with the notions of integrity and honor that underscore the key justifications of militaries worldwide. At the same time, many soldiers and civilians act honorably in the midst of violence, but when the realities of the front lines are deleted, these acts too become invisible. There is a second layer to this: perhaps in recognizing that civilians die because they are in the wrong place at the wrong time, and not because they do anything to violate the rules of war, people face the unsettling proposition that no matter how they live their lives, they too may fall victim to violence. Chaos — the unpredictable and uncontrollable — is deeply disturbing to most. The myth of an orderly war is more bearable.

No matter who shoots whom, certain power elites make a profit. There is more to this than meets the eye. The man who was burned to death in his bullock cart — nameless and long forgotten for most in a roster of war dead that in Sri Lanka alone totals thousands, and in the world totals hundreds of millions in the last century alone — seems a long way from explaining war and its erasures. But this man lies within a web of connections that, followed out to their global connections, is a story that is as indicative of war, and as nameless, as he is. Upcoming chapters will consider where exactly we look for war, and what acts define the "everyday" of war. These acts take us through soldiers and civilians alike who run arms and run orphanages, who sell drugs or take them to forget the horrors of war, who black-market antibiotics and textbooks in acts that are simultaneously profiteering and altruistic.

Somewhere, in all of this, the lines between war and peace break down. Not only in the midst of people's lives, but in the trillions of dollars a year that war industries generate for people working in peacetime locales; for people shipping goods across various lines of political alliance and antipathy; and for people who walk the front lines more interested in making a buck than in making an enemy. These systems of trade and profit are far larger than any one warzone, and are in fact larger than any single era of war. To put this in perspective: in the mid-1990s governments spent 700 billion *legal* dollars on their militaries. This doesn't include the vast sums spent along extra-state, gray, and black-market channels. The illicit weapons trade alone is estimated at half a trillion dollars a year.[6] I have spoken so far only of weapons profits. Add in all the vehicles and gasoline, uniforms and food, medicines and tools, engineering equipment, communications systems, and computers, ad infinitum, necessary to war. From the legal arms sales through the negotiated oil futures to the illegal diamond trade, war is good for business in the cosmopolitan production centers of the world. The diamonds, oil, timber, seafood, and human labor that come from warzones from Angola to Burma, and the weapons, supplies, and services these valuable resources buy from cosmopolitan industries add up to considerable perquisites. As Karl Meier observes: "The international community is not in the mood to finance the Angolan peace process any longer than need be, in contrast with its eagerness to finance and profit from the civil war."[7]

In considering the staggering profits that accrue to war, I suggest that the "politics of invisibility" is not an accident: it is created, and it is created for a reason.[8] The casualties of war would find a tragic truth in Charles Tilly's characterization of "war making and state making as organized crime."[9] The modern state is as dependent on warzone profits as it is on keeping these dependencies invisible to formal reckoning. Part of its power rests on the optics of deception: focusing attention on the need for violence while drawing attention away from both the war-economy foundations of sovereign power and the price in human life this economy of power entails. This is the magician's trick: the production of invisible visibility.

SHADOWS AND INVISIBILITIES

The Mozambican soldier continued his conversation:

> Invisibility: it seems you all from the North are pretty good at it too. You ask how it runs so smoothly. It works because people share a goal: to some-

how prosper. It works because doing business is human nature. It works because that's how we make it. People may call me a scoundrel for doing some deals, but in truth, I'd rather be doing deals that help people than killing some poor sod and leaving behind a widow and his children who may starve.

You know those guys who take payment from families for getting back their loved ones who have been press-ganged into military service—the ones we call "jackals"? OK, they are profiting from people's suffering. But you know, they are the only way people have of getting family members back who might be killed. They give people hope who are desperate—often the only hope they have of getting their family back. People despise the jackals, having to sell off their goods to pay these guys to find their loved ones, but they like them, too. You should see the families' faces when their father or sister comes stumbling out of the bush looking like the living dead from their experiences, and finally realize they are home. Yeah, it's business. But would it be any better if that jackal were taking up arms, killing? How does this stack up against the guys flying in arms from all over the world? Even here, nothing is straightforward. Some say they are flying in food and Bibles and they are flying in arms, and some say they are flying in arms and they're bringing in food and Bibles. But a whole lot of them are flying in arms and flying out with war booty.

You can buy anything out here if you know what you are doing: from the latest videos and the equipment to watch them, the generators to run them, and the petrol for the generators to a Mercedes Benz and the mechanic to fix it. Thing is, you can usually get *cadonga* [unregulated goods] easier than you can get things on the legal markets. African, European, American, Asian, everyone's in this business—they're all here.

Illegal. Informal. Illicit. Gray-market. Brown-market. Extra-state. Extralegal. Underground. Unregulated. Subterranean. Clandestine. Shadows. These words tend to conjure up images apart from day-to-day life. We don't tend to juxtapose them with images of supermarket shopping, attending school, buying appliances, picking a stock, watching our congressperson speak on labor law, checking currency exchange rates, buying the latest DVD hit.

Just as there is a popular image of "war," so too is there an image of "the clandestine"; a young adult male dressed in dark colors and a leather jacket—someone *apart* from the normal workaday world, not someone who holds a regular nine-to-five job and wears a dress or a suit. One of the most pervasive of myths is that two things can't exist in one place at the same time. This myth confounds understandings of war, and it helps to keep the shadows invisible. There is the legal world, and then there is the non-legal subworld. Two realms, distinct. A clean portrait, but inaccurate. The shadows exist in the midst of formal state society and the minutia of day-to-day living. The shadows are an integral part of everyday life and global politics, and they represent a power grid as substantial as that of many of the world's states.

Michel de Certeau captures the complex interactions of non/state and extra/legal that I will develop in this book. De Certeau asks that we give up a singular attachment to abstract domains of epistemology to explore substance in action:

> The wordless histories of walking, dress, housing, or cooking shape neighborhoods on behalf of absences; they trace out memories that no longer have a place. . . . They insinuate different spaces into cafes, offices, and buildings. To the visible city they add those "invisible cities" about which Calvino wrote. With the vocabulary of objects and well-known words, they create another dimension, in turn fantastical and delinquent, fearful and legitimating.[10]

If approximately half of the economies of countries like Italy, Peru, Kenya, and Russia run through the shadows, if half of all revenues for such diverse commodities as weapons, software, and cigarettes run through extra-legal channels, then even determining where the "extra" in extra-legal is may be empirically impossible. But the dividing line is not that which is normal life and that which is *apart*. Instead, like de Certeau's cities, the visible and the invisible intertwine throughout the walkways and cafes, the department stores and governing offices, the objects we love and the people we fear.

In making these inquiries, it helps to understand what Marc Augé calls "non-places." Augé is interested in supermodernity and the vast spheres of transit it generates: superhighways and communications systems, airports and fast-food chains — the nondiscriminate, indiscriminate spaces that define the cosmopolitan present. He doesn't deal with the illicit, but his theories apply well to these realms: "The world of supermodernity does not exactly match the one in which we believe we live, for we live in a world that we have not yet learned to look at."[11]

The world is most often presented, in academic text, popular media, and fiction, as a world of places. We are animate beings in a world of objects arranged in a locale. Our geographies have mountains and rivers and landmarks; our civilizations have capitals and governing offices and schools marked on maps; our businesses have buildings with addresses on named streets.

Place is not given, but made. People make place for various reasons:

of belonging; of politics; of power and control; of meaning. But people move, thoughts progress, goods flow: we live in a world of refined movement. In studying war, and especially in studying the shadows, I direct my research not at a set place, but at fluid targets. The shadows as I define them in this book are, at core, about movement, not merely place. They comprise, in Augé's words, non-places. This is part of the way in which they are rendered invisible. It is place that is given meaning and substance, it is locale that is populated, it is site that is "seen."

> We can say of these universes, which are themselves broadly fictional, that they are essentially universes of recognition. The property of symbolic universes is that they constitute a means of recognition rather than knowledge, for those who have inherited them: closed universes where everything is a sign; collections of codes to which only some hold the key but whose existence everyone accepts; totalities which are partially fictional but effective; cosmologies one might think had been invented for the benefit of ethnologists.[12]

The recognition of place often hinges on the non-recognition of non-place.[13] Non-place is the *elsewhere* that is populated by shadowy figures in dark coats: the realms constructed in popular thought as the province of misery and danger . . . the homeless, the criminal, the illicit, the marginal. Battlefields are immortalized as short-term places/non-places, idealized as distinct from everyday life and the "safe" world. The illicit is banished to realms outside of known place, outside of locales on a map or sites we can survey.

Of use here is Stanley Cohen's studies on "states of denial," where he seeks to understand how people and states can elect to "not-know" about atrocities, suffering, and dangerous politics. Of course, Cohen writes, there are systems of denial that operate on both the personal and the official levels when governments seek to sustain the massive resources of the state. But in addition, there are systems of cultural denial, which are "neither wholly private nor officially organized by the state. Whole societies may slip into collective modes of denial not dependent on a fully-fledged Stalinist or Orwellian form of thought control. Without being told what to think about (or not to think about) and without being punished for 'knowing' the wrong things, societies arrive at unwritten agreements about what can be publicly remembered and acknowledged."[14]

Like Augé, Cohen draws a distinction between knowledge and acknowledgment. People can "know and not-know" simultaneously. Information can be available — stories of wartime atrocities, suffering, and the impact of extra-state markets in our lives all circulate in modern media, myth, and conversation — but people may not fully acknowledge or act on them. Profound complexities mark this process: Cohen documents how Jewish people in World War II avoided "recognizing" the mortal danger they were in even though the facts of genocide were visible; they thus failed to escape to safety. Denial, then, isn't a simple process of disaffirming the problems of "others," but may well include denying those that threaten our own lives. Cohen discusses Primo Levi's explorations of why German Jews failed to see the dangers they were in despite so many warning signals, quoting the old German adage *Things whose existence is not morally possible cannot exist.*[15]

Linked with these beliefs that the morally dangerous or reprehensible should be — and therefore is — impossible is a concept Cohen calls denial magic: "The violation is prohibited by the government, so it could not have happened."[16] It links with denials that blame the victim for being politically partial, blame the reporter for being biased, and blame witnesses for having an agenda. "Magical realism" thus emerges as "a method to 'prove' that an allegation could not possibly be correct because the action is illegal."[17]

De Certeau's invisible cities are of course clearly, and visibly, situated in the midst of our everyday lives: deals made in coffee shops for both noble and ignoble ends; goods both legal and illegal moving innocuously down city streets; warehouses and stores doing layers of business along the un/regulated spectrum; illicit monies laundered through respectable practices.

In their 1994 book *Invisible Governance,* David Hecht and Maliqalim Simone describe the overlap between legality, illegality, and magic in a world where "place" is an especially shadowy notion:

> Although the bulk of this border economy is illegal, it is policed sporadically. . . . The murkiness and uncertainty of the border provides a text for magicians to decipher — is it a propitious time to buy, and if so, what items?
>
> Due to the important role these magicians play in the border economy, many people come to see them even though they have no intention of buying anything or going anywhere. Both sides of the border are often crowded with people who briefly step out of one nation with no intention of entering any other. People come to settle disputes, seek cures for fevers, put curses on villages, or regain lost virginity. With the acquired wealth, magicians frequently become traders, and many traders become magicians.
>
> Magicians foster disparate allegiances among the border police, often leaving national designations irrelevant. The resulting disarray is the only protection available to both buyer and seller. . . . Although both governments repeatedly try to

bring order and normalcy to the border, they find it difficult to change a situation where everyone can win some of the time.[18]

The state and the extra-state, the legal and the illicit, the violent and the peaceful intertwine along the streets and the cafes, the offices and the shops, the politics and the profits shaping the world as it unfolds into the third millennium.

PART TWO

WAR

Sun-tzu, the famous Chinese military expert, began his book *The Art of War* with the words "Warfare is the greatest affair of state, the basis of life and death, the Way (Tao) to survival or extinction. It must be thoroughly pondered and analyzed." Centuries later, we have come little closer to understanding why humans will or will not point a weapon at another and pull the trigger in the pursuit of politics.

In the twentieth century alone, over 250 formally declared wars took over 100 million lives. Undeclared wars — political repression, communal violence, and tribal genocide — took millions more; for example, between 50 and 100 million tribal people have been killed by forces and citizens of states in the last century. As we enter the third millennium, one-third of the world's countries are engaged in some form of political violence. In addition, approximately two-thirds of the world's security forces routinely violate human rights. Wars today are longer in duration, deadlier, and kill higher percentages of civilians than wars of preceding centuries.

Yet such numbers tell us little about how war is lived, felt, and died. What words carry a soldier into battle; sustain a fourteen-year-old bearing an assault rifle; evaporate as a mother falls dead at the front; are cried by her family in watching her die? War is defined differently by the winners and the losers; by historical perspective; by soldiers and pacifists — and in each case the definitions are more politically charged than factually correct. War is felt differently by those doing the killing, those being attacked, and those observing. The five-year-old, the adult schoolteacher, the soldier: all see a unique war unfold as they watch a gun fire and wait for the bullet to hit.

If we are to follow Sun-tzu in the pursuit of knowing war, we must pursue it to the front lines, where survival and extinction are inescapable truths.

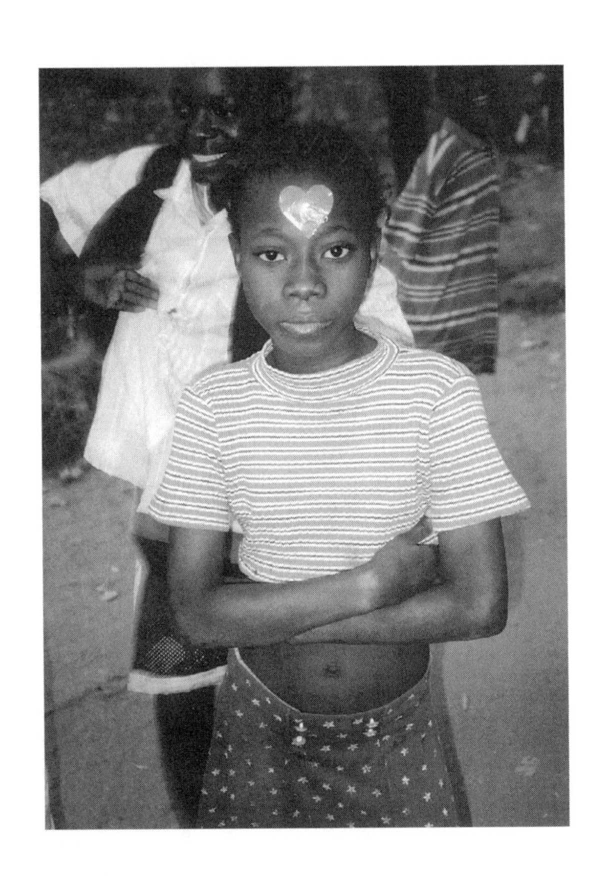

"REMEMBER TO HAVE SOME HEART," SHE SAID, REFERRING TO THE IMPACT OF THE WAR. ANGOLAN GIRL IN HOMELESS CAMP.

CHAPTER 4

FINDING THE FRONT LINES

> The "real" business of politics is taking place where analysts are often not looking.[1]

> There are essentially two types of armed conflicts in contemporary Africa: the political and the criminal. They are in effect nothing but the continuation by other means of the violence of everyday life.[2]

I made my first trip to Mozambique in 1988. The country was embroiled in a war that had taken nearly a million lives, most of them civilians. I can't say what images of war I thought I would first encounter, but I can say that my first encounter with violence wasn't at all what I expected. I flew into Maputo, the capital, from Harare, and checked into my hotel after evening had fallen. Settling into my room, I heard pounding at what I thought was my door. The hotel had hallways that led to short corridors with doors to two rooms side by side, and a shared bathroom. I opened my door and saw that a man was knocking on the door next to mine. He turned to me abruptly and told me to go back inside my room and shut my door. I did. A bit later I went out to wash up in the shared bathroom. I found a man lying in the bathtub, bleeding and clutching the remains of the shower curtain. Kneeling next to him, I saw he had been stabbed a number of times. I told him to hold on, that I would go find medical help. I went down to the front desk and told them there was a man in my bathtub who urgently needed medical help. When I returned to my room, he was gone.

At breakfast the next morning I asked the hotel staff who the man was who had been stabbed the night before and how he was. They looked at me blankly and said, "No one has been stabbed here." I replied that I had seen the man, that in fact I had found him in my bathtub.

They responded with the same closed expressions: "Really, no one was stabbed here." I rephrased my question: "OK, no one was stabbed here last night. But *if* someone had been stabbed here, who would they have been and how are they?" "Ahh!" The men relaxed and smiled, "That guy would have been the Angolan. Another Angolan came through and carried out their war here, the one guy stabbed the other — different sides of politics, you know. The guy, we don't know how he is, he disappeared, maybe he ran off, scared; or maybe he was carted off — he just disappeared."

In the middle of the war in Mozambique, the war in Angola intrudes. It intrudes not on some distant battlefield, not in the bush savanna, not on streets cordoned off, but in a hotel room, and in my bathtub. And each act of violence, even if it involves Angolans, affects the war in Mozambique, with reverberations that can travel across borders and political causes as easy as sound waves do. I was left wondering: where, exactly, are the battlefields, and who are the players in any war?

I was tempted to subtitle this chapter "Looking for War in All the Wrong Places." Before beginning a study of war, a researcher must decide where to look for it. In much of academe, I have been encouraged to find war in libraries amid tomes of second- and third-hand accounts of "politics by other means." These tomes themselves (mis)locate war in a powerful way. Military science locates it in the acts of rational soldiering and political science locates it in the acts of mostly rational political elites — and both do it in a largely irrational world. If there is even an iota of truth in Alfred Vagts's claim that military history is consistently written with "polemic purpose for the justification of individuals or armies and with small regard for socially relevant facts,"[3] then an analysis restricted solely to the institutions of war and politics will not provide a comprehensive understanding of the realities of war and peace.

Of course even an institution-based analysis of political violence raises the question: which institutions, which leaders and supporters, whose ideas and policies? The men and women in the military I have met who are dedicated professionals seeking to protect their homelands from violence? The troops who are engaged in drug running, weapons black marketeering, even cattle poaching? The soldiers who are torturers, who burn entire villages, who drink themselves into oblivion after raping women in front of their children? The child soldiers carrying guns bigger than they are? The kindly veterans who set up orphanages for war orphans? The troops who secretly warn villagers that an attack against them is pending so they can flee to safety? The generals who grow rich on war while others go broke? Those who go insane, or those looking for a brighter dawn?

While military power is instrumental in crafting national security ideology and action, a caveat attaches to this. The idea circulates in popular culture that interviewing political and military representatives in their offices (that is, away from the front lines) represents an accurate portrayal of the events taking place. There is often an implicit assumption that military and political leaders may not admit to certain forms of warfare taking place under their jurisdiction, but that they do know of it. This may be crediting people with more knowledge than they in fact have. Few people pass easily between the borders of power politics and front-line realities. Most grunt soldiers and civilians do not have free access to the corridors of power; if they do, many are loath to talk openly of battlefront truths that give lie to the carefully crafted belief systems about "the war" that circulate in society. And at the higher levels, people begin to believe their own propaganda.

The Mozambican photojournalist Joel Chiziane brought this fact home to me. In 1988, Maputo, the capital city of Mozambique, was largely devoid of consumer goods and public services; but there was an exhibit open to the public. It contained Chiziane's photos documenting the war in his country. The photos were riveting.[4] What struck me the most was how Chiziane had humanized the face of war. It had something to do with the way he captured eyes, and the human spirit:

— A hungry child sitting on the dirt floor of a mud hut war-emptied of all possessions except for an empty cooking pot over an unlit fire. The child has found a single grain of rice, and as he picks it up to eat, he stops and looks up at the camera, his eyes reflecting his knowledge of the depths of suffering and the size of hope that can fit into a grain of rice.

— A refugee mother who has set up a "home" under a parked train car between the tracks trying to coax a fire to warm her two young children while reaching out to caress her youngest, who has burst into tears. In mid-gesture, she looks up to give Joel a poignant smile; a mother, somehow any mother, who continues to cherish the idea of family love and a better day in the midst of a bad one.

— Burned-out cars reduced to pieces of twisted metal lining what was once a major national highway, now unsettlingly devoid of life and movement, like a scene from a post-apocalypse movie.

— A young girl lying on a hospital cot who has been burned over her entire body in the last attack on her village looking at the camera with the eyes of an adult and the humanity of childhood.

— A man gunned down in the doorway of a train car: all the photo shows is the view of the entrance taken from outside that shows the dead man's foot in the doorway as he collapsed back into the train, and his briefcase fallen open at his feet — the personalized generic death — any one of us.

— A soldier walking down the road with his assault rifle over his shoulder and his cooking pot dangling from it, who somehow reminds you of your brother or your neighbor.

Chiziane didn't glorify war; he didn't preach against it: he simply showed the realities of war on the front lines in a way that no one could dismiss or propagandize. He showed not generic images of casualties or perpetrators, but living, breathing people and the tragedies of death. It was a powerful indictment of war. I asked Chiziane how he had come to do this show. He was one of a handful of journalists who traveled out to the front lines at considerable risk, for this was at a time the rebel forces were targeting professionals, especially those exposing the war's severe human rights abuses. He replied: "The government and the people here in the capital don't really know what the war is like for the people in this country. They need to see it, to understand what it is really like out there, before they can broker a real peace accord. This is the best way I know to bring the truth of war home to them."

Chiziane challenges us to question what is taken to be the objective work of war: Where, exactly, do we get our statistics on war-related policies and casualties? On human rights and their violations? No researcher I know walks battlefield after battlefield counting casualties. No grunt soldier I know who does walk on battlefields walks through firefights, napalmed towns, and military prisons documenting casualties, or has the power to oversee what officers do with the reports he or she turns in. Political and military leaders do not want to advertise their own vulnerabilities in battle or the ways they ignore the Geneva Convention.

One of Chiziane's pictures portrays a woman in a tattered wrap standing in a recently dug hole several meters deep, trying to scoop up a bit of water collected at the bottom. This makeshift well commands the center of the image, and reaching out into the horizon in all directions from the well is a parched and barren landscape, broken only in isolated places by single shriveled stalks of corn, unable to bear food.

Wars don't occur in isolation from other tragedies of human existence. Indeed, they often provoke them. Under normal circumstances, the impact of a drought can be lethal to humans and livestock alike. But in war, resources are often channeled away from civilian support and into the war effort. In Mozambique, untold numbers of people perished from the drought, deaths that might well have been prevented in peacetime with adequately functioning infrastructure and resources. Deaths were further provoked by "the other side" disrupting emergency aid supplies to the drought victims — a military tactic to undermine "the enemy's" ability to support its own population. Drought deaths/war deaths — the dividing lines are indistinct and politically blurred. Where do these people, Chiziane would like us to ask, fit into the larger picture of war's impact and its reporting? These people, he fears, are left uncounted — their lives unrecorded, their deaths invisible in formal reckoning.

Many, perhaps even most, of the war-related casualties I have seen will never be recorded as such. Yet all represent the nucleus of war. The day after I first met Joel Chiziane, I had an experience that widened these considerations. I had met a group of people working in the Ministry of Tourism — a ministry that had little work during the war. They declared that since I was the closest thing to a tourist they had seen in years, I should accompany them on a multi-day trip to inspect a crumbling and largely unoccupied "tourist resort" on an island. About eight of us made the trip. At lunch, we were eating alone in a cavernous empty restaurant built to feed hundreds. A man who I had never seen before and who wasn't traveling with us came up during the meal, leaned over a woman in our group, and whispered something in her ear. There was a strange combination of friendly camaraderie and menace in his behavior, and Gella, the woman, seemed to shrink into herself, terrified. He briefly showed a knife, and I heard him say, "I can cut you, I can do the same to you." What was perhaps most disconcerting was that in complete contrast to his words, he leaned over her as a friend would when talking to a good acquaintance. He smiled and clapped her on the back, she turned gray, and he sauntered off. Everyone gathered around Gella to support her; everyone except me clearly knew what was going on. As she calmed down, one of the men looked at her, she gave him a nod of approval, and he began to explain:

> That man killed Gella's brother recently. He killed him with a knife and threw his body in the street. He threatens Gella now, perhaps to keep her quiet, perhaps just to show his power, perhaps because he moves in a world of violence.
>
> He is not a soldier, but he is not really not a soldier either. He's not in government, but in a way he is. You see, while he isn't in uniform—maybe he once was, or maybe he still is, it really doesn't matter—the point is, he has strong friends and contacts in the military, and they back him. He really doesn't hold a government job, but he has very strong alliances there too. He does "business" here. People in the government, in the military, they benefit from his work, his "business" associates, his ability to get things done. He's one of those people who has access to both daytime hallways and nighttime paths. He's a petty thug, he works the war.
>
> Gella's brother knew him, they were friends. He's dead now maybe because of this man's jealousy over Gella's brother, maybe because of some business gone bad, maybe because Gella's brother found himself on the wrong side of a political argument, or the wrong side of a military line, maybe all of this.
>
> The worst thing is, Gella can't get away from him. Every time she sees him her brother's death and her own fear become like a raw wound. Gella's war.

For this group the death of Gella's brother, and the threat to Gella herself, all existed within the framework of war. It was war that made such deaths and threats possible, and if the threat wore a uniform or medal of office, it mattered little to the victims. Such deaths as these are the uncharted casualties of war.

At the time Gella was threatened I thought the island was largely deserted; it had always been presented to me that way. I couldn't figure out how the knife-wielding killer came to be on the island at all. That night, when I took a walk along a "deserted" island path and inadvertently ran into a refugee camp arms bazaar, I discovered yet another example of the "strategically unmentioned" in war: the island was home to thousands of refugees, soldiers — or what seemed more like quasi-soldiers — bootleggers, smugglers, various quasi-military factions linked with quasi-business racketeers, and a host of other survivors washed up on the shores of war. Gunfire erupted throughout the night on the island, and we heard about the casualties the next day. No one in the group found this unusual. They had long since figured out the answer to the question as to where the front lines are — the next day, the man who had explained Gella's story continued:

> They extend out, from Gella and her brother, from the pain in her family, out to the military, and all the troops, militias, renegade bands of troops and armed troop bandits, out across the political fighting, and all the foreigners

who come in supplying and fighting the war, out across the "business" of war with its thugs and big leaders, out across the deals cut with different countries, out across the killing and chaos and right back inescapably into our homes and lives.

ZENO'S PARADOX: HOME FRONT AND BACK

> I wish I could write something about the way the full moon rises, yellow, over the high buildings; how it glides up silently from behind the forlorn office blocks, but I can't.
>
> Instead I feel the hot breath of war puff into my face and make my eyes sting with the ash of burning villages; ash from the burning of thatched roofs; ash from the torched corn stores. War has crept in on its belly through the long grasses of the dry season and crossed the dry riverbeds to come close, close to me here in the city where bush war should not reach. War wants me to see that it is more powerful that anything good, that it cannot be held at bay by non-war. Non-war is just a butterfly or soft petals. Strong wind or beating sun shrivels it.
>
> But war, war howls with the taka-taka-taka of machine-gun fire tearing up the edges where sunset meets night; tearing up the curtain behind which life is supposed to be safe. It is the numberless refugees marching down like a column of ants to reach Skyline and safety. It is Bernard's untold nightmare. It is the terrible stories unfolding next to a steaming enamel teapot and baked maize bread in Princess's flat.[5]

When researchers conduct studies of war in its midst, where, exactly, is that? Is war situated with the power brokers and the state; or alternatively, with multinational hegemonies and global politico-economics? With the front-line actors of all kinds, from troops to transnational actors? The maimed bodies of the persecuted, whether in torture chambers or barren backstreets? The militarization of the mind and the suffering of the spirit? The profound creativity average people employ in surviving war and forging peace? Do we consider the actions of the arms shippers who craft transit paths designed to avoid sanctions; the beliefs of skinhead mercenaries from Germany and Serbia found on the battlefields of Sudan and Rwanda? Do we follow the plight of war orphans forced into illegal underage labor by international war profiteers? Do we investigate generals' private lives to see if they maintain profitable connections to arms manufacturers, secretly authorize torture, or engage in racist or misogynist violence? Do we study the efforts to stop bloodshed that civilians with no political voice have instituted on the front lines? And, if so, how do we find these people and gain access to their stories? How do we give them human depth and empirical relevance at one and the same time? How do we ourselves stay safe in the process of doing front-line research?

Even if we begin situating the "Where is war?" question with the stereotypical (male) soldier, the realities of such a person's life carry the definition of war to greater complexities. This is guaranteed to play havoc with traditional military science and conflict resolution. For example, if a soldier fights in a battle, that is definitely war. But if a soldier goes home and interacts with family and friends, business partners and enemies, this must also be recognized as constituting part of war's reality. If he loots civilian goods because he has a gun, or donates books and help to war orphans, it is part of the war. If he sells pilfered weapons for money, if his brother-in-law sells drugs for arms, or if his wife is kidnapped and tortured by another army, this is part of the war. If his sister's ex-husband's cousin, a seamstress, lives in a town a thousand kilometers away that is bombed, that is part of the war story, as are all the stories of the civilians maimed and killed in the attack, the pilots who flew the bombing run, the industries that supplied the planes and the fuel and the maps, the commanders who chose this town to bomb, the propagandists who hid the number of civilian casualties, the refugees who escape, and even the anthropologists who document these realities. If that town is bombed because it holds profitable resources worth millions, perhaps billions, of dollars of profits, that too is part of the war story.

Looking for a line that distinguishes war from not-war is like seeking the line that divides zero from one in Zeno's paradox.[6] As John Keane notes:

> For citizens living in the so-called democratic zone of peace, alas, the world is not so neatly subdivided into peaceful and violent zones. Nor can it become so, thanks in part to the links between the two worlds forged by global arms production and the violence-ridden drug trades. Mass migrations, pauperization and prejudice also ensure that rootlessness, ethnic tensions, and violent lawlessness are features of nearly every city of the developed democratic world.[7]

Looking for such lines of war and peace, of barbarity and civilization, is as much a battle over ethical claims as it is a pretext to theory, a fact Valentine Daniel grapples with in his writings on the violence in Sri Lanka:

> I have called this an anthropography of violence rather than an ethnography of violence because to have called it the latter would have been to parochialize vio-

> lence, to attribute and limit violence to a particular people and place. Granted, the events described and discussed in the body of this work pertain to a particular people: Sri Lankans, Sinhalas, and Tamils. But to see the ultimate significant effects of this work as ethnographic would exculpate other peoples in other places whose participation in collective violence is of the same sort; even more dangerously, it could tranquilize those of us who live self-congratulatory lives in times and countries apparently free of the kind of violence than has seized Sri Lanka recently, could lull us into believing that we or our country or our people were above such brutalities.[8]

Daniel's words call to mind a conversation I had with a Mozambican at the end of the war in his country. He was explaining why many Mozambicans thought state-led truth and reconciliation commissions (which they subsequently declined to hold) raised thorny issues:

> So who all do we try? How far along the chain of associations that made war possible and atrocities a reality do we go? To the military soldiers? Of course. But also to the leading commanders? To the politicians who forged war policy? To Chissano, our president? To the military and political leaders in other countries who lent aid, advice, weapons, and manpower to the war? All the way to George Bush and Bill Clinton, your presidents? Where does the chain of responsibility end?

Where then, do we locate the study of war? The military, yes — but which aspect of it? Civilians, yes — but who? The businesspeople who burn out a competitor and blame it on the rebels, and the criminals who ply their trade across peace and war, are as likely to assist the military or their fellow citizens as to exploit them, depending on the "fortunes" of war. The traders who black-market in arms, food, medicines? And how far do we follow these traders? Do we follow the chain of procurements all the way to the cosmopolitan centers, continents away, that host munitions plants? Do we ultimately interview the CEOs of these industries? The transporters who bridge the borders between legal, gray, and black-market transfers? The professional consultants who actually make a business of telling people how to smuggle illicit goods? The weapons scientists who fashion these instruments, and the public/governmental debates about the legality and morality of using these weapons? Or, as Cynthia Enloe asks, in the can of Campbell's "Star Wars" soup, with its little patriotic missile defense weapons made of noodles?[9]

The answer to all this should be yes, and more.

DAILY REALITIES OF VIOLENCE: TANK IN RIVER AT THE FRONT. OUTSIDE CAMACOPA, ANGOLA, NOVEMBER 2001.

CHAPTER 5

VIOLENCE

> Among the paradoxes of this long century of violence is the paucity of reflections within contemporary political theory, including democratic theory, on the causes, effects and ethico-political implications of violence. . . . While there are certainly plenty of case studies of wars, civil wars and other violent conflicts, political reflection has lagged far behind empirical events. Of course, the sheer quantity of violence heaped by the twentieth century upon itself is enough to make even the most cheerful philosopher pessimistic, and since "optimists write badly" (Valéry) and pessimists tend not to write, the silence of those parts of the political theory profession which have been shocked by this century's cruelty is understandable. Elsewhere in the profession, the silence is simply inexcusable, for it is as if professional political theory is incapable of learning to think in pain or even that it has forgotten the experience of pain, that it has succeeded in doing what people normally cannot bring themselves to do: to overcome the animal pity that grips those who witness or hear about the physical suffering of others.[1]

In 1990, at the height of the war in Mozambique, I visited a town in the middle of the country. It was remote, but of strategic importance: the area contained not only the rich farmlands of a strong and independent group of Mozambicans, but also gem mines. The war had rolled over the area a number of times, and a sea of tiny hastily constructed mud huts housing the bombed out and the displaced spread from the unoccupied center of town. The center, which been reduced to ruins, apparently had been home and staging-ground to each set of occupying troops. The barren walls poking up from the bombed-out buildings were all covered in charcoal graffiti that told the story of war from the young bush soldier's perspective. There were pictures of battle plans; of helicopters strafing villages and villagers; of soldiers proudly holding the latest in automatic weapons. There were pictures of the human tragedies of war: soldiers raping women and grandmothers carrying the wounded on their backs. [2]

Perhaps figures etched onto broken walls in some distant Mozambican town don't fully convey the complexities of the inter/national and extra/state powers that define war. Looking into the reason why this town was so heavily targeted may tell us more. The paths that led out of the town center passed graveyards of heavy equipment bomb-twisted into useless scrap. Mining equipment. The pictures and the stories of the displaced contained numerous references to foreigners who passed through to collect large quantities of precious gems. When one military's control of the region was threatened, they sought to destroy the conquering side's ability to mine the region. And when they lost control, they sought to regain it. This remote spot had seen one side and then another take, lose, and retake the area in ongoing cycles, always hosting an international cast of actors. No locals were ignorant of the vast networks that kept the war afloat and the profits that accrued to this.

. . .

They arrive without money but with stories written on the parchment of their hearts which they don't recite easily. They are stories which have crept out of the edges of civil wars and scattered into the fleeing wind. You can read the words in their eyes, stained by despair; in their mouths, silenced and tightened by horror. You can even read the words in their torn and weary clothes.[3]

It isn't a simple task to figure out how to write about the front lines. Each story is woven in unending layers of obligations. Obligations to protect those who have given us their confidences, obligations to readers not to shock and betray, obligations to ourselves to stay safe, obligations to tell the story without telling so much we'll cause trouble. And the conundrum remains: how do we write an honest war story? One of my favorite answers comes from the American Vietnam veteran Tim O'Brien:

In many cases a true war story cannot be believed. If you believe it, be skeptical. Often the crazy stuff is true and the normal stuff isn't, because the normal stuff is necessary to make you believe the truly incredible craziness. In other cases you can't even tell a true war story. Sometimes it is just beyond telling.[4]

And O'Brien concludes:

> And in the end, of course, a true war story is never about war. It's about sunlight. It's about the special way that dawn spreads out on a river when you know you must cross the river and march into the mountains and do things you are afraid to do. It's about love and memory. It's about sorrow. It's about sisters who never write back and people who never listen.[5]

Those ideas are closely echoed by O'Brien's erstwhile enemy, North Vietnamese soldier-turned-author Bao Ninh. In *The Sorrow of War,* Bao Ninh describes his alter ego, Kien:

> Every evening, before sitting at his desk and opening his manuscript, he tries to generate the appropriate atmosphere, the right feelings. He tries to separate each problem, the problem of paragraphs and pages. . . . He plans sequences in his mind. What his heroes will do and what they will say in particular circumstances . . .
>
> But the act of writing blurs his neat designs, finally washing them away altogether, or blurs them so the lines become intermixed and sequences lose their order.
>
> Upon rereading the manuscript he is astounded, then terrified, to read that his hero from a previous page has, on this page, disintegrated. Worse, that his heroes are inconsistent and contradictory, and make him uneasy . . .
>
> He dares not abandon himself to emotions, yet in each chapter Kien writes of the war in a deeply personal way. . . . Kien refights all his battles, relives the times where his life was bitter, lonely, surreal, and full of obstacles and horrendous mistakes. There is a force at work in him that he cannot resist, as though it opposes every orthodox attitude taught him and it is now his task to expose the realities of war and to tear aside conventional images.
>
> It is a dangerous spin he is in, flying off at a tangent, away from the traditional descriptive writing styles, where everything is orderly. Kien's heroes are not the usual predictable, stiff figures but real people whose lives take diverse and unexpected directions.[6]

Most people think that violence simply "is" — enduring, unchanging, eternal. We talk about different wars, we don't speak of different violences. We distinguish between the Russian and American revolutions, but we don't talk of Russian and American violences. We differentiate the Thirty Years' War and World War II, but we don't differentiate the experience of violence in the seventeenth century and the twentieth century. Violence is categorized along a continuum: from necessary to extreme, from civilized to inhumane — but in each manifestation, it is recognized as sharing the same fundamental character.

But does it?

There was a time when people used to study war, up front and close. Journalists, poets, and researchers used to go to the front lines of wars like the American Civil War to document the battles. They set up chairs and sat with paper and pen to record the volleys that were unleashed and the bodies that fell. This wasn't an act of life-threatening heroism: in these historical periods, battles were circumscribed. Or at least some were.

But the dynamic of war has changed. Today, only the foolhardy few go out to the front lines to record battles with pen and paper in hand. Camera crews give us glimpses of life and death at the front lines, and journalists, poets and researchers still try to capture some essence of political aggression, but these acts of observation are as circumscribed as war once was. War itself now spills across the landscapes and cityscapes of prosaic life. The image of the complete battle, separate from the civilian life around it, is antiquated, unreal.

The images that we carry about any given topic shape our approach to that topic. War is no different. And the images of war, so carefully handed down through the decades and centuries — outdated as they may be — still shape our theories. The words that spectators wrote as they sat in chairs at battles' edges may be lost to time, but their approach remains. What are these legacies?

First, the very place researchers choose for studying war is shaped by their notions of what constitutes, and does not constitute, political violence. The people who documented war from its sidelines, pen and paper in hand, went to the *sites* of military battles. They watched immediate and sometimes immense physical carnage. They were far less likely to trace all the circumstances that led each and every actor to converge on the battlefield; to follow these soldiers as they pursued their lives after the battle. They seldom passed the sites of physical fighting by to document less honorable activities — the profiteering among commanders, the lies and deceits among soldiers, the torture behind closed doors. They documented the heroic and tragic. Nor did they find the lives of the soldiers' wives, sisters, and daughters as interesting as the lives of the soldiers themselves. And even if they wanted to, in the act of observing alone, they could not document the hopes and fears, the complexities of emotions, that animated the soldiers.

Today, even though 90 percent of war's casualties across the world are civilians and battles rage across people's hometowns,[7] the practice of studying soldiers and the immediate carnage of battles continues. And this shapes our understanding of violence. There remains a tendency to see a soldier shooting at another soldier as constituting war's violence, while the shooting of a civilian, or the rape of a woman as a soldier returns to the barracks, is seen as peripheral — an accident, an anomaly. The civilian casualty and the rape are understood as different orders of violence situated along a continuum that demarcates both severity and im/morality.

It would seem as if a hierarchy of violence is invoked in war, with harm against soldiers and the actions of those in uniform seen as greater acts of war than harm against civilians.

But there are aspects of these centuries-old models of war that are more difficult to challenge. Actions such as violating civilians' human rights in torture, looting, or rape still constitute the realm of immediate and physical carnage. This is the same genre of violence "witnessed" by the spectators of bygone centuries. Their academic gaze rested on the letting of blood and the dismemberment of the human body, and its relationship to political conquest among contending political parties.

Certainly, war at its most basic entails pain, dismemberment, death, and the politics of force. But people don't engage in or avoid war because of the sheer *fact* of death, dismemberment, and the politics of force. The mere *fact* of death is largely meaningless in and of itself. It takes on meaning because of its emotional content. We *feel* death as meaningful.

> "If I were to ask you what the single most important thing to know is to best understand this country, what would you say?" I asked Mia, a nurse in Kuito, Angola, in November 2001.
>
> "You need to understand death," she said. "Everyone here is on intimate terms with death, everyone has lost someone they love to the war—death walks everywhere with people."

People don't kill soldiers and civilians in war to reduce population numbers; wars aren't won that way. Wars are lost and won because people fear death, because they have a horror of dismemberment, because they feel the burdens of oppression so strongly they are willing to risk life and limb. People don't fight or flee war because of the sheer fact of violence. They fight or flee war because of what violence "feels" like.

And how does violence feel? As we will see, it feels like existential crisis, like hopelessness, like the loss of the future. It feels like impossible contradictions of resistance within oppression, like the struggle of humanity within terror. Violence is about im/possibility, about the human condition and the meaning of survival. This is why wars are fought with bloodletting, why torture takes place, and why neither violence nor war is limited to the physical carnage of the battlefield.

The researchers who sat at the sides of battlefields taking notes tended to see the end of the battle as the end of their observation. When the immediate carnage ceased, so too did war. But people on the front lines themselves tell a different story. Violence is set in motion with physical carnage, but it doesn't stop there. Violence reconfigures its victims and the social milieu that hosts them.[8] It isn't a passing phenomenon that momentarily challenges a stable system, leaving a scar but no lasting effects. Violence becomes a determining fact in shaping reality as people *will* know it, in the future. So while a study of violence may begin with direct and immediate carnage, it shouldn't end there.

If violence has enduring effects on the whole of a society, effects that will shape postwar as well as wartime life, then we must rethink the whole issue of who are winners and losers, and even what the terms *winners* and *losers* mean. We have long had the image in popular culture of military leaders presiding over a desolate pile of rubble — the kingdom they have decimated in order to wrest control of. This is perhaps nowhere as developed as in the case of nuclear war.

But there is another reality less easily captured in popular image or academic proof, and that is the leader presiding over a broken and maimed society, a decimated cultural stability, a tortured and traumatized daily reality. Researchers are still in scientific infancy in charting the progress of cultural trauma on the body politic. We are far from knowing if cultural wounds lead to ongoing cycles of social instability and violence.

One thing is certain: the most common definition of being human is being culture producing. Culture not merely in the sense of the products like systems of justice and the arts, but in the more profound sense of that which animates our life-world, and ourselves in it — the very knowledge by which we know ourselves and the world, and recognize both as meaningful. If our cultural foundations are undermined, what happens to our very sense of humanity?

What, then, is violence?

The rending of flesh with the intention to harm has become the foundational definition of violence. But this is misleading. As a person living on the front lines of a devastating war explained to me:

> I can't say it is the physical carnage that is the horrible thing about war, the worst thing about being subjected to violence. People see physical carnage all the time in life: we see accidents, accidents that can tear up the body horribly; we see illnesses and misfortune that leave bodies disfigured and broken. No, violence is something more than this, we fear what the war has made us become, we fear losing our humanity, we fear what people can become in war.

If someone is hurt in an accident, we don't tend to describe the accident as violence. Violence comes with intent, the willful decision to harm another. And if accidents that mangle the body don't involve political will, the purely physical act of harming another doesn't in itself constitute a struggle over political will. It is the intent, and thus the emotive context of the act, that defines violence and its relationship to political will.

Violence isn't intended to stop with the crippling of physical bodies. Violence is employed to create political acquiescence; it is intended to create terror, and thus political inertia; it is intended to create hierarchies of domination and submission based on the control of force. As Elaine Scarry writes, it "unmakes the world."[9]

An example of the social and emotive context of violence occurred just before I sat down to write these pages. I was walking back to my apartment in Angola before the war ended when a man came up to me and wanted to know if I could give him anything. He looked like a street person: shabby, unkempt, and psychologically scarred. I was surprised, however, when he spoke English to me, even though I had responded to him in the national language. As I listened to him speak English, I realized he spoke with a soft and formal correctness that didn't seem to fit with his street person appearance. During the conversation, I noticed that his hands were horrifically disfigured and deformed. At first I though it was leprosy. I realized, as I looked more closely at his hands, that it was not leprosy, but I was at a loss to explain the shape and location of fingers and knobs that almost defied the bounds of the normal human form. He noticed my questioning glance and said, simply, "I used to be with X" [naming one of the militaries]. Encouraged by my listening, he continued. "I used to stay in that hotel over there. It started in the hotel over there. They [the forces of the other side] tortured me. That's what happened to my hands."

I continued listening, and he stopped momentarily to look me in the eyes. I saw a clear mind there, as if it were peering out at me from shutters momentarily opened and ready to slam shut should the pain of reality became too severe. Torture creates such shutters. It seemed almost inconceivable how hands could be so deformed, or how someone could continue to walk and talk in life after undergoing such trauma. The man finished the story of his hands and shyly explained they tortured him all over, opening his shirt to show massive scars on his chest and then pulling his trousers up above his thigh to show extensive scars on his legs. We finished our conversation, I helped him purchase some food, and then I walked off.

As soon as I was out of the man's sight, out of the arena of hurting him with my reaction to his story, I felt the world turn on its axis, so to speak. For a moment, I couldn't conceive of living in the world with such horror perpetrated by humans, nor did I want to. This wasn't a fleeting feeling, it was profoundly existential — the world was simply too ugly to be in, and I felt it in the core of my being. Then, as I continued walking down the street, I felt that shadow of fear: *what if this happens to me, to people I know and love, to the place I call home?*

I knew this feeling, I have written on it extensively: it is the reason people employ violence—it is used to terrify populations into withdrawing from the world, or at least the political and military part of it, the part that effects power. I want to underscore that in the last sentence I chose the word *feeling*—for it is *not* the "logic" that torture is a possibility that shapes our actions. Logic tells me that I face a far greater chance of dying of malaria or a land mine than of torture. Logic tells me this man's story isn't my own. In many ways, logic is a protective garb in which we cloak ourselves. Torture and violence carry the impact they do because feeling weds with logic to produce the fear and the resistance seen on the front lines of harm anywhere. This was a stranger in a country not my own in a war affecting none of my own personal family, and violence could elicit this response from me. How much more would it affect this man's countrypeople, his acquaintances, his family? His torture is an enduring reality that lasts a lifetime and crosses vast social spaces. It is intended to stop people anywhere anytime from challenging the political and military authorities: if war were to break out in my country and in my lifetime, this man's ordeal would be in my political consciousness. The reality of his torture would challenge me to consider my own political involvement: what if this happens to me, to my loved ones? One unknown man's pain from another war, another time, and another continent survives to influence other people, other wars, other political outcomes.

Looking at the extent of this man's deformities, it is hard to conceive how harmful torture can be. And herein lies the crux of my point. As a medical anthropologist, I have worked in hospitals from America to Asia, and have seen bodies severely deformed by accidents, illness, and microbes. And in these cases I feel compassion, sympathy, and sadness that people have to suffer so. But I don't feel the world tilt on its axis. I don't want to escape from a world too ugly to contemplate living in. I don't suffer a crisis of existential proportions. It is the violence one individual willfully does to another that causes this powerful reaction. *This is the emotional content of violence.*

Though this chapter is concerned with the many manifestations of violence—physical violence being only one of many—it's important to recognize that physical violence itself carries complex sociopolitical messages. I have documented elsewhere the tactic in Mozambique of cutting off ears, noses, and lips, but, curiously, never blinding a person.[10] The message isn't subtle: "You will not hear what we don't want you to hear, you will not speak out against us, you will not have sense—but you must see this terror to know it." Of course, the attack against human senses is an attack against sense in the larger, intellectual, meaning. People with sense are political actors, and agency depends on sense-fullness. The senseless, torturers postulate (however incorrectly), are as domesticated as herd stock. This is an analogy I heard many times on the front lines: "They are trying to turn us into animals."

In Sierra Leone, troops cut off voters' hands and arms in attempting to impose an election boycott.[11] The political message is equally painfully obvious: the voters are "dis-armed." This is also true of the technological violence of land mines. Beyond the fact that civilians — especially children and women — are the most common casualties, many "anti-personnel" mines are constructed to blow off limbs, not kill people. Even in the bush, far from medical attention, many land-mine victims survive to crawl or hobble on crutches through the rest of their lives. Another common tactic is the mutilation of genitals, in part, as Suàrez-Orozco notes, to act as a symbolic assault on the *reproduction* of political resistance.[12]

Rape stands as a powerful example of physical assaults that are intended to carry deeper, supraphysical, impacts. I have listened to hundreds of accounts of rape, and few focus primarily on the physical pain. It is the emotional trauma, the social shame, and the violation of humanity that is conveyed most strongly in these accounts. What makes rape so grievous an act isn't just the assault against the body, but the attack against family, dignity, self-worth, and future. I have seen women suffer tremendously, even die, in difficult childbirths. I have seen devastating vaginal infections women have carried for months, even years, on front lines devoid of medicines. The physical pain involved in these is often as severe as that suffered in rape, and the grief over the deceased and the infirm as great as any war casualty. But these don't invoke the horror of rape and the intent that underlies such aggression.

Solutions to violence must address its myriad manifestations. Common wisdom has long recognized that psychological violence can be as devastating as physical violence. But the impact of violence extends beyond both the physical and psychological. I have found that people working directly with the victims of war tend to be fluent in the complexities of violence. In one example among many: I stopped by the UNICEF office in Angola one day to ask about their programs for war-afflicted and homeless children. Two Angolan women, Casimira Benge and Lidia Borba, head the Program for the Protection of Children (also labeled Children in Difficult Conditions). Shortly into the conversation, Casimira made the comment that there are many different kinds of violence. I asked her to explain. She and Lidia spoke without pause, each adding to the other's thoughts:

Well, obviously, the war is violence. It really is many violences. Physical aggressions, well, these are more obvious. But lack of assistance from the government is also a kind of violence, and this can be as important as physical aggression. Being sick or hurt or wounded and not having medical assistance is violence; as is not being able to get the vaccinations that will prevent common illnesses. To have to pay for your education is a kind of violence: these poor women in the barrios, they go to take their children for "free" education and are told they have to pay for this entrance exam and that text, for this thing and that service. Even to have to pay for your identity card is a kind of violence. You are stateless, you are completely vulnerable without your papers.

Violence, it goes on. Sexual exploitation is a kind of violence. Child labor. Street children. The war-dislocated and orphaned who have to go live with foster families, some no better than slaves.

And there is a kind of trauma with each of these kinds of violence. If a person is raped, it is violence, but it is not the only violence. This woman may live in a context where she has no water, no electricity, no food, no resources. She is raped and she has to return home to a place where she can't meet the minimum for talking care of herself. This is violence.

And you know, it is violence when society doesn't teach ways to live other than violence. When people live thinking violence is normal, well, this is one of the worst kinds of violence.

One might expect the war-afflicted to focus on the physical toll of violence, because this group more than any suffers wounding, maiming, torture, and murder. But their stories of violence plumb the depths of human experience. Their stories, whether from unschooled farmers or noted poets, are explorations of the philosophy of the human condition. Consider the words of author Bao Ninh:

Yet only a few of his heroes would live from the opening scenes through to the final pages, for he witnesses and then descried them trapped in murderous firefights, in fighting so horrible that everyone involved prays to heaven they'll never have to experience any such terror again. Where death lay in wait, then hunted and ambushed them. Dying and surviving were separated by a thin line; they were killed one at a time, or all together; they were killed instantly, or were wounded and bled to death in agony; they could live but suffer the nightmares of white blasts which destroyed their souls and stripped their personalities bare.[13]

Through his protagonist, Kien, Bao captures the thin line between survival and death, between war and peace, between today and tomorrow:

Seeing how sluggishly Kien ate, the driver sighed and says, "It's because you slept back there, with nearly fifty bodies [on military duty to collect slain soldiers]. You'll have had nightmares. Right?"

"Yes. Unbelievably horrible . . ."

"No doubt," the driver said, waving his hand in a wide arc. "This is the Jungle of Screaming Souls. It looks empty but in fact it's crowded. There are so many ghosts and devils all over this battleground! I've been driving for this corpse-collecting team since early '73 but still I can't get used to the passengers who come out of their graves to talk to me. Not a night goes by without them waking me to have a chat. It terrifies me. All kinds of ghosts, new soldiers, old soldiers, soldiers from Division 10, Division 2, soldiers from the provincial armed forces, the Mobile Forces 320, Corps 559, sometimes women, and every now and again, some southern souls, from Saigon." The driver spoke as if it were common knowledge.

"Met any old friends?" asked Kien.

"Sure! Even some from my own village. Blokes from my first unit. Once I met a cousin who died way back in '65."

"Do you speak to them?"

"Yes, but . . . well, differently. The way you speak in hell. There are no sounds, no words. It's hard to describe. It's like when you're dreaming — you know what I mean . . ."

"If we found a way to tell the news of a victory, would they be happier?" Kien asked.

"Come on! Even if we could, what would be the point? People in hell don't give a damn about wars. They don't remember killing. Killing is a career for the living, not the dead."[14]

Bao carries us into a world where violence disrupts the taken-for-granted; the timelines between yesterday and today, the immediate and the eternal. Time itself becomes a casualty of war, one that has serious repercussions. Bao captures a further truth of people's lives in battlezones that I have heard people speak of in every war I have worked in. That concerns the ability of violence to destroy the future.

Todo o angolano sente, no corpo e na alma, os efeitos directos e indirectos da guerra. Na verdade, a guerra mata, mutila, empobrece, destrói e avilta, transformando os angolanos em Homens sem amanhã.

(Every Angolan feels, in body and soul, the direct and indirect effects of war. In truth, war kills, mutilates, impoverishes, destroys and debases, transforming Angolans into Humans without tomorrow.)[15]

The present has meaning because it is embedded in a matrix of past realities and future possibilities. Our sense of self comes from memories (history) projected onto the (future) horizons of our lives. To choose one action (over another) is to choose a goal (over another); and that is to craft a future. Life takes meaning through these choices — through the directions chosen and the reasons for the choice; through linking the here-and-now and the imminent. We plant crops to harvest them, get pregnant to enrich our families, tell stories to pass on cultural wisdom, laugh to forge camaraderie. But in war, in the face of ongoing violence, the future itself becomes a casualty. Crops are destroyed, children killed, stories rendered meaningless, laughter silenced by grief and terror. Planting crops, making families, telling stories all give life its measure of certainty. War disrupts this certainty. And this lack of certainty disrupts a sense of future. Planting crops may not produce food, getting pregnant may not produce a family, stories may not produce useful wisdom. Violence changes the very sense of a meaningful outcome of life's plans. And it is in our sense of the future, people frequently told me, that our morals reside. In the words of an Angolan who had suffered the war firsthand:

> Do you think these soldiers would commit these atrocities if they had any sense of a tomorrow? No. The war works to kill this very notion of a tomorrow in soldiers. If they thought about the fact that one day the war would end, that they would have to face the families of the people they harmed—or worse, that they would have to face their consciences, account for their deeds, build lives in peacetime in the recognition of all they had done, would they do these things? No. But war, very precisely, kills their sense of the future. It is a kind of living death.
>
> And their victims? It is as bad, this death of the future. How can they run from war if war lies in every direction? Whatever choice they make they run into war, and then they take that responsibility on themselves: I made this decision that got my family killed, or harmed, or starved, or whatever. Nothing a person can plan has any meaning, for the war can come and take it all, obliterate the best plans and intentions. There is no future. The truth of it is that this very lack of future can kill.

The obliteration of the future affects not only the battlefield soldiers and civil society caught on the front lines but also the very organizations set up to bring humanitarian relief. In 1996 I visited a country (unnamed, as I discuss specific people and programs) suffering ongoing cycles of political violence. I was impressed by the vision of the head of the United Nations humanitarian wing. The policy of this country-wide effort was to rebuild society. As the person in charge said to me:

> If people have no confidence in a future, they will not work to create anything. We can't just feed the starving, we can't just sink wells, we have to work with people to improve their confidence that the war can end, that things can get better, that their acts can make a difference. If you merely provide infrastructure for a traumatized community, you have a community using structures in traumatized ways.

Two years and many re-eruptions of political violence later, I returned to find a disheartened United Nations humanitarian community. The work to rebuild society had given way to a focus on providing basic humanitarian relief. "Why?" I asked. "What happened?" The program director responded:

> Because it looks like everything we said was a lie. We said we would help, and no matter what we did, the political violence continued, the suffering continued. All this talk about constructing a culture of peace, it looks like a big scam, a big lie. I guess we've become disheartened ourselves, we've given up on believing we can change these things. People are habituated to thinking in terms of war; there are so few resources to change this. We believed, but it didn't work. We've gone back to basics.

It does little good to point out that two years is a short time to solve the problems put into place by decades of political hostilities, that a re-eruption of war doesn't mean that humanitarian plans have not worked, or that such goals were far from misguided lies. It does equally little to point out that maybe the original humanitarian vision is the only way to finally solve the horrors of the war, and that giving in to hopelessness and discouragement plays into war's very hands. The sense of a viable future had become a casualty of war for the humanitarian INGOs (international nongovernmental organizations) as certainly as it had for the civilians on the front lines the INGOs were working to help. As one of the UN staff summed up to me: "It's hard to make any plans when you don't know what the future will bring."

The death of hope is an equally traumatic war casualty. Unbearable circumstances become bearable only if there is some belief that they will come to an end. How do people bear up under the unendingly unbearable? How do people project themselves into a future that holds only more of a present defined by threat, deprivation, starvation, brutality, and violence? In the words of a man caught in an embattled zone:

> To hope for a military solution, and to have war cut across your life time and again, you begin to fear to hope for a solution, for each time war comes again, the pain of crushed hopes is devastating. You hope the violence will calm down a bit so you can have time to harvest your crops, so your children can eat; but after a momentary lull, a lull where you got your hopes up, the violence erupts again, and you can't harvest your crops, feed your children, stave off that sad and hungry look in their eyes.
>
> So you begin to fear hope, because it hurts so much. You begin to stop hoping. But this is a kind of death. People just give up, that's the giving up of hope. Some people just wither up, like walking dead.
>
> Aggression comes from a lack of hope too. People give up hoping and begin raging against it all—like the violence and the hopelessness is all there is, all there will be. People can't see a way out, and they become like it, fight-

ing against hoping as a kind of broken response to having your hopes ruined again and again.

Hopelessness also serves to cripple political will—making it militarily strategic. A population divested of hope is likely to be a politically acquiescent population—or so dirty-war theorists posit. The ramifications are extensive. The man continued:

> Someone without hope for a better future, will they plant their fields? Will they work to develop industry? Will they devote time to helping others, work to resolve conflicts, work to repair damaged towns, and build up their societies? Will they work to staff hospitals, build new schools, open new trade routes? No. All that depends on a sense that things can be better, that these actions will have some benefit in the future. People have to have confidence, a sense of hope, in their future. Without this, people don't build up something so it will be destroyed. So people stop working, and society stops progressing.

This man's words, and the larger recognition that violence undermines core foundations of a society, harken back to the point that while much of western theory is conversant in the physical ramifications of violence, we know far less about the wounding of culture, social dislocation, and the destruction of the very epistemological and ontological tools by which we construct our world and ourselves in it.

A final observation on violence concerns its ability to escalate and to insinuate itself into the fabric of everyday life. The idea that battlefields are self-contained zones of violence and that life proceeds normally outside these circumscribed areas is a powerful myth, but a myth nonetheless. From average people caught in life-threatening situations of war to theoreticians like Michael Taussig, we are cautioned about the ability of violence to reproduce itself.[16] Relatives of torture and murder victims don't necessarily become paralyzed by fear; they often join in the fight against those who have perpetrated these horrors on their loved ones, sometime reproducing the same violence against the families of those who harmed their relatives. I have witnessed this many times.

One evening in the mid-1980s in Sri Lanka, I was invited to have dinner with a family I knew. Several other people from the town were there as well. As we sat down to the meal, a man came in to join us. He was highly distraught. I had not met the man and did not know his circumstances; everyone else seemed to. Listening, I began to piece together that this man's family had just been massacred by "the other side." The murders were intended to both kill and horrify: the wife had been stabbed and then covered with a mattress that was set aflame, and her infant had been thrown on the burning mattress. The rest of the family in the house had met equally brutal deaths. As the story came out around the table, everyone became more and more agitated, an agitation that turned into a desire for revenge. At first, profoundly moved by what this man had suffered, I responded with sympathy, and was rebuffed by all the men. In the spirit of revenge, it seemed, people did not want to lose their anger to pain. Perhaps the pain was too great to bear at the moment, and the fury of revenge offered a more bearable response.

By the end of the meal, the anger had turned to action: the men at the table decided to leave immediately to exact revenge with the same kind of violence as had befallen the man's family. The men began drawing and inspecting weapons. As the only woman at the table, I assumed the role of noncombatant, and tried to raise the point that this action would set in motion further cycles of retaliation that might end in the deaths of more of these men's families. It had come out that the killing of this man's family was a revenge killing for a previous murder of a family on "the other side" by "this man's side." My words fell on deaf ears. The men, guns drawn, left to exact revenge. These events brought the contradictions of war home to me: I felt powerfully for the man who had lost his family to such violence, and I felt equally powerfully a horror that he was to do the same to another. I saw him simultaneously as deeply wronged and wrong. I saw clearly the onerous difficulties of stopping entrenched cultures of violent revenge. And I saw the ridiculousness of dirty-war strategies that assume terror-warfare will cow a population into acquiescence.

From this vantage point on violence, the entire concept of winners and losers takes on a new hue and tone. In some ways it becomes moot. Victor and victim alike stand not only on a charred battleground, but upon charred hopes and dreams. If "future" becomes a war casualty, it comes not of "losing" or "winning," but in the sheer fact of violence. Societies, as well as individuals, can become "dis-abled." Of course, as the following chapters will show, societies, through the individuals who comprise them, heal as well as crumble. But neither the impact nor the amelioration of violence will make sense if violence is configured only as a physical act. It is in the more intangible realms of the "existential" — the meaning of existence — that violence takes its definition and its toll. It is here that resolving violence must begin.

"TAKE MY PICTURE," HE COMMANDED, POINTING HIS GUN AT ME.
MALANGE, ANGOLA, 1999.

CHAPTER 6

POWER

It was a sprawling party in a town in southern Sri Lanka, the kind where everyone from the political and economic movers and shakers to starving artists looking for a decent meal congregated. The year was 1985, the war between the government and the Tamil separatist forces was full blown, and Amnesty International was preparing a report that would cite the Sri Lankan government as one of the worst human rights violators in the world. I was surprised when a high-ranking military officer attached himself to me; I hadn't cultivated relations with the state's forces, focusing instead on the daily life of war: the tortured, the fearful, the rebels, the refugees, the people caught in more cross-fires than seemed humanly possible. The commander talked banalities with me, but with an intensity and seriousness that belied something else. I couldn't shake him. He was nervous, full of energy — could we take a bit of a walk, he asked me? As we moved out of earshot of the partiers, he began to tell me about the war up north against the Tamils:

> It's crazy, it's completely crazy. I can't control my troops. It's awful up there. One of the soldiers [government, largely Sinhalese] is hit by a guerrilla [Tamil], or they run over a land mine, or a bomb explodes, and they go nuts. It's been building up and building up, and they just go wild. The guerrillas have long since melted away, and the soldiers turn their fury on the first available target. Of course, the only people around are civilians. They open fire on everyone, they destroy everything in sight, they rape and torture people they catch on the streets or in their homes, they lob bombs into homes and schools, markets and city streets. I've tried to stop them, I try to control the situation. I can't. None of us commanders can — though god knows some don't try. The troops just take off like this and there's no stopping them. We can't dis-

> cipline them. We can't prosecute them. We can't dismiss them—we'd have no army left if we did. The situation up north is completely out of control, and there isn't a damn thing we can do about it.

The commander wasn't looking for a response from me: this was delivered as a monologue, delivered with a specific purpose. I understood his words, but I was less clear on what his purpose was in telling me. It didn't seem appropriate to ask.

I have met any number of soldiers who were disingenuous and given to Machiavellian motives. This man appeared genuine in his words and preoccupations. At the time I thought that he really did want to stop the appalling human rights violations taking place in the Tamil regions. He explained that he knew every time his soldiers harmed innocent people they were creating new enemies, new battles down the road, new impossible antagonisms. Militarily, it was bad strategy. But there was something more. My take on it was that the man found maiming and killing the innocent offensive. Struggling to make sense of why he was telling me this — this definitely wasn't something openly talked about, quite the opposite — I remember wondering if he just needed to express himself, and for some reason a foreign woman provided a relatively safe outlet.

It was only later I thought his words might be connected to the fact that I had traveled by myself up to the north and seen the human rights violations firsthand. Maybe he anticipated or feared some question, or more likely some accusation, from me — from all of the people he thought were judging him — and needed to answer it. Maybe he thought the whole thing would blow up internationally with the release of the reports of atrocities, and he wanted to distance himself from responsibility for them. I was left with the impression that he just didn't want people to think he was like that, that he authorized this kind of warfare. But beyond all this, I began to realize, and to study, the ironies of power. Power, it would seem, isn't at all what we generally take it to be.

Writ large, the story of war is the story of power. Power, in its most basic terms, is the ability to exercise one's will over others. Of course, exercising one's will involves controlling the very definitions of power. For the most part, the privileged and the elites of the world control the means to disseminate the definitions of power; few peasants, cab drivers, or grunt soldiers craft legal policy, publish their definitions of power in academic presses, or write interviews for the general media. Steven Lukes's classic statement that power is essentially contested is now generally accepted.[1] But my research suggests it is far more contested than even Lukes acknowledges. In fact, if the distance between the institutions and the manifestations of power is as great as I will suggest in this chapter, Lukes's assertion that power is essentially contested takes on a fundamental internal irony.

Power isn't a monolithic construct. Like all human endeavor, it emerges from complex human relations: continuously challenged, subverted; negotiated and renegotiated over time, space, and interaction. Definitions do not come easily. Following the now-classic works of Michel Foucault and Antonio Gramsci, most scholars accept the theorem that power is decentered in and through society.[2] Simply said, no single or supreme font of power exists in the social or political world, and no single top-down power rules lives and politics. In this view, power is exercised not only through societies' formal institutions, but through communication and action, and the cultural knowledge that grounds them.[3] The dynamic nature of power is highlighted with Nietzsche's call to focus on the *performance,* and not merely the sponsorship, of power.[4] For Nietzsche, it wasn't the institution but the actor who was relevant, and no simple lines of authority align the two. In his words, "the doing is everything."[5]

Power comes in many guises and is expressed in a multitude of ways. Because power is reproduced not only in the institutional centers of power brokers but also in the many social and ideological relations that make up daily life for a population at large, the processes constituting power are full of competing and conflicting forces. Power, then, can't be accurately thought of as a fully rational process, nor can it be conceived of as an irrational one. For power is a cultural product — embedded in cultural convictions, sociopolitical relationships, and interpersonal actions propelling societies whether at war or at peace. These relations of power are in large part subjectively enacted and are at best only partially recognized.[6] Power relations become part and parcel of the taken-for-granted world.

What happens when these philosophies of power are uprooted from their academic homes and situated on the front lines?

I pondered the words of the military commander at the party in light of a visit to Jaffna I had made earlier that year. Though not sure who I was or why I had traveled to the Tamil north, the Tamil leaders of the main military forces wanted to show me what their life was like in the besieged Jaffna Peninsula and along the route to the town of Trincomalee in the east — I think to help counteract government-dominated media.

They told me at the time that in two years only one BBC correspondent and I had visited Jaffna, and that because of this, government reporting predominated in national and international presses. As we toured the environs of Jaffna, I remember inventing the word *rubble-ized* to describe a number of communities I saw where shelling and mortars had reduced everything, absolutely everything, to pieces of rubble no bigger than stones you could hold in your hand. Houses, schools, clinics, trees, bicycles, books, TVs — everything.

As we returned to the town center, a government army patrol unexpectedly opened fire at a bus stop; we saw a number of civilians wounded or killed. The people accompanying me wanted to follow the victims to the hospital to verify what had taken place. While it seems unusual that a stranger would be asked to go into a personal scene of tragedy and political tension, there are times when people want the truth of their stories told to the outside world. When no one but troops visit a warzone, atrocities are whitewashed, and suffering silenced. Veena Das writes about a war-impoverished man who offered to pay her to tell the truth about what happened in the riots against the Sikhs after the assassination of Indira Gandhi in India.[7] In this case, I spent the morning being shown the bodies of the dead, listening to the next of kin, and speaking with the wounded and their families. None were members of any military or political group. All were involved in distinctly nonpolitical activities at the time of the attack:

> My husband was at the bus stop waiting to ride to work this morning. He is a simple man, he works in a bakery. He has never fought with anyone, he has never taken up with politics. He was killed for trying to feed his family.

> My sister was waiting for the bus to take her to the market so she could get household supplies. She wanted to do a good cleaning of the house because we have a birthday to celebrate in the family, and she wanted to get a few nice things to eat. She had put on a nice sari today. She is like our grandmother that way: if you are going out you should look nice. She was just a kid, she was in her teens.

> My daughter was going across town to visit some family members. She had taken along some of the food she had made, knowing that it was one of the favorite dishes of her cousin. She wanted to help out a bit; she knew one of their children hadn't been feeling too well.

> My mom was waiting to come home after going to a market on the outskirts of town to get some food.

> My son was going to town.

and so on . . .

There was no discernible provocation.

The sole possible explanation I could uncover for this attack was that someone mentioned hearing a car backfire before the troops opened fire. Or perhaps, some suggested, it was a distorted notion of power.

The classic theorem of a direct link between the source and the implementation of power would have us believe that political leaders forge ideology to determine action, that military commanders forge strategy to carry out this political vision, and troops act to accomplish these ends. A neat but quixotic scenario. Analyses based on such heuristic constructs are divorced from the proclivities and the complexities of human action, social interaction, individual will, personal foibles, competitive vested interests, and the constantly negotiated tension between the intended and the wildly unexpected.

Once we put human actors into the power equation, we find that power is constantly being reformulated as it moves from command to action. Where, then, does the power of war lie? On the larger level, military commanders act according to national tactical and ideological paradigms, and according to the transnational politico-military and economic alliances supporting them. Battlegrounds are international, and notions of power are transported along manifold lines of alliance and aggression.[8] National need, necessity, history, and mythology join with internationally forged dogmas in the creation of any given military's ideology for action.

And what motivates the actions of ground soldiers? Personal ideas of violence, interpersonal loyalties and antipathies, individual gain, and responses (often spontaneous and unreasoned) to immediate threats more than generalized conceptions of political conviction. Military "tactics" thus become infused with the particular life histories and personalities of the soldiers themselves and the local sociocultural traditions in which they operate.

The logic of power is turned upside down. Perhaps my favorite example of this is the response of an underage soldier on a battlefield when I asked him why he was fighting. With a profound seriousness, he looked at me and replied: "I forgot."

All the political warmongering, the nationalism, the treaties and alliances, the military ideologies and training so carefully forged, all the saber rattling of the power elites don't make war. This young soldier who pulls the trigger — who enacts violence — makes war a reality. His power is predicated not on political rationale, not on fervent nationalistic belief, not on military dogma, nor even on a basic defense reaction to threat: "I forgot." What does this say about the logic of power? About the rationale of command? About war? I had the following discussion with a soldier I met on the front lines:

Soldier: I'm with the troops.

CN: Why? *[Meaning, did he join or was he conscripted?]*

Soldier: I wanted to come join up with them; I want to protect my people.

CN: Are you fighting with the others? *[A battle had recently taken place in the area.]*

Soldier: Yeah, the fighting's been going on all around us here, and I'm fighting too.

CN: *[I nodded at his gun, an eyebrow raised in question.]*

Soldier: *[Holding up his assault weapon]* I carry it all the time, it's mine.

CN: Where'd you get it?

Soldier: Commander gave it to me, told me to learn to shoot.

CN: Do you mind not having much in the way of clothing? *[The soldier was dressed in a tattered shirt and baggy shorts much too big for him.]*

Soldier: No, I'm a soldier, what do I need with fancy things? I'm here to fight for my people.

CN: Do you like the life of a soldier?

Soldier: No.

CN: You scared of the war?

Soldier: No. *[Said quietly and hesitantly, with large eyes that conveyed otherwise]*

CN: How old are you?

Soldier: Eleven.

If, in Clausewitzian terms, war is the extension of politics, can we speak of politics being extended through the arms of an eleven-year-old? The question isn't rhetorical: What, exactly, does this say about the nature of power? Of force? And of political participation? No state code in the world today recognizes a child as an adult political actor. So what politics are forged in the conveyance of war through nonpolitical actors, through underage soldiers? The United Nations estimates there are some 300,000 child soldiers under arms today.[9]

War is not a paragon of Camus's absurd, comprised of children and soldiers who fight long after the reason for doing so has escaped them.

But this is far more common than traditional political and military sciences and nationalistic philosophies recognize. The following quote expresses a fairly common sentiment, articulated in different words but with similar sentiments in many warzones of the world. The speaker and I were traveling in an area undergoing heavy fighting. We were both hitching a ride on an NGO pickup, sitting and talking in the back of the truck. He was saying:

> You want to know why people join in this war? Look around you. A guy is walking down the dusty road and a nice big car flashes by him, leaving him eating dust, and he thinks, "Why him and not me?" And he knows the answer is that the guy in the car is on the right side of politics—the side that controls the goods. He knows he is on the wrong side. No matter how smart he is, no matter what a good worker he is, no matter what his ambitions, he won't get where he wants to go. The other guy, the guy with connections to the politicos in power, not him, will get the job; the other guy, not him, will get the chance to go for advanced education; the other guy, not him, will get the good piece of land to farm. No matter how much he wants or deserves it, it won't be him that gets the scholarship to study abroad. And that reality stretches out in front of him to cover his whole life: there's no changing the politics of it. It won't be him riding in that car; he'll be walking the rest of his life. So he eats that other guy's dust and he thinks, "Why not join the opposition and fight, that's the only way I can improve my lot in life."

The complexities of power extend to another level. This level revolves around the inescapable fact that people occupy many roles in life. No soldier is only a soldier. He or she is entangled in scores of interpersonal relationships with other people, each with a set of norms and rules, demands and possibilities shaping action. A soldier is a family member, with parents, siblings, and children. A soldier has friends and enemies far from the scope of war as well as within it. A soldier has school and business partnerships, age group associations, drinking pals, and dangerous rivals.

All this plays out on the front lines of wars. The front lines are a veritable cornucopia of human endeavor. Many activities other than warring occupy a soldier's time. Stand in any battlezone: you are as likely to see soldiers selling military stores out of their tanks like convenience stores; as likely to see soldiers turn their guns on civilians to extract food, money, goods, labor, or compliance as to see them turn them against other armed forces; as likely to see soldiers help rebuild damaged homes and schools and read to sick children; as likely to see a good deal of war-related damage has been done, not by the military, but by one business competitor burning out another in the midst of firefights. Commanders — and humanitarian aid organizations — variously run everything from strategic planning sessions to international arms sales, gem dealing, and cattle-rustling. Family matters are settled on the front lines; class, clan, and tribal loyalties are upheld in battle; profiteers band together to form predatory groups within troops. And the kindhearted carry orphans to new homes, assist at hospitals, aid the needy and traumatized.

These complexities extend worldwide. It is only convenient lore that a set of troops and a nation's military are comprised of members of that nation. This myth is satirized in a joke:

> There was a joke going around Angola a time back. "Our Cubans are beating their South Africans"—or vice versa. We talk about a civil war here, about the MPLA [government] and UNITA [rebels] . . . but for a while the [apartheid-era] South Africa Defense Force troops fighting for UNITA and the Cuban troops fighting for the MPLA were doing a lot more fighting between themselves than actual Angolan nationals were. There was a time when they were the war. Then Executive Outcomes [former South African Defense Force troops privatized for hire after the end of apartheid]—who used to fight for UNITA against the government—are hired by the government to fight against UNITA. In the meantime, we send troops to DRCongo to help them in their war. Oh, I won't even mention all the others who have stopped to pick up arms here in Angola, from the Russians to the Americans.

Let's return to Nietzsche's point that "the doing is everything." This means that war only comes into being when an act of aggression occurs, and that act of aggression takes place, not in the offices of military commanders or political leaders, but on the front lines, usually by the lowest echelon of grunt soldier. Power manifests itself in "the doing" of war. What, then, is war as a soldier shoots out of a scientifically unfathomable combination of personal convictions, historical circumstances, interpersonal loyalties, and emotional needs?

And herein lies the fundamental irony of power.

The soldier clearly gains the legitimization (power) to act and continue acting by his or her association within a recognized set of political and military institutions. Without this legitimization a person's aggressive actions would be decried as individual banditry or crime. Yet if the soldiers bring their own ideals, ignorances, and interests to the fore of their actions, and if these play out in the actual context of the war among others with their own personalities, traditions, and vested interests — they are essentially constructing the reality of power's expression and the enactment of war.

"The doing is everything." If you take the bullet from the gun and the soldier from the front, the power elite loses their means of control and power becomes an empty exercise. At the ground level, power is constantly negotiated — by the interrelationships among soldiers, political officials, civilians, rogue troops, paramilitary, international associates, profiteers, family, friends, and personal foes. Military force, sadism, charity, greed, bribery, clan loyalties, family ties, friendships, sexual liaisons, business transactions, illegal trade, envy, love, anger, compassion, confusion — these are the forces that define the realities of war, the ebb and flow of conflict and survival, of barter and control, of terror and negotiation, of peace, possibility, and power.

There is one final aspect of the irony of power, one most clearly visible in the way leaders respond to individual will on the battlefield. The unusual nature of the military commander's words that began this chapter illustrates this. Few of this man's colleagues spoke in the same way. Most echoed the words of another commander I spoke with who ran both overt and covert "cleansing operations." At this time, some videos were circulating among commanders and were being shown to create support for their military missions. These videos showed gruesome carnage, both on battlefields, and, perhaps more commonly, in terror assaults on civilians and civilian centers — committed by both the government troops and the Tamil separatist militaries.

The Sri Lankan commander swung his arm out to encompass the videos, and by extension, the entire war effort facing him. We were sitting in his living room, and the video was showing on his TV. The real atrocities, he implied, were done by "the other side."

> How can you fight against this? This kind of fighting, this kind of barbarity of these terrorists *[referring to the Tamil militaries]* will threaten the very foundations of our Sinhala nation. And how can you defeat this? How can we defend our nation? By standing by and watching them maim and kill, our arms tied by policies and conventions and diplomats that have no idea what is really going on here? Standing by and letting them kill our soldiers and then disappear into the houses and schools where they put on an innocent face? Our troops are here to control. We don't kill indiscriminately; we are not here to harm civilians. But when those supposed civilians kill, or harbor killers, what choice do we have if we are to protect our nation? Our soldiers get a bit hotheaded sometimes, but they know how to handle it. Those videos of some

> of the Tamils killed—they were involved, and this stands as a warning to all the others. It's not a pretty fight, but they started it, and we'll finish it.

The irony of power, then, resides in the fact that power brokers, political and military alike, have the option of accepting responsibility for ground-level actions or of risking the appearance that they aren't in complete control, that they don't represent the font of power.

The latter, in the context of the state and the military, is unthinkable. It violates the most basic premises upon which the state and the military function: that governing structures operate top-down, and that elites tame the Hobbesian beast of the masses. To avoid giving the appearance that they don't have power, leaders often prefer to act as if they intended ground-level actions, even, "offensive" ones. This means they would prefer to take responsibility for objectionable military violence than to admit they do not control their troops — that they do not wield ultimate power. To do this, leaders invoke a (mythologized) time sequence whereby they take sponsorship for the actions after the fact "as if" the action had actually derived from their institutional authority.[10] To play on Kipling, these are "as if" stories.

Curiously, little discussion takes place regarding acts of heroism that don't fall within the ken of military control (saving a fellow soldier is part of the formal ethics of war, saving a town from military targeting isn't; carrying civilians to safety is part of the military ethos, setting up social services outside of the purview of the state isn't). Altruism, it would seem, is also carefully controlled: to act in ways that undermine state authority, no matter how positive, is suspect. The state, not the private individual, provides "social good" through social services — this too is part of the power equation. As South African advocate Justin Wylie said to me:

> What is the difference between a barroom brawl and a boxing match? Nothing, save that the one is recognized as legitimate based on certain fictions (no one will get hurt, etc.).
>
> What is the difference between the Cosa Nostra and state sovereignty? Nothing, save that the one is recognized as legitimate, but based equally on a series of fictions.
>
> This is why violence is kept at arm's length—the carefully crafted notions that war takes place on "battlefields" and that criminal violence is constituted of marginal elements that can be contained . . . the illusion that violence is "outside society," and that the state keeps society, keeps *us,* safe.

The entire fabric of state and military leadership is rooted in the belief in top-down governing power structures. The state's raison d'être ceases to exist if war and peace are authored in any sense from the ground up, if power is wielded in action, if the state can't act except through the acts of those outside of the purview of direct control. And in all of this, in the grand narratives of state and nation, power can be forged by a young man who forgot why he was fighting a war.

PART THREE

SHADOWS

Legality at first glance appears a straightforward concept. There is a line dividing what is legal and what is illegal; rules define those lines, judicial codes institutionalize these rules, and enforcement agencies guard justice.

Yet there is no biological imperative marking crime from legitimacy; borders between the world of the licit and the illicit are conceptual. As concepts change, so too do borders. And as cultural categories, borders are fraught with ethical implications. Are running weapons across sanctions to the military your country supports as serious a crime as running nuclear components? Human trafficking? How do we compare smuggling illegal narcotics to smuggling antibiotics for desperate people in warzones? What relationships hold between the informal trade that sustains a country's population during war and the massive profits that transnational corporations and business kingpins ultimately make from the ashes of political violence?

Answers are not easy: they are obscured in the shadows; hidden by the power of profit, blurred by shifting borders of il/legality. But they are not impossible. Fieldwork along the borders of il/legality is not common to economics nor to studies of power. But it uncovers a simple truth: every action is enacted by a person; a person who moves according to a complex set of values and orientations. People walk the shadows, and they tell their stories.

There are many stories to convey: trillions of dollars move outside of legal reckoning yearly; millions of people are involved. Most of the world's countries cannot boast a GNP that high.

"JOE'S COLLEAGUE": RUSSIAN HUMANITARIAN AID HELICOPTER PILOT.
MOZAMBIQUE, 1990.

CHAPTER 7

ENTERING THE SHADOWS

Veteran military pilots from "the rebel side" flying emergency relief goods for the government in their fight against the rebels. Emergency relief planes paid for by international governmental and nongovernmental institutions that sometimes fly black-market goods for powerful business interests. Relief planes, funded and supported through the government, that sometimes fly supplies to rebel bases . . . This isn't the plot of a bad B-grade novel, but the reality of everyday life in war.

At the epicenters of conflict, emergency relief cargo planes play a host of roles. They are a lifeline of essential foods, services, and goods; they afford the opportunity to travel free from political affiliations, and, as will become clear, they may well straddle numerous extra/state divisions. Often, outside of military transport, they are the only travel resource available to the front lines of conflict, especially given the large-scale land mining of roadways. These emergency airlifts are quintessentially international enterprises: they are generally run through international organizations with goods and by personnel from around the world. They often receive aid money, both from governments and from large international nongovernmental organizations (INGOs) that require international alliances — airlifts are very expensive, and cross a host of political, legal, and technical jurisdictions. An old DC-3 airplane, the oldest and probably least expensive workhorse still flying, costs several thousand dollars an hour in aviation fuel and service fees alone. Add institutional overhead, pilots' salaries, mechanics' wages, parts, permits, communications gear, and of course, the goods being transported.

In one country, I hitchhiked frequently on relief planes, and the pilots would alert me to cargo planes going to destinations they knew I would be interested in visiting. One evening the pilots who had invited me on a run the following day stopped by to tell me that the flights had been canceled.

CN: What's the problem? Is someone sick, was there a crash, were they downed?

Pilots: Everyone is fine, thanks. No, the planes are not down. Yes, we are flying tomorrow. No, we don't know where to. No, you can't come.

CN: How can you not know where you are flying to? You have to make flight plans.

Pilots: We don't know, it will be sorted out tomorrow.

CN: Maybe it will be a good research place for me to visit. Can I stop by the airport tomorrow and see where you are going and maybe jump a ride?

Pilots: Not possible. The plane has other requirements.

CN: Other requirements, what other requirements?

Pilots: Don't know . . .

All of this, from the answers to the silence encoded in them, was out of the ordinary. Flight plans may not exist, pilots may give anthropologists unauthorized rides, but information is a commodity that tends to be freely exchanged. I became curious about these flight cancellations, and searching for the facts turned out to be a study in power. After some delicate digging, the story began to emerge. Chipping away at the walls of silence my questions evoked, someone (after considerable whiskey) finally explained:

A group of businessmen requisitioned the plane for this day. They do business, big business. Big enough to be able to take this relief plane, cancel five or six emergency relief runs, and use the plane for their own purposes. This time, they are flying goods into the interior.

It may seem like the towns have been bombed and attacked to a standstill, that the entire population has been reduced to hungry refugees without the means to buy even food. But big businessmen, big not just along the lines of this province and this country, but big along international lines, they live and work and run business all over the country. They fly goods across the country; they do "business": in shops, in black-market trade, in the businesses they are developing.

Business goods, telecommunications equipment, war-related supplies, [stolen] motor vehicles, VCRs, luxury items, precious resources, food, ciga-

> rettes, liquor, petrol, you name it. They provide the latest movie releases not even available on video in the regular stores yet, and they provide the sets to play them, the generators to run them, the petrol to fuel them, and the jobs to get the money to pay for all this. You can get a beautiful Mercedes Benz, or perhaps you prefer a Land Rover, here in the middle of the bush in the middle of this war. You can order the parts you need to repair it when it hits a land mine. If you are one of this crowd.
>
> These men have fortunes; they are powerful. Powerful enough to requisition these planes when they need them, and to tell the pilots to fly them where they want to go—with no questions asked.

These people not only had the money to "requisition" an airlift plane for personal use, they had the power to make sure the entire machinery that supported the airlift—from governmental to intergovernmental aid organizations—was kept uninformed or beholden. In this case, USAID, among others, was providing monetary support in the millions of dollars, though I doubt it was aware of the non-aid uses the plane was being put to. Not all such flights originated within the country, as this one did. Some nights, under cover of dark, planes were "requisitioned" to fly over the border, collect state-of-the art computers and weapons, and fly the goods back into the country to a military base. And we aren't talking about pounds of cargo, but tons.

Such unregulated flights offer a view into the deeply international character of extra-state shadow activities and power systems. For example, in one case I followed, a major emergency airlift was being run by an international organization, flight-licensed and aircraft-registered in an African country outside the scope of the airlifts. It was paid for by superpower governmental and nongovernmental donors (who, I am sure, were unaware of any untoward activities), and was headed by a European man through a European organizational base who was both a humanitarian aid professional and an international smuggler. This airlift operation grossed a lot of money, though few know the exact figures. The planes actually did fly many tons of cargo to bombed-out townspeople for months on end, but a number of other less altruistic activities were taking place as well.

These transport flights operate on commodity and service circuits, and in the world of business, a weapon, a diamond, a Mercedes, and a bag of rice are all valuable commodities. Drawing distinct lines between business and war supplies becomes impossible. Distinguishing between "businesspeople," "military," and "political officials" is equally difficult: power often resides in the associations holding among these roles, positions, and alliances.

Ethnography is a jigsaw puzzle researchers piece together, and in today's globalizing world, we do so across long distances and stretches of time. Years after the fieldwork that took me on the flights I described above, I was in Nairobi at a restaurant having lunch when I ran into "Joe," one of the pilots who had given me rides in the preceding war years as he delivered humanitarian supplies. In the curious way of people who work internationally, Joe picked up the conversation where it had stopped years ago as if no time had intervened. Except for one difference. During the time we knew each other in the war, Joe seldom explained anything. He would only hint at shadow activities. If listeners were sufficiently informed to pick up his lead, they could do with it what they chose, as long as they didn't ask him anything further.

I remember one day during the war when Joe dropped off his cargo at a site recently beleaguered by attacks where I was working, and offered me a ride back home. By happenstance, no one was in the empty plane but the two of us, and Joe told me to ride co-pilot; he would give me some flying lessons. I knew the flight should take about an hour, yet after an hour we were nowhere near home base. I asked Joe about this and he waved off my questions. Some time later, he told me he wanted me to practice circling in downward spirals. I saw we were over a town that had been completely wiped out; every building was burned to the ground. It was a devastating massacre, and one far from the eyes of the media and human rights observers. It had been a silent death, a death in the shadows, committed by sanctioned weapons no one would admit having.

Joe never made mention of what he had discovered and shown me. Yet that day in Kenya, some years after the fact, he opened up and talked for several hours:

> We flew endless tons of food and medicines into those bombed-out towns. Sometimes we'd fly in and the military would just show up with their guns and take everything we had; sometimes we'd fly in and the local strongmen would take everything we had. An entire economy from the aid. Yeah, and then there were those flights we had to make for the businessmen. We'd show up one day and be told our flights were being diverted. No one asks questions, no one interferes. This goes a whole lot higher. Cars, electronics, industrial equipment, computers, communications, appliances, big stuff, small stuff—fortunes moving across these battlezones. Business. We'd be

> paid the same to fly emergency supplies to towns under attack and for flying hot cars and electronics on those unannounced routes.
>
> That isn't the whole of it. Remember some of those nights we'd just be gone? *[Night flights were not legal at the time.]* Some nights the planes would be loaded—computers, arms, you know, the lot—and we'd do an uncharted run to a main "enemy" base camp and unload the stuff. These goods come in from all over the world. All this stuff going around all the sanctions and laws. You meet the whole world, see it all out there on some dark runway off the map out in the middle of some war.
>
> Here we are killing ourselves flying five or six runs from dawn to dark to get essentials to starving bombed-out people under the good auspices of one side, and then find ourselves flying weapons and supplies to the other side that night. The guy—that European—who ran the company that chartered out to humanitarian aid . . . what an operator! He played all sides of it. Aid by day, running goods for the businessmen at noon, flying for the other side at night. And you know, thing is, he's the one that got food and medicines out there to those people on the front lines; he really did. No one else was risking their ass to fly that stuff out.

As we were talking, Joe introduced me to several Executive Outcome pilots who happened to be sauntering by. (Executive Outcome is the formal mercenary organization founded and run by former apartheid South African Defense Force soldiers.) Joe knew them — pilots working in warzones are a coterie, and they have to share information to maximize safety — but he wasn't overly comfortable with them; they had different work philosophies. In their presence, Joe reverted to his previous taciturn style. He gave me a lead, and I could follow it where I chose, as long as I didn't ask him questions. War and the shadows were still hand-in-hand partners: he, the Executive Outcome pilots, and all the rest of the other private pilots in the restaurant that day were waiting for clearance to fly into the Democratic Republic of Congo. This day's hot spot, this day's fortunes of war.[1]

. . .

In late 2001, the news was running stories that two Mozambican privatized state banks — the Banco Commercial de Moçambique and Banco Austral — "lost" $400 million. Two people were murdered who were working to uncover the truth behind this — Carlos Cardosa, a Mozambican journalist investigating corruption, and António Siba-Siba Macuácua, interim president of Banco Austral, who was just launching an audit. The story caught my attention for two reasons. The first was that Carlos Cardosa was one of the first people who befriended me when I arrived in Mozambique in 1988. He told me he would help me understand the war then raging in his country — that he would make sense of it; and that the only way to do that was to make sure I understood that if I ever made sense of the war, I would never understand it. He taught me how to melt crayons in an oven to create art; and over Rice Krispies cereal (a rare commodity in warzones) he spoke for hours of the war. And corruption. It was a conversation we continued whenever I saw him in subsequent years. The last time I saw Carlos we were both writing on extra-legal profiteering, and he spoke of his research into the state banks and their relationship with "big" interests. He spoke too of the threatening environment in which he did his research.

The second reason the news story caught my eye was that it symbolized something my research data continued to highlight: corruption is often portrayed as a national problem, when in fact it is profoundly international. The $400 million "lost" from the Mozambican banks is of course a key part in understanding the shadows, but this money does not stand in isolation. Along with the many millions and billions siphoned off in like manner from banks, industries, and political institutions worldwide, this money shapes both local possibilities and global economies as funds flow back and forth across lines of legality. These illicit dollars influence hegemonic relations as they are laundered into legitimacy, brokered into power, and rendered variously visible and invisible in political and economic accounting. Carlos was not killed merely because of Mozambican motives — but because of the ways these motives linked to much larger interests set in international contexts and profits. It is too pat to say, "These countries/regimes/leaders are corrupt." Such a focus can obscure the larger linkages that give extra-state activities the power they have. In speaking of the shadows, then, my interests rest more with the international character of extra-state networks and the ways in which these intersect with multiple governments, businesses, and development interests.

My inquiry into these issues began with the basic question: How do governments and rebel groups alike obtain extremely expensive weapons, communications, and security systems and the entire range of supplies necessary to wage war when they don't have a sufficient tax base to cover these purchases, many of which are sanctioned? Furthermore, how do these war-related systems move from the industries of the cosmopolitan centers of the world across all known forms of il/legality into the hands of soldiers, and how do the precious resources that pay for these goods move back across all these equally complex lines of il/licitness? How is business, both local and international, configured in these equations? Why are illegal drugs, precious gems, weapons, and basic foods simultaneously moving along entangled routes, and why can one see the same international cast of businesspeople, profiteers, and black-marketeers transporting these war-related supplies across the warzones of the globe?

The answers to these questions lead to a series of powerful economic, political, and social extra-state networks—networks that are non-state, non-legal, and non-formal—that span the globe from cosmopolitan centers to rural outposts, across war and peace, and through key power, financial, and development grids of the world. In war the illicit trade in weapons, the illegal trade in drugs, the extra-legal trade in luxury items such as gems and seafood, and the informal trade in food and clothing all become siblings. These arenas of shadow activity share the same proverbial house and family name. The name is profit and survival, and the house in this case is war.

Armaments must be purchased with hard currency. Many wars are fought in states whose currencies don't trade on the world market, so luxury items and key commodities become the equivalent of hard currency. These goods may be tangential to the running of states, such as drugs, or they may be central to the world's monies, such as gold. They run the gamut from the trade in key energy sources, such as petroleum, to the trade in human flesh, as with forced prostitution and indentured servitude. Even countries whose currencies trade on the international markets face problems in acquiring what they need to conduct warfare. Quite simply, war's goods are very expensive, and few countries' tax bases and governmental revenues are sufficient to pay for war's outlays.

As we will see in a later chapter, the Truth and Reconciliation Commissions hearings in South Africa showed the surprising amount of illicit and illegal activities the apartheid government was involved in to procure military finances, goods, and services. Consider also the case of Turkey: in order to finance Turkey's wars at home and abroad, especially the Kurdish war, which by the mid-1980s was costing Turkey $8 to $10 billion a year, the Turkish state gave the green light to para-state organizations to take over the billion-dollar drug and casino business in Turkey.[2]

Such examples show the intersections of non-state illicit international networks with formal state institutions and officials. At times, even a straightforward demarcation of state and extra-state or legal and illegal often proves impossible. Susan Strange writes:

> The fact is that while financial crime has grown enormously . . . it remains, legally and morally, an indeterminate gray area. The dividing line is seldom clear and is nowhere the same between transactions which are widely practiced but ethically questionable and those which are down right criminal. . . . The need to use such secret or covert financial channels is not only a prerogative of organized and economic criminal groups — but also of terrorist and revolutionary groups and indeed of many individuals and economic operators engaged in activities which are not necessarily illicit. Investigations into the biggest financial scandal of the last fifteen years, the bankruptcy of the Bank of Credit and Commerce International, showed that BCCI was engaged in "reserved" or illicit financial services for a very varied group of clients, including Colombian narco-traffickers, Middle-East terrorists, and Latin American revolutionary groups, as well as tax evaders, corrupt politicians and several multinational companies.[3]

These various spheres of legal and non-legal production and distribution work together to create interlocking grids of exchange and control. Roles themselves — the positions any given person holds in society — are often complex and multifaceted: a state actor can also function as a non-state actor, a sock manufacturer, a black-marketeer. A state actor can simultaneously vote sanctions into law and then ignore them for profit or power. A businessperson can lament clandestine sales while profiting from them.

Manuel Castells emphasizes this point in his observation that there is a "thin line between criminal traffic and government-inspired trade."[4] For both Castells and Strange, this isn't a product of happenstance or simple convenience, nor is it relegated to non-cosmopolitan locales: "Complex financial schemes and international trade networks link up criminal economy to the formal economy. . . . The flexible connection of these criminal networks in international networks constitutes an essential feature of the new global economy."[5]

Legal or illegal, the oil and gems (or timber, or minerals) smuggled out of southern Africa to pay for military supplies boost the arms industries of the world's industrial centers, the most successful of which correspond to the major UN power blocks (for example, the nations comprising the UN Security Council). A mercenary using an automatic assault rifle or a torturer using a solar-generated laptop computer linked to a satellite dish may well be decried by the governments of the world, and there may be sanctions in place to deny them straightforward weapons purchases and high-technology supplies. But mercenaries and torturers don't lack for guns and computers, or the full range of war-related supplies described throughout this chapter. Journalist Richard Norton-Taylor reports that "the trade in torture devices such as electric shock weapons, leg irons and serrated thumb cuffs is rising, according to Amnesty International, which says that 130 countries are now making them compared with 30 in the 1980s."[6] No matter how many layers of sanctions-breakers and black-marketeers purchasers have gone through to gain those weapons, the industries that made these supplies ultimately profit. A gun sold is a gun sold.[7]

Should any quaint notions exist that mercenaries and human rights violators only get weapons from "sources in non-democratic locations," anyone who has walked in warzones, myself included, can easily attest to the wide range of supplies available from all the major sellers in the world. In one square kilometer of land in central Angola I visited with Halo Trust (the British de-mining NGO), they removed land mines manufactured in thirty-one countries.

. . .

I asked a local entrepreneur from Southern Africa:

> "Who sets the real currency exchange rates—the street rates that underpin the core economy?"
> "Businessmen," he said.
> "The ones who use the relief planes?"
> "What do you think?"

The businesspeople who diverted emergency flights for their own extra-state purposes demonstrate another set of international power relations—those accruing to international currency markets. This is a form of power of considerable proportions.

In warzones, currencies often collapse, and "street" currency exchanges are the norm. Those who control the black-market money exchanges thus control key exchange rates. These change daily, the product of complex monetary calculations. "Street rates" are extra-state calculations. They don't run through the banks and the government institutions of the country, yet they are more powerful than formal institutions: they set the "true" currency prices for an entire nation. These currency markets are very international. Businesspeople are calculating money indices based not only on internal conditions but on a host of global market factors that range from the accessibility of goods and their worth to international exchange rates for hard currencies.

Mozambique provides an interesting but not unusual example of a country where the "street exchange" was taken as a baseline for both formal and non-formal economies. At the close of the war, a consortium of international aid organizations and the World Bank counseled Mozambique to take black-market rates — not the official bank rate — as the true economic indicator. The health of the formal economy was gauged on the relationship of the black-market to the bank rates: as the formal bank rates approached those of the "street" — not vice versa — the formal economy was deemed to be recovering. Formal exchange was set at street-calculated rates. Mozambique agreed to this. What these organizations didn't discuss was the vast network of international, political, and economic linkages, exchanges, and relationships that make black-market currency exchanges possible at all. The capacity to forge economic global currency indices constitutes significant power on the international stage, and these vast "street systems" are constituent aspects of shadow power.

These conditions can stimulate entire extra-state banking industries. In Angola in 1998, I conducted interviews at several major banks. The banking industry had largely collapsed: at that time the state banks were open only to provide salaries and monies to the state sector and its employees. No loans were available to citizens. When I asked how average people could borrow and bank the money they needed to build businesses and industries, the bank staff I spoke with just shrugged their shoulders. "Not with us." The formal banking system had no answers.

Solutions rest with the "informal" economy, but "informal" is far from the ILO's definition of small scale and low income. A "businessman" I spoke with explained:

> It is impossible to get money through any formal bank system these days. Even if money were available, which it is not, the restrictions would prevent most people from even getting a foot in the door: the "in-group" get in, and the rest are broken down with insurmountable restrictions, regulations, tariffs, and rates. How do you do business in these conditions? Development as a solution to war, everyone says—how do you develop without loans and banks?
>
> But systems emerge, people just take care of business. We take care of

> each other. I make loans. These are not small things. People need money to run entire businesses. Some need buildings and machinery, vehicles, and transport routes. There are sophisticated systems of development here, all run this way. Most of this runs like any business, on negotiations and collateral, on trust and associations. People just know: if they need money they come to me, to those like me. There just aren't possibilities in the formal state sector.
>
> For the most part, it runs smoothly, we all know how it works. And it works: we're holding the country up.

Worldwide, these unregulated financial systems can be found in many guises. Take, for example, the extra-state "banking systems" in Asia. People often think of offshore financial interests and their relationship to money laundering when discussing extra-state banking systems (though few recognize that some 20 percent of the world's financial deposits flow offshore).[8] But a far more mundane, yet powerful, "informal" banking system is in place throughout the world. A customer, for example, chooses an informal "bank" in one country in Asia and can send any amount of money to a receiving "bank" in another country to give to anyone the sender designates. This system may be non-formal, and the "banks" little more than storefronts, but the system is both vast and powerful, transmitting untold fortunes through family and ethnic linkages, business partnerships, and unregulated financial associations.

The informal banking system is centuries old and is found on every continent. But this alternative (or parallel) remittance system has recently come into the spotlight with the "war on terrorism." The *hawala,* as it is commonly referred to (called *hundi* in South Asia and *fei ch'ien,* or flying money, in China), moves money for good and bad: in the massive flow of *hawala* transfers for individuals (for example, sending money home to families and businesses making payments across borders), the funds of a terrorist group or the transfer of very dirty monies leave few footprints. But, as noted in *Time World*, funding terrorism is not a priority for the *hawala* dealers. "The big money comes from defrauding trade regulations."[9] In fact, according to an Interpol report, "The delivery associated with a hawala transaction is faster and more reliable than in bank transactions."[10] This report explains that alternative remittance systems are successful because they are cost-effective, efficient, reliable, nonbureaucratic, lacking in paper trails, and useful for tax evasion.[11] The "war on terrorism" is unlikely to affect the many billions of dollars moving throughout the world along largely untraceable hawala channels. But economic markets are shaped in this way.

. . .

The global nature of the shadows can be seen in the following quote from a conversation I had with a pilot and a "businessman" in Southern Africa:

> On one of the "uncharted" cargo runs you can find a veritable global supermarket. Look at a typical run for today: (German-made) cars and lorries stolen in the capital city and neighboring countries, (French- and Japanese-made) industrial equipment for their factories and (Russian-made) weapons for the militias guarding their interests, some (United States–made) computers and (Chinese-made) electronic equipment both for their own use and to sell or barter, and luxury items like (European) alcohol, (American) cigarettes, (western and Indian) videos, and (globally produced) clothing and foodstuffs.

How many networks operate at any given time around the globe? Pat answers are, obviously, impossible. But several key observations are possible. Small-scale subsistence markets (from food to fuel), informal economies (from clothing to pirated software), large-scale gray and black markets (from arms through luxury items to oil and freon gas), and state industries and personnel (from sanction-breaking technology to corrupt customs officials) are more interrelated than neoclassical theories suggest.

Profits are immense. Yet the largest profits often come from unexpected arenas. We assume that high-profile goods like drugs, weapons, and gems bring in the most money. But these often ride along with daily necessities, and the latter may well give the "sexy" commodities a run for their money. In Angola today, a chicken and a bag of tomatoes are often more scarce, and more precious, than automatic weapons. It isn't unusual to happen across a truck unloading bag-loads of potatoes and tomatoes on the road in an impromptu market—a market that can fold up at the hint of trouble. Truckers may also trade for assault weapons and other big items, but the vegetables are the more valuable commodities.

There has been a tendency in both popular and academic analyses to place the following extra-legal commodities and related services into separate conceptual arenas of investigation:

1. illegal luxury items such as drugs;
2. illegal military items such as weapons systems;

3. sanction-breaking high-tech goods like state-of-the-art computers and industrial equipment;
4. informal sector foods and goods like grains and clothes; and
5. the economic, political, and social associations that undergird these systems of power and exchange.

Neoclassical economic theory tends to postulate non-state networks as quite discrete: smugglers, official corruption, and informal subsistence economies each occupy a separate and largely unrelated realm.

The difficulty of even finding a term to represent the full spectrum of related "extra-state" exchanges demonstrates this tendency. Most texts define informal markets as small-scale, rural, and low-tech; they rarely recognize that the transactions can be worth many billions of dollars a year. When political actors engage in extra-state actions this is simply labeled "corruption," which misses entirely the complexities of power-defining global systems, and the intermingling between legal and non-legal systems. While arms and luxury black-market items such as drugs and precious resources are the classic examples of extra-state exchanges, it's important to keep in mind that traders carrying rice or cigarettes outside of state-licensed channels are as basic to, and can be as lucrative as, shadow enterprises like battle-ready solar-generated laptop computers or chemical weapons.

The example of the businesspeople commandeering aid flights and setting international currency exchange rates — I'll discuss gem and commodity running in countries like Angola later — shows how basic goods and luxury items like gems link within larger international exchange networks ranging from armaments through high-tech computers and industrial equipment to core energy sources. The lines between state and extra-state power can easily blur here. Smugglers commandeering INGO relief planes may carry sanctioned telecommunication equipment, VCRs, and stolen cars, yet by day these marketeers are often upstanding members and officials of the country. In fact, the returns on such "enterprises" can supply the wealth, industrial base, and influence to gain political office.

While extra-state networks aren't all-inclusive — while no single overarching criminal or extra-legal network mentality exists — these networks are more complex, interrelated, and governed by shared norms of conduct than traditional and neoclassical economic theory holds. Manuel Castells writes : "Crime is as old as humankind. But global crime, the networking of powerful criminal organizations, and their associates, in shared activities throughout the planet, is a new phenomenon that profoundly affects international and national economies, politics, security, and, ultimately, societies at large."[12]

The people involved seem to feel that creating associations among extra-state networks internationally is desirable. For example, some drug-smuggling networks based in Latin America and Southeast Asia send drugs to Europe via Africa. Any number of ports, from remote Namibia to urban Nigeria, broker these drugs on their way to western destinations. Market logic and rational analysis suggests a route straight from Latin America or Asia to Europe makes the best sense, instead of routing the goods through so many transit points, with the associated higher risk. No matter how easy it is to get illegal goods into an intermediate port, in the end it's just as hard getting them into Europe. So why route them through Africa?

A part of the equation might be that the heavy flow of precious minerals and gems, ivory, weapons, mercenaries, food, and medicines in and out of Africa provides more avenues for other types of goods to travel along, which speaks to the interrelated nature of diverse networks. But that's only part of the answer. Another part is that associations of extra-state networks (and their state linkages) are more productive and powerful than smaller, isolated coalitions of people and profit. Routing drugs through Africa links Africa with the goods and power politics of Latin America and Asia, and provides the latter with the rich resources and human power of Africa. Each country and continent gains more by its association with others than it could hope to achieve alone. Much like multinationals.

This phenomenon isn't isolated to drug shipments. As Susan Strange observes:

> What is new and of importance in the international political economy is the network of links being forged between organized crime in different parts of the world. While the Sicilian and American Cosa Nostras were the growing point, as it were, of this network, they no longer operate alone. There are half a dozen other major transnational criminal organizations. . . . The expansion of illegal markets has fostered a wider and more frequent interaction among the major organized gangs. Drugs, arms or illegal immigrants often pass through the hands of up to ten or twelve different operators attached to various national gangs. Inter-group bartering of illegal commodities has also become very common since such deals help conceal the origin of the profits for the state authorities. As various criminal groups (like the multinationals) have expanded their activities outside their home terri-

tories, the illegal markets within state boundaries have joined together horizontally to form a single world market.[13]

Strange goes on to discuss the institutions, logistics, and social norms that have given rise to the "transnational diplomacy between national mafias" that operates worldwide today. The people forging these non-state networks set up the transport routes, communication linkages, and banking systems to sustain their interactions.

Drugs are good illustrations of the complex interplay of legal, illicit, and survival economies. The term "drugs" tends to elicit images of marijuana, cocaine, and heroin linked with callous trade practices and immense profits. But along warzones, through collapsed economies, and on the streets of daily life, a whole different economy of drugs exists. Here, it is not the dreams of an addict that beckon, but the burdens of illness. Some of the most important "drug dealers" today are flogging antibiotics, cancer drugs, AIDS treatments, birth control pills, dialysis machines, and surgical equipment. It is here that the links between licit and illicit economies, state and non-state practices, and local and multinational industries intersect in the most fundamental ways.

Along the streets of most major cities, if you know where to look, most people bypass the cannabis and cocaine dealers to buy pills marked with the logos of major international pharmaceutical companies. Soni, who runs an unregulated market for pharmaceuticals and medical equipment in Southern Africa, explained:

> Of course we get the stuff from all over the world.
>
> We, well, most of us try to get the real thing. We study how the trademarks and production marks are made, and try to spot counterfeits. It's best to get them from the containers coming in. Or from out the back doors of the hospitals and warehouses here. Or from dealers you know and trust. We all have our favorites: the antibiotics from France, the Chinese treatments for liver and kidney diseases, the new AIDS drugs from India. . . . We know the industry worldwide.
>
> 'Course, you know, there are factories all over the place putting out counterfeit drugs. It's a huge industry. We work with it. Hey, I have a reputation. I have a family, I don't want to be running and hiding and trying to figure out how to set up a new shop somewhere else if I give people bad drugs and they don't get better. What does it do for me to sell crap to people? I'm just out of a job. Oh sure, there are those who do, but the consequences can be harsh. So some of these counterfeit factories put out decent stuff. It's our job to know. Hey, this is a huge business.
>
> Me? I never went to school, but lots of people thank me for their health.

Soni works at the level of the local market. He buys his goods from a much larger "businessperson" — the kind of person who might be able to requisition humanitarian cargo planes, help set currency exchange rates, and run an "informal" banking network that crosses any number of international borders and moves billions of dollars. A man like Leo.

Leo gave me a glimpse into his world one day when I bumped into him buying a warm Fanta in a small, poor, neighborhood shop in Mozambique. We sat outside on rickety plastic chairs that had seen much better days drinking warm Fantas out of the bottles. Leo had on a simple pair of slacks and an open-neck shirt. Sitting there in front of a poor street shop, he looked like the average anyman, not a person who commanded an economic empire:

> I love this country; it's suffered a terrible war, but it's my home. So I'm trying to start up this business. Do you have any idea what that means? I have to get Chinese cables, European machinery, Indian software, a reliable source of energy . . . just keep going. I need to cut deals all over the place that don't often match the letter of the law. Throughout all this friends say, "Hey, we need some X, Y, or Z from [another country], can you bring it in with you?" and then we are bringing in everything from ball bearings to software to some goddamn weird new winepress someone thinks can make a fortune here. Coming in legally can be a death sentence. Taxes and all are bad enough, but honestly, I don't have time for endless paperwork and whatnot.
>
> I have to protect my businesses from attacks, so I have to arm my guards. I sent a request for protection to the military about this once, and given my businesses' "importance to national development" they sent, honestly, I'm telling you, they sent several convoys of weapons. Old weapons, new weapons, broken weapons . . . all just slung into these trucks. Took us endless days to sort through that mess. They even sent armor-piercing tank killers—like we were going to wage a full-scale war. They sent enough weapons for me to outfit my own militia. I told them to come and take back about 90 percent of it. I'm still waiting to hear from them. 'Course, I'm not going to let a bunch of weapons sit around inviting attack: they were good barter for some business supplies I needed.
>
> The stories just go on. It's a constant juggle. Hey, drop in for dinner; I just got a load of Russian caviar.

Networks, like the markets and the politics that gird them, are constellations of economic, political, demographic, historical, and cultural processes. As such, they are dynamic, not static, phenomena. As the constellations of factors that define networks change over time and circumstance, so too do the defining characteristics of the networks. Perhaps the very extra-state nature of the exchange systems I am speaking about attests to their success. The more formal nature of state-based systems is vulnerable to bureaucratic gridlock, while non-formal systems can more easily and flexibly meet demands. I'm not making an ethical statement here that in any way supports non-state and non-legal activities. To say these networks are often successful isn't to support their claims to authority. The simple ethnographic fact is that they are successful, right or wrong.

STORE IN NORTHERN NAMIBIA, NEAR THE ANGOLAN BORDER, 2001,
JUST BEFORE THE END OF THE ANGOLAN WAR.

CHAPTER 8

A FIRST EXPLORATORY DEFINITION OF THE SHADOWS

An example, one that links a hungry war-orphan street child to the vast international networks operating in the shadows, will help set the stage for the definitions to follow. I met this boy in Angola, in a town that had been completely bombed out during the 1993–94 battles. The fighting took place in the center of town; a dividing line down the main street marked the division between the MPLA government forces and Jonas Savimbi's UNITA forces.[1] The loss of civilian life was extensive, numbering in the tens of thousands. War orphans are one of war's more brutal legacies. One day, I struck up a conversation with the boy; he was about ten years old. He was selling foreign-brand cigarettes, and I asked him about this.

> "One of the businessmen sells them to me and I sell them on the streets for a little profit," he said.
>
> "How do you start out if you have no money to buy?" I asked.
>
> "He gives them to you to start with, and you must come back to share the profits," he said.
>
> "And what if you can't make a profit, or if some larger street kid takes your cigarettes?" I inquired.
>
> "Then your life can be short, like in the war."

As we walked down the street, he showed me the shop of the man who "sponsored" him. In a bombed-out building, gleaming new television sets, VCRs, and other luxury items peeked out from darkened backrooms. In a town bereft of basic foods and electricity, much less a table to put a television set on, cosmopolitan dreams from the world's urban centers called out to passersby without shirts or shoes. But someone had to have the means to buy these luxury items, and to use them. People who did not deal in *kwanza,* the local currency.

I stopped, sat on the crumbled curb, and asked the boy:

> "You mean," I asked, "that if you didn't sell cigarettes for this shyster, you would not be able to eat?"
>
> "What's a shyster?" the child replied.

A question that cuts to the heart of the matter in war-torn societies. Simple divisions of children's rights so clear in peacetime comfort lose that crystal clarity in the midst of shattered worlds.

This child selling foreign cigarettes on bomb-cratered roads far from the world's economic centers links into extra-state global economies that reap trillions annually.

The man who fronts cigarettes to street children — from Angola to Los Angeles — is a prime example of a lynchpin in the intersection of shadow transactions, business development, and political power. Like the businesspeople in Mozambique, the man is linked to international networks capable of bringing valuable goods across international borders; he is linked with networks that produce the resources that convert to the hard currency to buy these goods; and he is linked with formal state systems in running his industries.

With financial and business success this man also has political power. He can back politicians, he can formulate policy through major state institutions, or he can run for office. He can also work in INGOs, become a UN representative, sit on multilateral trade boards, or attend forums on international law. He will not be likely to give up his extra-state alliances when he enters a formal state role. Why would he want to? As the young cigarette vendor reminded me, that's where he acquired money and power in the first place. As Manuel Castells notes, there is a "thin line between criminal traffic and government-inspired trade."[2]

. . .

Shadows, as I define them, refer to the complex sets of cross-state economic and political linkages that move outside *formally* recognized state-based channels. I use the term *shadows* (rather than "criminal" or "illegal") because the transactions defining these networks aren't confined solely to criminal, illicit, or illegal activities, but cross various divides between legal, quasi-legal, and downright illegal activities. This isn't a study of individual people operating in the shadows, but of the vast networks of people who move goods and services worldwide — networks that broker power comparable to, and in many cases greater than, the power of some of the world's states. I have come to this area of research through the study of warzones, where non-state actors and transactions are perhaps most visible. But, as we will see, extra-state networks extend across war and peace, and across all the world's countries.

This study of the shadows isn't merely a study of extra-state transactions. The finances and power wielded by these shadow networks challenge academics to rethink theories on states, sovereignty, and the loci of power.

The following are core features of the shadows as I define them:

— Extra-state political economies are more than sprawling, value-neutral international market networks.[3] They fashion economic possibilities, they broker political power, and, importantly, they constitute cultures, for these networks of power and exchange are governed by rules of exchange, codes of conduct, hierarchies of deference and power — in short, they are governed by social principles, not merely the law of the jungle.

— The networks are by definition international. They blur the distinctions between discrete nation-states and recognized political and national borders.[4] They are societal systems that cut across national, linguistic, and ethnic collectivities.[5]

— These networks are more formalized, integrated, and bound by rules of conduct than is implied in studies of gray and black markets focusing on high-risk items like armaments and narcotics, or on basic informal markets like foodstuffs.

— The term *informal* is not the same as *non-formal,* the word I use to characterize the shadows. In many definitions — including the classic one by the International Labor Organization — the term *informal* refers expressly to small-scale, low-income, low-tech, and subsistence level economic activities.[6] The traditional use of the word *informal* has confounded an understanding of the relationships among (small-scale) survival economics, (large-scale) corruption, and (international) extra-state empires. Writing on Mozambique, Mark Chingono observes:

> The International Labour Organization (ILO), the agency that has formalized the term "informal economy," characterized the informal economy as "a sector of the poor" in which "the motive for entry into the sector is essentially

survival rather than profit making. . . ." On the contrary, not all of those who participated in the grass-roots economy were poor nor was their motive for entry merely to survive. Corrupt bureaucrats and professionals used their office, influence or contacts to acquire via the grass-roots war economy, through for instance, smuggling, fraudulent export, barter, speculation, bribery, and embezzlement, and invest in building houses, hotels/restaurants, or in transport. Similarly corrupt commercial elites, religious leaders, international agency personnel, as well as international racketeers and their middlemen, smugglers, money-dealers, pirates, and slavers and abductors, not to mention soldiers in the warring armies and foreign troops, were among those who yielded substantial benefits, and in many cases, became obscenely rich, by participating in the grass-roots war economy.[7]

— Extra-state phenomena are not marginal to the world's economies and politics, but central to them. Scant in-depth work exists estimating the amount of money generated per year through extra-state activities, but initial inquiries place it in the trillions. The following examples show how these figures add up; they run from the tragically exploitative to the remarkably mundane:

As much as 20 percent of the world's financial deposits are located in unregulated banks and offshore locations.[8] The United Nations estimates the annual value of illicit drug traffic at $500 billion. The illicit arms industry is estimated to be of comparable size.[9] Human trafficking, considered to be the third-largest illicit activity after arms and drugs, brings in hundreds of billions of unregulated dollars a year. Of comparable size is the empire of gain from the unregulated sex trade and pornography industries. In a study on money laundering, Pasuk Phongpaichit of Chulalongkorn University in Bangkok estimated that people-smuggling earns $3.2 billion a year in Thailand alone — and that solely from Thai women smuggled into Japan, Germany, and Taiwan for prostitution. People-smuggling for illegal immigration and labor also adds up to huge sums. Profits to Chinese triads smuggling illegal immigrants into the USA alone are placed at $2.5 billion a year, and this represents merely a fraction of people-smuggling worldwide.[10]

While there is a tendency to focus on the dramatically criminal in looking at extra-state activities, it is estimated that in the USA alone, just three categories of corporate crime — consumer fraud, corporate tax fraud, and corporate financial crime — cost between $247 and $715 billion annually.[11] The black economy in a single country — India — in the early 1980s was placed at more than $60 billion, and has grown since then.[12] India is not unusual: in Peru, 48 percent of

> the economically active population works in the "informal sector." That figure rises to 58 percent in Kenya, and perhaps even higher in Russia.[13]
>
> South Africa's Truth and Reconciliation Commission hearings showed the world that taxes often cover little of a government's expenses, especially in financially demanding wartimes. The apartheid South African government was involved in such extra-state activities as gem, gold, ivory, and arms smuggling — and even bank robbery. In the world's smaller states, a single non-formal industry can add up to significant sums. Estimates of Sierra Leone's extra-state diamond earnings on the world market in the late 1990s have been placed as high as $500 million a year.[14] At the global level, some 20 to 40 percent of all diamonds are smuggled, reaping a billion dollars a year.[15]
>
> Cargo in other shadow activities may be more mundane, but its scope can be dramatic. One million tons of oil was smuggled into China in the first six months of 1997; on a *single* standard cargo of 30,000 tons, smugglers make $1.8 million. The infamous Lai Changxing of Fujian Province smuggled $6.38 billion worth of oil and related goods from 1996 to 1999.[16] Freon smuggling is a classic example of the mundane and often overlooked that reaps huge profits. In Miami alone, illegal freon smuggling has exceeded drug trafficking in volume and may rival it in revenues.[17]
>
> Finally, illegal proceeds need to be laundered in order to produce usable money. Michel Camdessus, former managing director of the International Monetary Fund, estimates that money laundering accounts for between 2 and 5 percent of the world gross domestic product.[18] According to Charles Goredema, money laundering specialist at the Institute for Security Studies in Cape Town, South Africa, such commonly used figures significantly underrepresent the true size and scope of money laundering because they are based on the most dramatically illegal activities, such as arms, drug, and human trafficking. Such figures do not include the widespread, but less "sexy" and thus less investigated laundering coming from such unrecorded proceeds as food, clothing, art, minerals, information technology, and the like.

It is anyone's guess how much money is actually generated each year through the sum total of all extra-state activities, though, taken as a whole, it represents one of the larger monetary and power brokers in the contemporary world. Nor does anyone know how many people are involved in these exchanges in total, though the number will run in the millions. The power the leaders in these extra-state empires wield can rival that of state leaders, and these networks can shape the course of international affairs as much as the formal state apparatuses of some countries do. The revenues generated can far surpass the GNP of smaller nations. Importantly, we do not know how these vast sums affect global (stock) markets, economic (non)health, and political power configurations. What we can surmise is that these extensive transnational transactions comprise a significant section of the world's economy, and thus of the world's power structures. We are discussing a series of power grids that shape the fundamental econo-political dynamics of the world today. If all these industries were to collapse overnight, the world's economies would be in chaos.

INTERSECTIONS AND IL/LEGALITIES

> The Roque Market was born in a conversation between two businesspeople expelled from the city. Two miserable marginalized people who after many setbacks met one another outside the city, not far from the ocean, at a clandestine locale to sell and earn what they could so that they could help maintain their families. So began everything. . . . From the fresh foods of the sea to the fruits of the land, all could be found, including the small trinkets people buy that always get lost in the house. These people joined with others who came from afar, fleeing the rigor of the city and of the society imbued with laws and norms that they could not or did not know how to carry out and of prejudices they could not accept.
>
> The nature and diversity of products that could be found, and above all the practical prices attracted the people of the surrounding neighborhoods, not only to buy, but also to sell that which they did not consider essential to their basic needs. Afterward, given the rapid growth whereby it became a true market, and because of the fact that people met outside of the jurisdiction of the police, products imported clandestinely from neighboring countries that complemented what was being sold in Luanda began to flow in, arousing the attention of the Luandans. In this way, tempted by the confidentiality of the commerce (guaranteed by the absence of forces or order), businesspeople came to traffic goods they acquired honestly

> or fraudulently in their workplaces. The Roque continued to flourish in the hypnotized eyes of the authorities, who, also, began to come, little by little, to get supplies, purposely ignoring what was taking place. "If you want something, go to the Roque, where everything is bought and sold!" All of the urbanites came to the Roque. And so was born an oasis of liberty, a free zone, social, spiritual and commercial, a true escape valve from the pressure that life and its rules exert over many. . . .
>
> Some individuals, more active in the import business and who had links with the superstructures, discovered other continents, such as Europe, offered better opportunities and better prices and "opened the routes" to Asia, to the Americans and to other, more stable, African countries. And so the Roque became a place all could come, carried by diverse circumstances and driven by misery or by ambition.[19]

Everything from radios and children's textbooks to spare parts and energy sources are necessary to sustain a society at war or at peace. The legality of these commodities is often fluid, negotiable. More than the dramatic examples of illegal drugs, these basic goods may define the deep interweavings of formal/state and non-formal/non-state economies and power. Often a single commodity moves across the lines of legality, illicitness, and informal marketing a number of times in its commodity-life.

The intersections of formal and non-formal trade routes I am considering here are myriad, and perhaps these associations can be used by traffickers to "tame" the dangerously illegal — as when drugs and contraband arms move alongside the fluid il/legality of mundane commodities. Guns ride as often with bags of grain through international ports as they do with state-authorized arms shipments through military channels. Software for war-related computer technologies is bootlegged along with smuggled VCRs. The dangerously criminal, the illicit, and the informally mundane cannot, in actual practice, be easily disaggregated, as Manuel Castells reminds us:

> In addition is everything that receives added value precisely from its prohibition in a given institutional environment: smuggling of everything from everywhere to everywhere, including radioactive material, human organs, and illegal immigrants; prostitution; gambling; loan-sharking; kidnapping; racketeering and extortion; counterfeiting of goods, bank notes, financial documents, credit cards, and identity cards; killers for hire, traffic of sensitive information, technology, or art objects; international sales of stolen goods; or even dumping garbage illegally from one country to another (for example, US garbage smuggled into China in 1996).[20]

These intersections of power, il/legality, (questionable) legitimacy, and non/formal are characteristic of shadow networks. Key to this analysis is the fact that smuggled medical supplies are as much a part of the dynamics defining shadow states as illegal narcotics and arms. Understanding how these informal, illicit, illegal, and legal networks form and reform in conjunction with one another and across the boundaries of the world's states is crucial to illuminating not only the processes of war, but also those of postwar reconstruction, a topic I will explore in later chapters.

THE IRONIES OF DEVELOPMENT AND EXTRA-STATE GLOBAL NETS

> Forgive the trickster and the tribe will be happy, but kill the trickster, the tribe will be ruined.
>
> *Yoruba proverb*

> The market is a place where fortunes are won and lost. In the Yoruba pantheon of deities, one finds Eshu, trickster and god of the marketplace. The Yoruba say: "Eshu can turn shit into treasure." But he just as often turns treasure into shit. Like a deconstructionist, he reworks relationships between gods and men while occasioning the necessity of such reordering. He destabilizes speech and spatial arrangements just so that he can speak with reassuring tones and theories, only to subvert the terms once again. He makes the normal monstrous (or, more precisely, makes the act of assurance monstrous by making it normal). He is an imp. Depicted in Yoruba sculpture, he is all cock and mouth; the one who dares to connect disjunctive forces, aware that failure is inevitable.
>
> With a feather in his cap, Eshu can be found at crossroads, where nothing is sure but everything is possible. And at the cemetery where everything is sure and nothing is possible. Eshu turns life and death in on themselves. The Yoruba are both terrorized and amused by the sheer extravagance of attempting to bring together things that don't belong, and consider Eshu their favorite deity. Although most at home in the marketplace — that anarchic swirl of bodies — he prefers to talk about what's going on in the bush, about swamp fevers and torrid passions seeking the cover of all the forbidden, boring, banal, and empty territories where new generations are procreated. He reminds people that their everyday experience is embedded in an intricate network of visible and invisible forces. . . .

> The African trickster shows that the "really real" is incessantly multifaceted and ironic. Every social reality is fraught with an extravagance which is both its forcefulness and undoing. All attempts at closure, necessary in order to determine what's in or out, what's incorporated or "free," must eventually burst out, become a laughing matter — a bursting of the seams.[21]

Non-formal markets comprise a much larger section of the world's true economy than formal indices document. In Luanda in 1998, senior UN and World Bank economists told me that Angola's economy was about 90 percent informal. Given the fact that the country had been enmeshed in continuing cycles of political violence and war, and that its economy had collapsed, this may not seem a surprising figure.

But the example of Angola raises another point about extra-state transactions: they are fundamental, and possibly necessary, to development in devastated communities. This turns conventional wisdom on its head. Such wisdom views extra-state transactions as undesirable, generally because of the associations with illicit goods, criminal networks, and a failure to produce state revenues. As Clement Jackson, a senior United Nations Development Program (UNDP) economist, explained: "The whole point of development is to move economies into formal state-based frameworks and stop nonformal activities."[22]

But it would be virtually impossible for countries like Angola to piece together a society and economy from its war-torn legacy without relying heavily on non–state-based development. This relationship between non-formal economies, postwar transition, and development is in no way restricted to the African continent. Consider the case of Cambodia:

> It was not just rice that Cambodians wanted at the end of 1979. In the preceding ten years an incalculable amount of their national and personal wealth had been destroyed. Every Cambodian family had lost what much of the world considers essentials. Now the nation began to restock itself — in a unique, open-air bazaar along the Thai border at places like Mak Moun and Nong Samet. It must have been the greatest open-air market in the world. Almost everything you can imagine was available there. . . . The sums of money that changed hands were staggering, almost unbelievable. On some days up to $500,000 worth of gold poured out of Cambodia across the border.[23]

There is a general tendency to postulate that the non-formal markets of Eastern Europe, the former Soviet states, Africa, and Asia are the result of a combination of changing political regimes, social transitions, and economic opportunism. The belief is that as these countries settle down in the course of normal state development, their economies will become increasingly defined by state-regulated formal economic structures. Though illicit markets and mafias will always exist in the countries of the world, this reasoning goes, they comprise a marginal part of the world's real power structures and economy. My research to date suggests we need to rethink these assumptions.

I can stand in the most remote warzones of the world and watch a veritable supermarket of goods move into and out of the country along extra-state lines. Tracing the supply routes of these goods takes one through both major and minor economic centers: the sanction-regulated laptop satellite-linked computer (or Mercedes Benz, or land mine, or surgical kit) on the battlefields of Africa was made in a major cosmopolitan center of the world, and the gold, diamonds, ivory, and seafood that paid for it move along the same channels back to those cosmopolitan centers. At the bottom line, it would seem that non-formal economies play a formidable role in countries like Japan, Germany, and the USA as well as in areas of more rapid economic and political change and development.[24]

Statistics place Italy's extra-state economy at up to 50 percent of its gross domestic product, and the United States extra-state economy as high as 30 percent.[25] One-third of Canada's population participates in informal economic activities.[26] The Russian Ministry of Labor in 1995 estimated that 40 percent of the country's economic activities was in the shadows, another 40 percent was generated through the visible economy but hidden from taxes, and another 6 percent was of unknown origin.[27] Even the non-formal economies of developed countries are turning out to be more sophisticated and developed than classical economics or popular academic conception assumes.

TILLY'S ORGANIZED CRIME/STATES

> If protection rackets represent organized crime at its smoothest, then war making and state making — quintessential protection rackets with the advantage of legitimacy — qualify as our largest examples of organized crime.[28]

State-based ideology sets a strong demarcation between legal/state and non-legal/non-state activities. In fact, most of the state's raison d'être rests in honing the health of the nation in opposition to the "anarchic" non-state forces challenging it. But perhaps, obscured in layers of crafted political invisibilities, the state is defined in part by its intersections with the extra-state. In "War Making and State Making as Organized Crime," Charles Tilly argues that war making, extraction, and capital accumulation interacted in shaping the development of the European state, and asserts that "banditry, piracy, gangland rivalry, policing, and war making all belong on the same continuum" in this state-making process.[29] Distinctions between legitimate and illegitimate force are of little importance in this process. States seek to monopolize the use of force over all others — and what, Tilly asks, distinguishes the violence employed by states from the violence produced by anyone else?[30] Eventually, the personnel of states enforced violence on a larger scale, more effectively, more efficiently, with wider assent from their subject populations, and with readier collaboration from neighboring authorities than did the personnel of other organizations. But it took a long time for that series of distinctions to become established.

Tilly is discussing the period of state-making in Europe, a time now relegated to the historical past, but he observes: "In our own time, the analogy between war making and state making, on the one hand, and organized crime, on the other, is becoming tragically apt.[31]

Perhaps the links of war making, banditry, and extraction are necessary to the continual success of the state. A number of studies have explored such links for Africa.[32] I will ultimately argue that in fact the cosmopolitan centers of the world depend in part on "shadow" economics and politics, and are intricately linked with resource wildcatting in warzones like Angola.[33]

Essentially, a country's political institutions — and the ideologies shaping them — must support the cause of political control by removing distinctions between in/formal policies and il/legal actions when it is politically and militarily expedient to do so. Hence extra-state and criminal activities become embedded in the everyday functioning of a country's governing institutions. This isn't to say everyone is implicated; they are not. Nor is it to say that the institutions are fundamentally criminal; they are not.

But I am suggesting that in the most conventional sense the modern state is configured around both the formalization and the informalization of economic and political power. The question then arises: Are the millions of people and the trillions of dollars that flow across nebulous demarcations of legality — moving goods, people, and services around tariffs and controls and laundering them back into formal economies — central to the grounding institutions of the state itself? Confounding this question is a second one: Do the power formations of extra-state economies run parallel to those of the state — do they provide alternate routes of access to social success, economic empires, and political power?

STATES, SHADOWS, AND FUTURE POWER CONFIGURATIONS

> People have historically struggled for spaces of operation, spaces where they have some autonomy. Western power seeks to bring order to Africa — order to the process of accumulation and stratification; it seeks the repayment of debt and the perpetuation of economic dependency. Its information gathering penetrates deep into the African interior. Resistance, if it is to have a chance, must be murky and chaotic; demonstrate a willingness to occupy the unoccupiable. There is seldom judicial recourse, constitutionality, or legal protection of life or property. But there Africans can redefine the political realm to encompass activities and territories in which those with power might prove reluctant players.[34]

There is a tendency among analysts and policy makers, as well as in popular culture, to view states and international alliances such as the United Nations, powerful INGOs, and multinational corporations as the only real power brokers determining political trends and economic realities. The non-state organizations are considered only as they function through recognized state and interstate authorities. Non-state players, from barter exchanges among poor citizens to large international mafias, are usually seen as operating at the "sub-state" level. No matter how powerful, they are ultimately posited as marginal to the hegemony of the state.

Anthropologists have long worked with multiple nodes of power defining any given site.[35] The state represents one such model: a form of power that coalesced after the Middle Ages along territorially bounded, legally codified lines. Concurrent systems, such as the shadow powers I discuss here, operate coexistentially across time and space. No single system of power reigns supreme, no ultimate hegemony prevails in the world.

Joel Siegel, an attorney in Berkeley, California, told me that the phrase "shadow networks" reminded him of the merchants in the Middle Ages who developed international commerce systems intended to stand apart from kingly rule. These merchants developed trade agreement and dispute settlement methods on the basis of arbitration, not bloodshed. They instituted functional courts in marketplaces. These actions were radical at the time — indeed they were extra-legal to kingly law. This, of course, is the basis of customary law and the foundation of contemporary commercial law.

The merchants of the Middle Ages were instrumental in reshaping global politics. They operated internationally, and to a large extent outside the direct rule of "king-doms." The commercial laws they developed were direct challenges to royal authority. As they gained wealth and power, these merchants and markets set the way for the introduction of the modern state and international law as it replaced traditional kingdoms.

In this light, the "shadows" of today may foreshadow new power formulations barely emergent on the horizons of political and economic possibility. It may be convenient to think that internationalization is situated most powerfully in the world's cosmopolitan centers. But perhaps Mozambique and Angola, Africa and Asia, are the sites where new configurations of power shaping the world are most visible, as Ngũgĩ wa Thiong'o implies in his book *Moving the Centre.*[36] For it is here that flexibility, the breakdown of entrenched institutionalization, the politics of survival, and the realities of development meet in the most direct of ways.

MARKETS RISING FROM THE ASHES. KUITO, ANGOLA, 2001.

CHAPTER 9

THE CULTURES OF THE SHADOWS

THE MEAT, POTATOES, DIAMONDS, AND GUNS OF DAILY LIFE

This is ultimately a tale of meat and diamonds, no potatoes. But it is an anthropologist's story, and as such takes flavor only in its full context, so bear with me. It is a story in four parts that starts with a camera, moves through a betrayal, visits a birthday party, and coalesces with meat and gems.

It was 1989, my second visit to Mozambique and my first to the coastal province of Zambézia. The war was reaching a peak. The minister of health had asked me to do research with the *curandeiros* — the indigenous doctors. He said: "This form of medicine and these healers are illegal, and if I ask a Mozambican to do this work, it might harm them politically, but you, as a foreigner unaffected by our internal politics, I can ask." At that time, I was pretty much a novice to the complexities of the country. I had asked a man who worked for a well-known INGO to accompany me on interviews in Zambézia because while I could work in the national language, I thought it would be good to have help with the indigenous languages. During one of my first interviews with a group of curandeiros, I asked if I could take a picture of them. A man stepped up to me and said sure. As I tried to take the picture, the man began to make all kinds of faces at the camera, and the automatic focus of the lens opened and closed continually, unable to take the picture. I laughed, he laughed, and he said, "Come, take the picture." Again, the faces and the opening and closing, until finally the machine broke completely, the shutter freezing closed over the lens. As I walked back to town, I laughingly said to my companions, "Well, he didn't have to break my camera to prove what a powerful curandeiro he was."

The next day I hitched a ride with a humanitarian cargo plane inland to a town that was situated on the crossroads of the front lines. All medical facilities and resources had been bombed and looted into closure, and only curandeiros operated to patch broken bodies and souls. The man from the INGO accompanied me, but kept disappearing once we arrived. At one point, on my way back from talking with an ancient healer, I saw him collect a bag from another man, and, when he turned and saw me, quickly hide it. We didn't speak of the bag, though as I found out later, he did with someone else, changing the story in an important way.

Back in Quelimane, the provincial capital, on the recommendation of the Ministry of Health, I joined with some of the men who worked at the local branch of the Mozambican umbrella organization that coordinated all emergency relief funds and work. Everyone called it "Disasters," for short. We set out on a work assignment, but one of the men was having a birthday the next day and someone had told him of a pig available for the festive meal. We had to detour to bargain for the funds to get the pig, then detour to barter for gas to get to the next town, and then detour again to find the owner of the pig and strike a deal. As we set off to do the work — with the live pig — we came across some shipments of what might be called, in times of peace and stability, black-market rice and supplies. Now it was just called "necessity" — dinner. Another set of detours. Some six hours later we heard of some attacks at the coast, and went off to collect the stories. When we got there, a man arrived carrying a guitar, and another found an old discarded tin, and soon a band had formed. We hadn't even come close to beginning the work we had set out to do. I gave up my attachment to my time schedule and joined in the dancing, which of course lasted well into the night. We never did get the work done.

The following day I was walking down the street by myself, the man from the INGO having suddenly disappeared, leaving a note he had gone back to the nation's capital. One of the men from the day before came up to me, suffering from a terrible hangover, and said:

> You danced with us, so I'm going to tell you that the man from the INGO told the political boss here that you were carrying rocks. You've got some trouble.

Carrying rocks? When had I "carried rocks" and what kind of trouble could that entail? And then it dawned on me that the slang, as in English, translates as "smuggling gems." Lacking a better plan, I simply went to the political leader and said:

> I understand I'm in trouble, what should I do?

He asked me if I was running gems, and I responded sincerely that I was not, but that he didn't know me from a hill of beans, and I could understand his concern. He smiled and said,

> No, I don't think you are doing anything illegal here. You never carry a camera [I had thrown the broken camera into the bottom of my travel bag and left it there], you take no improper pictures, you never carry a [camera] bag. I've decided to let you stay and continue with your work here.

To this day I have wondered about that old curandeiro and my camera breaking. But as I began to learn more about war and survival, the incident took on deeper overtones. The city I had traveled to with the INGO man — who obviously was running gems — was on the crossroads of the front lines because it hosted gem mines. These gems reside in the midst of bombed-out buildings and refugee mud huts in Mozambique, but they radiate out to powerful economic and political circles of the world. Pigs, too, circulate. Survival requires meat and rice, gas, and bargaining currencies.

Economic viability may depend on this. Informal transfers happen beneath the radar of formal economic accounting. A woman trading tomatoes for antibiotics is often deemed too small scale to seriously affect national economic indices. But, as Alexander Aboagye, a senior UNDP economist in Luanda from 1998 to 2000, told me:

> Everyone is thinking in terms of "one person, one tomato." But everyone here survives by trading like this, and that's 11 million "tomatoes." Think in terms of all the commodities and services that circulate daily—moving around the country and across borders at any given time. Eleven million "tomatoes" comprises a formidable economy; but the irony is, no one realizes the sum total of this vast market, its definition of the basic economy of the country.

The pigs and tomatoes, the diamonds and military stores, are market transactions — rational if not always moral. But life amidst the shadows does not take its character solely from the logic of market systems. Lest anyone think these networks of power and profit are merely value-neutral transactions, it is important to hold in mind that for the actor in the shadows, betrayal, camaraderie, and the unquantifiable values of the human spirit impart a significance to their actions that plumb the depths of culture and identity. This chapter turns now to explore the larger ontological world — the dreams and realities variously captured or broken, and the communities that form around these fragile pursuits — of the shadows.

FOLLOWING DIAMONDS

There are endless stories of diamonds here, *the man in Kuito, Angola, said to me in 2001.* Take Marra: she lives by the River Kwanza, as do bits of diamonds. Her brother is doing some mining—working here and there in mines on either [military] side depending on circumstance and survival—to make ends meet. One day he manages to find a good gem, and he keeps it. At this point there is a government push against UNITA. In the attack, Marra's brother is killed. Marra takes the gem, puts it in her teeth, and flees with her children—and nothing else. It is a humanitarian disaster: but the *deslocados* [dislocated; internally displaced: IDPs] know food and humanitarian aid is available in Kuito, and those who still have the strength push on. Marra walks endless kilometers and countless days with no blankets or food or money. She and her children are malnourished, and eat plants along the way to keep alive. She is shit poor. But she keeps the gem, she doesn't know what it is worth, but she knows it is worth something; some blankets and some food are what she critically needs.

There are guys in Kuito who have a bit of money: maybe they run the bar or a shop in town, and have a lorry. They know when the IDPs come to town, and they know that some are likely to have gems and other valuables. They give Marra maybe $20 for the stone. Then they have to sell the stone. It's still not worth an awful lot yet: they get maybe a couple of hundred bucks. The stone has to be laundered to be worth anything, and that's done down the line. The stone goes up the chain, to Luanda, Mozambique's capital, and on to Europe.

So how does this stone get to European gem dealers? Well, what comes into Kuito? Food. Mostly from Portugal. Portugal's connections are stronger in this area because of the enduring nature of the old trade routes from colonial times; it's habit. So stones follow this old trade route: Kuito–Luanda–Portugal–Europe.[1]

That's just one story, Marra's story. One person, one gem, one route. Multiply that.[2]

Bringing a diamond out of a mine in Angola (or gold out of the Amazon; hardwoods out of Southeast Asia; or drugs out of Afghanistan and Colombia) involves an extensive network of people. Start with the miner who extracts the gems, then add the toolmaker who makes the miner's tools and the cook who feeds him or her, and the teachers that tutor the miner's children. The view that miners in Africa are marginalized, poor, and uneducated is challenged by one of the few in-site studies of miners: Paul Richards found that in Sierra Leone during the war in the mid-1990s, a significant number of miners had some secondary, and sometimes even university, education, and thirsted for international news and goods.[3]

Equally important are the relationships of intimidation or taxation the soldiers have with the miner, the miner's family, and the mining community. Militaries use resources to raise the foreign currency to buy arms and supplies, but they also set in motion an extensive barter system that taps into global commodity flows. Global Witness (the London-based NGO dedicated to honing corporate and political responsibility in the face of resource profiteering and corruption) writes:

> In cash terms diamonds are cheaper in Angola at approximately US $100 upwards per carat, although UNITA seem keen to encourage barter for medicine, clothes, electrical equipment and other supplies. Again rates given for barter vary widely from a couple of pairs of trousers for a small diamond or a Sharp cassette player for a larger stone from an individual seller, to the agreement of orders in advance with UNITA officials for quantities to be brought in by four-wheel-drive vehicle, whilst placing a counter-order for diamonds at the same time. In Mwinilunga and Zambezi there is an established barter of diamonds for cattle.[4]

Because these gems do not leave the country as commodities, taxed and controlled by the state, a further network of people must be in place to take them out of the country and across controlled borders with maximum profit and minimum penalty. Vehicles are needed to transport the goods; and drivers or pilots, mechanics, loaders, and a host of other people, goods, and services are necessary to get these gems from the mine across countless legal borders to Antwerp, Belgium, for example. Global Witness reminds us that the final stage—laundering unofficial diamonds into world markets (the first two stages involve gaining authorization for access to the diamond regions and then acquiring the diamonds)—expands the number of people critical to extra-legal exchanges well beyond commodity production and transportation: "The third stage is somewhat easier than the second, and less fraught with risk, namely that of acquiring the necessary paperwork to turn the unofficial diamonds into a legal commodity and thus exportable under the terms of the UNSC embargo."[5] Today, there are specialist consultants who make a living by advising people how to transport and launder extra-state and illegal goods. There are also worldwide "businesses" making illegal, but fully reliable, insurance available to protect against the seizure or loss of contraband goods.[6]

Other businesses exist to forge such documents as customs receipts, lading bills, shipping levies. Some "talented and reliable" forgers have international reputations, transnational businesses, and Web sites. Further networks of associates must be in place to buy the gems, convert them to hard currency, and trade them for other valuable items. The same kind of networks exist to purchase armaments and supplies, and to transport them across borders, into countries, and into the hands of the (extra-state) buyers.

Who thrives in such economies? From urban centers to remote rural communities, there are people who do well in such conditions, who profit from the political instability or social chaos that reduces normative and legal restraints. Mafias and international cartels function smoothly in these circumstances, as do multinational industries and consortiums willing to undertake wildcatting enterprises. In many ways, these non-formal market(eer)s parallel, and even make use of, colonial-style market systems: simple extractions of labor and resources channeled along equally simple routes to cosmopolitan centers around the world.

These are the conditions of a frontier: the perilous transport of daily necessities to the millions who need them; the wildcatting of vast fortunes; and the systems of protection, usury, and domination that see these various ventures to fruition. From kindly women trading tomatoes for medicines, through syndicates trading in gems, drugs, and high-tech computers, to violent gunrunners selling postwar weapons to urban criminals, the non/formal sector steps into the limelight in these transitional times.

THE SMUGGLER'S SOCIAL WORLD: THE CULTURES OF SHADOW NETWORKS

> For António André the day was a true success: eight thousand dollars of sales. For several months now he had been doing good business in diamonds with an individual coming from the Lundas and he would receive a commission of around ninety thousand dollars. Never had he seen such money and he didn't know how to manage it. First he bought a car for fifteen thousand dollars. After that he spoke with a fellow countryman from Humanbo, Quarta, whose extensive experience of Luanda, according to what he said, gave the impression he negotiated big business deals and would help him. He spoke of Portugal, of South Africa, and also of Hong Kong, explaining that many people become rich by buying merchandise directly from these countries. He said he had friends in South Africa and in Portugal, but it was preferable to begin in South Africa.
>
> António went there with five thousand dollars for an initial investment, and stayed at a luxurious hotel in the suburbs of Johannesburg, because he was told upon arrival that he should not stay in the city center because of the high level

> of crime and the many armed assaults. He searched through many warehouses in the company of one of Quarta's friends who also saw in this a good opportunity to make some money, and also because he had plenty of time given that he was unemployed. They spoke only of fabulous profits and António fell under the influence of this chatter.
>
> Returning to Luanda, without informing his wife, he didn't hesitate to hand over fifty thousand dollars for his orders. When the goods didn't arrive, two days later, the friend called by telephone to say that he had been assaulted near the airport, and that he had been robbed of all the money and that he needed a thousand dollars to pay for his stay and to buy a new ticket.
>
> "I was swindled!" António thought, filled with panic. He didn't know what to do. He explained what had happened to his wife, who didn't faint only because she was strong. But he sent the thousand dollars to Quarta, because in truth he didn't know if the man was telling lies or speaking the truth. When his friend returned to Luanda, he gave him a copy of the police report from Johannesburg that certified the assault. There was nothing left for António to do but to recommence his life intensively: he sold the car and with what remained of his trafficking in diamonds, close to five thousand dollars, he returned to the Roque Market, which in reality he had never really left. As regards Quarta, he opened a clothing store in association with a Portuguese. After some time, when the business began to prosper, he got it all when his foreign partner was expelled from the country because he was an illegal resident. Quarta became a rich man.[7]

Profiteers, smugglers, and black-market merchants are not isolated actors loosely linked into a web of profit. The very term *smuggler* conjures up notions of young adult males with dark demeanors, dark clothes, and a potential for dark violence. They are alone, or with others of their ilk. But in truth, the farmers who plant drug-related crops and the miners who harvest gems have families and children they must provide for, from paying mortgages to celebrating birthdays. Truckers who transport illicit goods need tires and tune-ups for their trucks and dental work for themselves and their families the same as if they were ferrying Post Toasties cereal. Pilots trained at accredited flight schools fly smuggled goods, often wearing professional pilot's emblems and uniforms. The banker who launders money and buys a smuggled diamond-studded Rolex watch, and the college student who deals drugs to pay his or her tuition, may not fit the image of the dangerous drug lord, but they are as essential to the whole enterprise as the growers and the transporters.

All of these people are deeply enmeshed in the tendrils of daily civil life: they have families; they belong to civic organizations; they hold community offices; and they set up pension funds for their old age. (The mercenary organization Executive Outcome provides pensions for its soldiers.) From interpersonal relations to illicit transactions, "smugglers" interact in social worlds that cross legal and illegal divides in ways that follow codes of conduct and rules of behavior as developed as those followed by people interacting within the legally recognized institutions of a society.[8] And they don't tend to see themselves as smugglers.

— Leo, the businessman I quoted in the previous chapter, doesn't consider himself a smuggler — though he is well aware of the international laws and regulations monitoring the flow of goods and people. "I am helping my country," he says honestly.

> We all try to work amidst endless strangleholds. Ruined infrastructure, land mines, corruption, excessive taxes, contradictory regulations, slow and inefficient bureaucracy, loaded and slanted international trade policies, patronage—you name it, we struggle with it. If you wanted to make sure a country has problems developing, you'd invent this. Without development, this country dies; the people starve. We make things work, we're bringing goods, industry, employment, into the country. We are setting up trade systems, kicking up production, getting essentials into the country. We're providing work and jobs. Honestly, the systems we work with are a lot more organized than the governments we work with.

— The pilots like Joe who flew the humanitarian runs into front-line towns under fire, and who also found themselves asked to fly contraband and war supplies for both sides in the war, don't consider themselves smugglers, though there is no doubt in their minds that they ferry goods across all kinds of legal and international borders. In Joe's words:

> We're paid to fly a plane. We're given our flight plans. That's our job. From start to finish, we don't make the decisions—not what humanitarian cargo to carry, not where to ferry it, not how many runs to make a day. Hell, we're overloaded by a ton or two practically every humanitarian flight, and we can't even do anything about that, and that's our lives. We work, we fly, but we don't call the shots. You don't like something, you don't fly, you don't work. It's as easy as that. Look, I have my stripes—I'm a pilot; no one can take that from me. We fly in here where no one else in their right mind comes, and we keep people alive. That's what we take home at the end of a long day.

— The man from the INGO who accompanied me to Zambézia and who "unofficially" ran gems doesn't consider himself a smuggler either. He knows the laws and the penalties for breaking them, but the war and its deprivations, and the monies to be made, are a far greater force in his life. When I returned to the nation's capital I tracked him down and asked him why he ran gems and why he had fabricated the story that I was smuggling gems. He told me:

> I was thrown into prison for being on the "wrong side" of the war. They called it a reeducation camp, but I was tortured and ill-treated. When I got out, I fled to a neighboring country for safety, never being sure if I would be found with my throat slit one day because of politics. But I missed my home—missed it like a physical pain. My family was there, my wife and children. My life and my lands and my memories were all in my home country. I loved it, and I feared it. So I watched and listened and asked questions, and when it seemed safe, I came back home. But I have lived a life of fear and anger. You have said at times that police are similar in many countries, but you don't know. You just don't understand. You don't know what these people have become, what the pressures have made them do, what they can do to a person, what a person becomes like subjected to this. And while they break us down, the rich ones become richer. And why? Why should they, and not I? I lost everything. First by joining the "wrong side," then in the reeducation camp, then living in another country, then being back here living always looking over my shoulder. When was I supposed to make a good job for myself? Build a house and provide for my family? Become a leader, gain a good position? When was I supposed to get my share? I watch my friends on the "right side" send their children to good schools, travel in nice cars, laugh and relax over a beer with friends without worries pressing their heads constantly. And I watch my children go to a school that doesn't have enough chairs, not to even mention teachers; I walk to work, and I live with constant headaches. How can you understand this? The world is a harsh place, and I will do what I have to do to survive and to provide for my family.

— The military official who "raises money" through unregulated trade and cross-border exchange, and who profits on controlling resource-rich areas does not think of himself as breaking any laws — far from it:

> What I do, I do for the good of this country. We've been fighting a war. To do that, we need resources, supplies, infrastructure. The government can't do this by itself, what government can fight a war all on its own? Everyone has allies. How do you think we get the stuff we need? How does anybody? It's what is essential to fighting this war, to keep the government stable. And my own gain? My control over access to prime "business" locations? That is how we keep control, how we keep the right

people in work and keep trouble out. You can't let just anyone have access to setting up business and industry. The wrong people can take their gain and use it to back those who fight us. Those of us who know the military, who have been here all along, we know what's going on, who to trust and who not to. We oversee these things in the interest of keeping the country stable.

— At cosmopolitan centers — the sites where weapons are manufactured, resources crafted into global markets, and money banked — little sense of responsibility attaches to the checkered history of goods and monies.

Weapon manufacturer: We make and sell weapons, there is no way we can control where they end up or how they are used.

Gem merchant: Sure, we see the "blood stones" come in, and people say they can tell the home mine of a stone, if it is from a site mined to purchase weapons. But the truth is, maybe you can tell and maybe you can't. And if it's a good deal, maybe you don't care.

Bank manager: Of course laundering is a prime concern of ours. But you expect us to follow the trail to the source of the deposits, as if this were possible?

At the front lines, where the resources are extracted and the weapons fired, smuggling is what the powerful and the elite do; the rest is survival. It is here a woman trades an assault rifle for a chicken to feed her family. It is here a man works in the mines (or logging timber, processing drugs, poaching game, or working in the sex industry) under dangerous and harsh conditions, either because he is forced to by military and business officials who need the proceeds, or because he hopes to make enough to improve his own lot in life. Without the poor and the powerless doing this work, neither the official nor the illicit system can be maintained.

My options? Get shot, starve, or do this work. . . . What would you choose?

TRUST AMIDST SHADOWS

One of the more interesting questions regarding international shadow econo-political networks is how such massive amounts of goods and money, which follow such complex exchange routes and political associations, flow as smoothly as they do. In plain words: Jonas Savimbi's gems got to Antwerp and from there onto rings on our global fingers without any more murder and mayhem than state-based transactions generally entail. The billions that flow through the informal banks of Asia function quite a bit like state-supported banks in that their customers generally don't lose their money. In a nutshell, the system works. But how it works is another matter. Many people I have spoken to about this respond that the system works because if it does not, people are simply killed. That may or may not be true: the fact is, it is an assumption; people have not collected representative data. We simply don't know how these vast billion- to trillion-dollar systems function on a day-to-day basis.[9]

One of the answers to the question of how these vast international extra-state networks operate as coherently as they do is that people in these systems generally trust that the transaction will occur as predicted, and that they will remain safe.[10] "Corruption," writes Diego Gambetta, "requires trust."[11] Gambetta observes:

> What is at issue is not the importance of exploring in greater depth the causality of those forms of cooperation which are independent of trust, but the fact that economizing on trust is not as generalizable a strategy as might at first appear, and that, if it is risky to bank on trust, it is just as risky to fail to understand how it works, what forces other than successful cooperation bring it about, and how it relates to the conditions of cooperation. Considering the extremely limited literature on this crucial subject it seems that economizing on trust and economizing on understanding it have been unjustifiably conflated.[12]

Ernest Gellner provides an interesting take on the place of trust amid chaos:

> The Hobbesian problem arises from the assumption that anarchy, absence of enforcement, leads to distrust and social disintegration. . . . But there is a certain amount of interesting empirical evidence which points the other way. The paradox is: it is precisely anarchy which engenders trust or, if you want to use another name, which engenders social cohesion.[13]

It's a powerful irony that even Hobbes recognized: networks of self-interest are grounded in cultural codes of trust. Right or wrong, Gellner asks us to understand how pattern and value become imbued in what is typically understood as anarchy.

By way of example, let's return to the humanitarian flights commandeered to make private business runs with (German) vehicles stolen in

Johannesburg, (French and Japanese) industrial equipment, (Bulgarian) weapons, (American) computers, (Chinese) electronic equipment, and (English) cigarettes. For a businessperson to pick up cargo at point X and fly it to point Y, an extended chain of associations involving a significant degree of trust must be in place. Entrepreneurs must trust that the middlepeople in the chain of shipments don't give their names to authorities or steal their cargo; they must trust that the border guards and customs officials don't arrest their minions or steal their cargo. These are international alliances, so people can't rely exclusively on family, ethnic, and national loyalties; they must forge associations across distinct language and identity groupings. As Janet MacGaffey and Rémy Bazenguissa-Ganga write in their study of the Congo-Paris second economy: "As the traders go boldly to strange countries, they need hospitality and help in buying their goods. They say: 'It is difficult when you don't know anyone: we need to help each other; we are helped and in our turn we help others.' For this help, they rely on personal connections, sometimes based on family ties, but more often on ties of ethnicity, nationality, religion and friendship from locality or workplace."[14]

Levels of trust in illicit activities extend exponentially from production through procurement to delivery: watchdog organizations must be kept out of the information loop; the officials that oversee transport, inspection, and border control must be bribed, kept in the dark, or otherwise compensated; workers must be trusted to do their work without breaking loyalties or absconding with the cargo. At the national level, to open an industry in a warzone, to have the only all-terrain vehicle in a town, and to have the means to set the currency exchange rates in a region all invite regulatory inspection—and violations of the law can result in confiscation, imprisonment, or a death sentence. Businesspeople must trust that their alliances with regulatory and security officials are strong enough to avoid any of these disadvantageous outcomes. They must also trust that at any point in this chain of transfers someone won't simply shoot them and take their goods.

At each step of the way illicit, gray, and legal institutions intersect: middlepeople transfer legal purchases across unmarked borders; pilots paid in Eurodollars fly uncharted runs with unrecorded merchandise; entrepreneurs evade taxes by bringing unlicensed goods into legal industries; government officials set regulatory law and simultaneously grease the flow of illicit goods into development industries. Without trust—and without denying the role violence plays in illicit economies—such vast enterprises are impossible, and networks could not function. The building of trust is a finely honed business survival strategy.

Writing on the war in Mozambique, political scientist Mark Chingono captures the paradoxes that inhere in the complex intersections of il/legality and the state:

> Although operating within these constraints, the grass-roots war economy was more predictable and rational in many respects than the official one. Illegal and unrecorded trade was not haphazard but institutionalized, operating according to a system of rules known to all participants. Examples included the standardized equivalences observed for barter transactions, the set rate for paying border guides, the arrangements set up for the terms of clientage, and the reciprocal obligations of other personal ties. The organization of a grass-roots war economy depended to a great extent on these reciprocal obligations of personal ties. The trust and confidence inspired by personal relations or common cultural background provided the reliability and predictability that were so conspicuously lacking in the official economy. To some extent, therefore, the grass-roots war economy generated alternative economic opportunities for people as well as an alternative society, with parallel religio-economic institutions alongside official ones.[15]

Whether in wartime or peacetime, extra-state networks are not haphazard collections of people in ad hoc groups circling like moths around the light of profit. There is an implicit assumption in many analyses of state and non-state actors that states are somehow supracommunities, born of unique institutions of leadership that are not replicated outside the formal institutions of the state. No matter how successful or large a non-state enterprise, it will never approximate the moral community of the state.

However true the existential answer to this might be, practical reality demands a more nuanced assessment. From diamonds to drugs, dominions exist that follow hierarchies of authority, rules of conduct, ways of punishing transgression, and codes of behavior. Within these dominions, communities form, ideologies develop, and worldwide alliances and antagonisms are drawn. These interrelated transnational industries shouldn't be confused with states, but they do have governing councils, laws, and security forces. They forge trade agreements, foreign policy, and currency exchanges. And they set up the transport routes, communication linkages, and banking systems needed to effect trade.

SHADOW COMMUNITIES

> "Nothing works, but everything is possible," says the Sudanese writer Abu Gassim Goor, and these sentiments increasingly seem to embody contemporary African realities where societies are simultaneously flourishing and collapsing.
>
> In thousands of small ways, African societies "play" with a

> visibility — fronting masks when nothing is hidden; deploying stark realities as covers for something more complex or uncertain. Take the shantytown communities of France, Angola, Texas, Cambodia, and Harlem — all part of a larger district, Umbadda, in Greater Khartoum. While North and South, Muslim and non-Muslim battle a slow war in which nearly a million people have been killed, these neighborhoods — a mixture of mud huts and tents in which almost every Sudanese ethnicity is represented — largely remain outside of state control. Here, there are internal conflicts between religious and ethnic groups reflecting national battle lines, but they primarily serve as pretext for collaborations among individuals of different groups for their own smuggling and trading operations.
>
> Religious convictions, ethnic identifications, distinct world views are very real — allegiances are not merely cynical convenience. Muslims take Islamic law seriously even when they are sharing alcoholic drinks with heathen Dinka hustlers in a car junkyard that serves as a makeshift bar. One set of convictions do not preclude other, seemingly, contradictory affiliations from taking place. Every smuggling operation in these shantytowns contains individuals from different national, religious, and ethnic backgrounds who bring to the operation different external alliances, resources, contacts, and access to competing interests at other levels.[16]

Underlying the rules of conduct, the values of alliance and exchange, and the ideologies that give these shape is the creation of community in its most basic anthropological sense. If transnational extra-state realities are to be understood, neither state nor market assessments alone will provide sufficient explanation. People survive in communities. Peter Vale, director of the Centre for Southern African Studies at University of the Western Cape, noted in a conversation in Cape Town:

> The work on the Southern African region tends to be scripted in a wrong ontology. Our point of entry remains the state, and this just does not provide an adequate understanding of the forces shaping political and economic relations. It is an intellectual challenge to rethink how to best answer the questions posed by power and profit. People do not want to take up the challenge because this is hard work. We need to go into the dark corners of social theory and shine light where people don't want the light to shine. We need to ask uncomfortable questions about the very nature of knowledge. We need to find honest ways to talk about identity—we need to emancipate identity from a simple way of understanding it through the state. We need to unpack the really difficult sets of relations holding between the state and capital. And we need to set our understandings in dynamic historical context.

> The solution? The way to approach these problems? Look at community. What, indeed, is the essence of community? Look at the relations that hold between identity, ecology, and borders.

There is no doubt that some of the communities that revolve around illicit exchange and profiteering are grounded in violence, fear, and exploitation. But others are invested in establishing ordered communities and stable relations. In either case, as Justin Wylie, advocate in Johannesburg's office of Public Prosecutions, said to me:

> Organized crime is more organized than the state.

What, normatively, defines communities that move in the shadows? In South Africa, I talked with a number of sources, from prosecutors to street vendors, and they made the same point about the deeply complex nature of non-legal groups and networks: gangs — or whatever name you want to use — have fully developed community systems, some rivaling any legal system. Each of the following men gives a differing perspective on what this "community" means, from dangerously exploitative to peacefully entrepreneurial.

Zaais Van Zyl, deputy director of Public Prosecutions in Johannesburg, South Africa, told me the following story during an interview in his office in 2002:

> Someone was murdered in prison some years back, and I had the case. The man who was murdered belonged to a gang, and had murdered plenty of people himself—as a matter of fact, I had dealt with him in a previous case. But now he was dead. When the guards came to his cell and found him dead, there was a card outside his cell. Simple as that, murder someone and leave your card announcing you did it. So we go to the guy's cell whose name was on the card and he is just sitting there calmly, and he says "I did it; it's me, boss."
>
> The murder itself entailed a complex process. First the prisoners involved held a kangaroo court to try the man, and judged that he would be killed. Then another prisoner cut himself, so he had a pretty bad wound, and he went to the infirmary to get it bandaged. When he returned to the jail area, they set up the murder: they took the bandage off the wounded man and wrapped it around the condemned man's neck, and with people on each side holding one end of the bandage, they strangled the victim. Other members of the gang sat around and sang hymns so that no one could hear.
>
> The prisoner who confessed to the murder belongs to the gang "the 27s." This particular gang is called the "air force" because its members are known for being great escapees. It was a bad case to try: the court ruled that his statement—"I did it; it's me, boss"—did not constitute sufficient confession.

When they brought the man in, I could see he had been in a long time; you could smell it, see it in his color. I tried to talk to the man, but all he would say was, "I'll tell in court what happened, but I won't talk now."

You see, prisoners have a fully developed legal system in the prisons. Before a prisoner goes to court, they have a lawyer in prison—another prisoner who has studied law, who knows it in and out. Maybe he has never been to law school, but his group has gotten him the books and whatever he needs to thoroughly study the law and the legal system, and then it is his job to prepare his fellow gang members in prison. These "lawyers" are good; some are excellent, better than some of the formal lawyers who will be trying the cases in court. So an entire case is tried in prison by the prisoners. They prepare the prisoner for any possible contingency. You have to appreciate how sophisticated this process is.

Consider the fact that there are gangs here in South Africa, gangs based in the prison system, that have traditions that date back over a hundred years—gangs that are older than the actual state [unified in 1910]. They have traditions more established, larger, more entrenched than those of the state. They have developed complex communities: they have sophisticated networks of communication, well-developed codes of honor, and secret social practices and symbols around which they organize.

Another lawyer in South Africa, who because of the nature of the story I will leave unnamed, told me the following story to underscore the kinds of power prisoners can wield:

There's a man in prison who is being tried for murder. He's one of the top men in a gang here. So he's here in prison being tried, but he moves in and out of the prison. People see him at clubs dancing with his girlfriends and meeting with others to do work. After a good night out, he goes back to prison. We have—well, we had—two witnesses against him, witnesses prepared to testify in his murder trial. He walked out of prison and murdered one of them recently. He has a great alibi: "How could I kill someone? I've been in prison!"

He has more power in our penal system than we have. How? Any number of reasons. The prison staff are scared of him. He's a big man, they are poorly paid staff; he walks out of prison and kills a witness. What might he do to them, to their families? At the same time some of the highest levels of corruption in this country are in the correctional system.

Peter Gastrow, who heads the Institute for Security Studies in Cape Town and researches organized crime in Southern Africa, told me about the more mundane aspects of the creation of community as a prime resource in strengthening criminal organizations:

This kind of research is challenging us to broaden the very notions of what economy is. The American-based notion of organized crime has dominated the research and policy world: the idea of a structured well-organized criminal group that focuses on areas of illegal specialization—the mafias. But South Africa shows a different system: here we see fluid networks that change and align themselves to pursue ever-changing objectives. They are highly interlinked. Sometimes in competition, but often acting cooperatively. In this way, the activities of these criminal networks expand across a wide range of transactions and illicit goods.

Look at a car stolen in Johannesburg. It's stolen by a less sophisticated person in terms of power in the criminal system, and then sold to the next level of organization with access to international markets. They will know that, say, someone in Mozambique is looking for a luxury 4 × 4, and they'll have it smuggled across the border. But that's not the end of it: they'll come back with Mandrax [a drug], assault weapons, Nike shoes, U.S. dollars, whatever the market is at the moment. It may be even more entangled than this: say they don't think they can recoup the price for the car given the costs of the trip across the border, so they might bring some diamonds along. So they drive to a guy's house and knock on his door and explain they want to run some diamonds across the border with the car. The diamond connection says, "OK, sure, but bring me a new BMW." So the driver takes the diamonds and at some point steals a BMW for the diamond dealer.

It does not stop here: there are informal hospitality systems as well. There are some 50,000 stolen vehicles smuggled out from South Africa across international borders a year. There are excellent network contacts throughout the region. For example, there is a nice house in Maputo [Mozambique] for the car runners to stay in. They drive across the border, and drop in to stay at the hospitality house. There is a great room, fine food, good wine, and plenty of women. But the big thing is that they meet other guys staying at the place from all over, and they share networks. They'll be sitting around the house having a drink and share stories: "Hey, I came across the border at X-stop and paid 1,000 rand to Joe." Another guy says, "Man, I came across and paid 500 rand, go to Sam, and use this crossing." Someone else says "Heard they need bakkies [small transport trucks] up north, and this is the guy to talk to." And someone else says, "Well if you are going to do a bakkie run, take along some Nikes, or batteries, or drugs, there's a good market up there." And finally: "Oh, you're heading back to Johannesburg? Want to take some cigarettes (drugs, weapons, minerals, people . . .) with you?"

This is the way work is done: like traditional wood and leather men's clubs and business associations. Traditional policing isn't working because it hasn't caught up to the fact that entire criminal economies need to be understood before they can be changed.[17]

A savvy street hawker enmeshed in cross-border trade leaned against a lamp pole and invited me to do likewise, suggesting a good story was coming.

I came in from the rural area. We didn't have anything. My dad got sick, you know [AIDS], and we could just barely get by. I figured if I got off to the city

> I could make some money, and my brothers and sisters might do better back home if I could help. Jobs here in the city are a lot of who you know. It's not easy getting work, it's not easy breaking in. But as I met people one by one, they began to explain to me how the system works: "There's a guy here who needs help with moving these goods; someone needs a person they can trust to do a run," that sort of thing. It's like a community: you know who to go to if you have a problem. I'd be starved to death now waiting for a break into some kind of government or office job. Here, I'm making enough to raise my family and help those back home.

This man articulates values similar to those Janet MacGaffey and Bazenguissa-Ganga found among Congolese traders in France: "Traders in the second economy have their own system of rules. One must not kill anyone but only take material possessions, and both break-ins and muggings are forbidden. La débrouillardise [the 'business'], they say, should avoid 'violent' money."[18]

Clearly, as Van Zyl's observations about gang violence show, community shouldn't be idealized. Gangs challenge state control by effectively managing violence — in a model not far removed from that of states themselves, who police their members and maintain their borders by controlling the means, definitions, and enactment of violence and legality. Yet as in any organization of humans, only a certain amount of violence and instability can be tolerated; breach that existential line and the community tends to collapse.

Laurie Nathan, director of South Africa's Center for Conflict Resolution, says his work in mediation clearly shows that people embroiled in violent relations prefer peaceful solutions, stability, and trust — they just don't know how to achieve them. For many unregulated businesses, Nathan notes, the ideal is to move into the stable, formal, and legal economy and political sphere. It is here that job and industry security allows businesses to expand and thrive. MacGaffey and Bazenguissa-Ganga say the same holds true for the Congolese traders working in the second economy: as soon as they have amassed the money to set themselves up in fully legal business, they elect to do so.

In my work in the field, I found that this is only part of the story. Like Mark Chingono, I have found that extra-legal activities thrive amid formal economies — layers of entangled associations that produce both legal and extra-legal empires at the largest and most sophisticated levels. Massive corruption at the state and inter-state levels would not exist if economic and political enterprise manifested a teleological tendency toward state legality. As I noted earlier, the man who ran the bombed-out shop full of state-of-the-art goods in war-torn Angola will find he can barter his economic power into political power as well, and having done so, he is unlikely to give up the very (non-formal) financial systems that allowed him to survive and profit in a violent and unstable war economy. MacGaffey and Bazenguissa-Ganga capture this:

> Through their trade and other activities, the traders protest and struggle against exclusion. In their search for profitable opportunities, we find them contesting boundaries of various kinds: legal, spatial, and institutional, and also the bounds of co-operative behavior. They are individuals who refuse to abide by the constraints of the global power structure and its alliances between multinational capitalism, Western governments and African dictators. They contest the institutions and norms of both African and European society which frustrate their aspirations for wealth and status. They resist the hegemony and control of the large-scale entities dominating the global scene.[19]

Yet economic successes do tend to move people into formal economies — from entering politics as a form of "protecting business interests" to laundering money, which requires moving illicit gains into formal enterprises. Success often comes from straddling and blurring these divides. As MacGaffey and Bazenguissa-Ganga write: "We avoid using the terms 'illegal' and 'legal,' since the boundary between legal and illegal is a political one, established by the dominant to maintain their power and control."[20]

For example, Mozambique has become a transit point for global drug shipments; coming out of a highly destructive war, the country does not yet have the infrastructural capacity to easily control borders and "business." In addition, in a decimated economy, illicit commodity flows provide access to hard currency and global networks that both formal and non-formal actors can profit from.

A profound contradiction lies at the heart of such exchanges. The vast wealth that is made on the drug money must be laundered — non-formal cash is useless on global markets. These days, one popular way to launder such cash is by developing the tourist industry. This industry can bring in substantial business revenues, but in the case of Mozambique, it was entirely destroyed during the country's war. In developing tourist resorts and infrastructure, illicit drug money is laundered in a way that provides jobs, services, and infrastructure for Mozambicans. The profiteering allows some dangerously unequal access to power and politics, which in turn shapes formal development. This situation represents a dilemma of considerable proportions for both development studies and security forces. The ironies and contradictions — that the dangerously illegal and the beneficially developmental coexist in this intersection of il/legalities — don't justify the extra-state, but they do define it.

PART FOUR

PEACE?

Peace is not the resting pulse of humanity, reestablished the moment a peace accord comes into being. It is the pulse of humanity — but it does not rest: it is wild, erratic, fragile, sweet, and too often elusive. Peace is not merely the absence of formal war. It is a child free from the hungers of the twenty-first century; a woman free from fear of assault from either friend or foe; a man who no longer has to look with confusion at where his leg was just a moment before he unwittingly stepped on a land mine.

Peace does not wait for the end of war to make its debut. It takes its greatest definition on the front lines. As one war orphan living on the streets told me during the years of war in Angola: *I carry a little bit of peace in my heart wherever I go, and I take it out at night and look at it.* Peace starts in the trader walking across the front lines to carry critical necessities to a town under siege; it starts in the teacher holding classes outside the bombed-out schoolhouse even though teachers are being targeted for attack; it starts in the songs and paintings of artists who envision ways to end the war; it starts in the belief for a better tomorrow amidst an unbearable today.

But the habits of war die hard. They can carry beyond the front lines and into the fragile pulse of peace. If peace starts in the midst of war, aspects of war continue past peace accords to affect the daily life of a society until they are dismantled, habit by habit. Such work is not easy: some have learned in the pursuits of war that power, profit, and militarized control offer irresistible rewards.

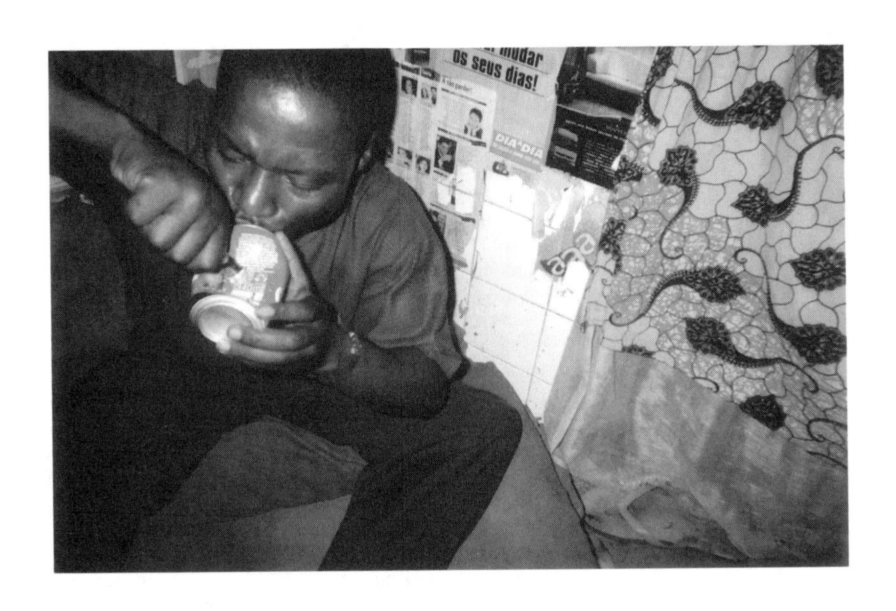

THE SUFFERING OF THE STREETS: HOMELESS WAR-DISPLACED MAN SMOKING CRACK.

CHAPTER 10

THE INSTITUTIONALIZATION OF THE SHADOWS

(HABITS OF WAR MAR LANDSCAPES OF PEACE)

When the truth is too dangerous to tell, people don't stop talking. Instead, they shape truth into stories. People who might be arrested for talking openly of arms transfers and corruption are far less likely to come to harm for telling parables about brothers and birds. But anyone with sharp ears "knows" who the brothers and the birds are, and in this way people gain the information they need to survive.

"The war is ending now, Carolyn, and with this will come many changes," a Mozambican woman I know told me in 1991. "There are things we all will need to understand. Come by my house later today. My children have a story to tell you." Later that day we settled in the woman's living room. I remember being surprised that the women had a sofa in her living room because I knew that the looting and poverty born of war had taken all her household belongings. "I borrowed it from a neighbor," she said seeing my look, "stories need a place to sit," she laughed. Her children gathered round, ready to share in the tale. Clearly this was a story everyone, children and adults, needed to understand:

> It is said at one time we were all brothers and sisters in the forest. Perhaps this is true, but that is another story. Change came to the forest: times of conflict set in. Some had more than others: more food, more anger, more desire. Many had less.
>
> Some brothers were walking through the woods one day, and they heard a bird sitting on the limb of a tall tree singing: "Here are riches, here are riches, here is enough for everyone to eat."
>
> The brothers followed the call of the bird, and found fine treasure for the

taking. It seemed no one's treasure, it was everyone's treasure. "If we took this," the brothers told themselves, "we could start that store we have dreamed of."

Overhearing this, a small bush pig said: "But that makes no sense. There is plenty for all of us. If you take this, the rest of us will starve, and what is the purpose to that? The treasure is of the forest, why harm what has given you this?"

Leaning close together, the brothers whispered among themselves: "What is this little bush pig's nonsense? Let us come back after nightfall and we will help ourselves to the treasure."

If the inhabitants of the forest suffered this loss, the brothers were not aware of it. They prospered, and then they began to fight among themselves. One day the youngest brother was sorting through their beautiful blankets and said, "You have taken more than you have given me; just because I am the youngest, you think you can take advantage of me." "You are mistaken," said the older brothers. "Come, let us take a walk and sort this out."

As they walked into the forest, they came to blows, and the youngest brother was killed. They wrapped him in a blanket, and buried him. But when they returned home, a forest bird began to sing: "Who has killed youngest brother? Who takes a blanket not for warmth, but to hide the dead? Look to the forest."

Infuriated, the brothers took shotguns and tried to shoot the bird, saying, "How dare a simple forest creature defile our names?"

But the townspeople followed the bird into the forest, where they found freshly turned earth, and began to dig. There they saw the blanket, and beneath that, the body of the youngest brother.

The truth was out, but what is the end of this? Did the brothers' store crumble and decay under the weight of the crime? Or are the brothers still thriving, still running big stores, using their fine blankets to cover the truth? These are difficult times, difficult to understand.

Sitting back in her chair, the storyteller reached into her pocket and handed one of her children some coins and said, "Please run to the store and buy us some biscuits, dear."

. . .

When a war ends, it makes less difference than we might think. No alchemy exists whereby state and society "naturally" revert to prewar realities with the declaration of peace. Even in a cease-fire, a country continues on war footing until its institutions and practices are actively redefined toward different ends. My concern in this chapter is with documenting the institutionalization of violence and corruption that can occur in war, and the problems of changing these institutions in the postwar period. This is not a topic restricted to a single war or locale; David Hesketh, who heads the International Assistance Branch of U.K. Customs, spoke with me about the persistence, or momentum, of illegality:

> Soldiers will smuggle. They are cannon fodder. Put people into a warzone and ask them to kill someone, and smuggling, well smuggling is a misdemeanor. You put these people into an environment based on immorality: drinking, drugs, smuggling, killing. How bad does smuggling look next to the killing?
>
> Now a peace accord is signed and someone says it is all over—do you expect this all to end? You expect these smuggling routes to suddenly close up and these people return home hungry and empty-handed?
>
> So what do you do? Bring in customs and police? Preshipment inspection companies? Do full inspection of goods and documents? When the best anyone in the world does is inspect maybe 10 percent of all the goods entering a country or port? This is going to stop the smuggling? The world is not a controllable place, we can't get a handle on it in its entirety—there are just too many factors. Add in the fact that this is now being transferred to globalized trade: companies exist today with the kinds of money and power that used to be exclusive to governments.
>
> And finally, supporting all this is the growing trend for the acceptance of illegal activities in general culture. People now just accept the place and role of illegal activities in their lives when a generation ago they would not.[1]

It's very hard to define the complex relations of a society or state that is technically at peace (by virtue of a formal settlement) while still operating through war-forged institutions (by virtue of practicalities instituted in conflict that have remained unchanged). Yet in these transitional times, we can uncover answers as to why war-style human rights violations continue after a war has ended, and why civil violence and organized crime frequently skyrocket with the signing of a peace accord or a widely supported political transition. In these conditions the complexities of power become apparent, as old and new forms of authority coalesce into hybrid and unexpected forms of governance.

South Africa's Truth and Reconciliation Commission (TRC) was one of the few political entities that publicly illuminated the routinization of violence and corruption marking periods of political hostilities. I choose this example not because these problems are worse in South Africa than in other countries of the world—they are not—but because South Africa's political choice to reveal information on militarization and criminalization supplies substantial information that other countries haven't made public. For this reason alone, South Africa's experiments with TRC hearings are groundbreaking in a political era in which, worldwide, military politics and economics remain largely non-transparent.

I was in South Africa for the opening of the first TRC hearings in 1996.[2] From abroad, it is hard to imagine the degree to which South Africa was caught up in the hearings. They represented a massive psychological as well as social and political evaluation of both the past and the future. It is also hard to imagine from a distance the tremendous impact the TRC disclosures had on South African society. Some of the confessions went beyond everyone's darkest projections. I returned to South Africa for the second year of the hearings in 1997, and the TRC confessions continued to rock the very soul of the country as people were exposed to the frightful extremes of which humanity was capable. This time is etched in my memory as the "*Brai* period." *Brai* is a South African word for barbecue, and several confessions involved soldiers torturing political prisoners with fire while *brai*-ing their daily meals. People who had lost loved ones in this manner, and people who had loved ones who conducted these atrocities, found their most core beliefs of *what is and what can't be* challenged in the most devastating ways.

To understand how these atrocities configure post-conflict politics, it is necessary to investigate as well how peace processes during the time of conflict configured the Truth and Reconciliation Commission. Apartheid's hold in South Africa was dealt a fatal blow in the early 1990s when a coalition of parties, both apartheid-government and anti-apartheid, formed the National Peace Accord to combat the rampant violence in the country.

An independent commission agreed to by all parties was formed to investigate the causes of the violence. It was headed by Judge Richard Goldstone, who opted for complete public transparency in the process. Goldstone had the names of all investigating officers published in local papers to see if anyone had issue with any of the selections. In a country where security forces had enacted serious human rights violations, he felt that anyone associated with his commission who had been involved in such abuses would undermine his chances of success. Perhaps more groundbreaking was his decision to publish materials he confiscated during a raid of military headquarters demonstrating that government security forces were routinely involved in human rights abuses against citizens, and that these actions had been directed by high-level authorities.

On this evidence, the government was forced to relieve from duty a number of security personnel, including some generals.

Goldstone also made public the commission's findings that senior police officers, including the National Deputy Commissioner of Police, were involved in contracting murders of African leaders and disrupting the peace process in the country as a whole. At the time I interviewed Judge Goldstone in 1997 post-apartheid South Africa, the minister of defense during the apartheid government and a number of the leaders of the South African Army were on trial for murder and other criminal activities, including fraud involving millions of rand.[3]

The tone set by the Goldstone Commission affected the country's decision to conduct the Truth and Reconciliation Commission hearings at the end of the apartheid government.[4] The TRC was set up on the principle that political and social reconciliation in the post-apartheid era required making public the truths of the human rights abuses and criminal activities of all parties during apartheid's political violence, as well as making restitution to victims and their families. Truth, it was said, allows for system change, and carries its own political penalty. Thus, amnesty was granted to those making full and public statements of illegal activities, from murder and torture to robbery and trafficking, within the rubric of political crimes.

The relative success of the TRC will likely be debated for years to come. Many think the amnesty process, with its full declaration of criminal activities, was needed to illuminate the corruption embedded in the society's formal governing institutions so that changes could be made. Others argue that justice can't be served without punishing perpetrators. And still others worry that the amnesty process — where all criminals have to do is publicly confess — reinforces the very culture of crime that the TRC sought to dismantle. These arguments are important, not only to South Africa, but to a world trying to come to grips with severe cultures of political violence and the difficult issues of postwar reconstruction.

The Goldstone Commission and the Truth and Reconciliation Commission clearly demonstrated that the level of criminal activities and atrocities institutionalized in politico-military structures is much greater than most people in society realize. Richard Goldstone told me in conversation that most South Africans were unaware of the extent and severity of the criminal activities in the security forces and were shocked at the disclosures. In fact, the expression "shocking revelations" often adheres to the TRC confessions. In 1997, when I was speaking with a man who had worked with the TRC since its inception, I noticed he frequently used the phrase "shocking revelations." I finally asked him if he, a person who had lived in this country and dealt with the problems of political violence all his life, a person who had helped forge the TRC and worked with it daily, did in fact find the revelations shocking. He replied:

> You know, I have worked with this from the start. I know of terrible political violence from my growing-up years, and I thought I was prepared for it all. But even I found some of the disclosures of these men shocking. Men with families, men who would go home and play with their kids, torturing and maiming and murdering people in the most horrific of ways during the day, and their families and neighbors saying they never had a clue until the man detailed his activities at a TRC hearing.

This discussion isn't intended to paint South Africa as particularly immoral; these activities take place worldwide.[5] Nor is it intended to paint members of the public as hopelessly uninformed wherever this occurs in the world. My point is that when people are largely unaware of the extent to which violence, human rights abuses, and criminal activities are operationalized within the political, economic, legal, and social frameworks of their society, they will be largely unable to correct them. Knowledge must precede action.

The TRC disclosures have shown an apartheid politico-military system whose criminal activities extended well beyond the torture, rape, maiming, arson, and murder that usually define individual human rights violations.

- — Members of the security forces engaged in drug, ivory, precious gem, and mineral running to raise money for their cause and to purchase arms and supplies.
- — Members of the security forces were involved in bank robbery, embezzlement, and money laundering.
- — Members of the security forces were involved in the falsification of records, the illegal sales of licenses, and the fabrication of evidence.
- — Members of the security forces acted to foment violence between the different anti-apartheid parties, by, for example, murdering members of one group dressed as, and proclaiming to be, members of another.
- — Some judges and courts issued politically and racially biased rulings.

— Certain key public sector businesses were linked to criminal activities such as running supplies, transferring armaments, laundering money, and implementing racist policies.

The list goes on.[6]

These criminal activities became embedded in the everyday functioning of the country's governing institutions. This is not to say everyone was implicated. Nor is it to say that the institutions were fundamentally criminal, for they were not. It is to say that these activities did not take place outside the scope of normal institutional life: where they occurred, they occurred as part and parcel of "the way things are done." Society emerges through these processes; they become institutionalized.

It is sheer naiveté to think these vast interrelated systems of governance and industry — these entrenched bureaucracies — can be changed overnight with an election and a change of government. The bureaucracy that defines a country actually changes little with a change of government. The key officials may change, but the day-to-day running of the institutions — the people involved in the minutia of everyday political, security, legal, educational, and economic activities — remain largely unchanged, as do the habits and policies that guide them.

Two things happen when power changes hands or war comes to an end. First, the people most marginalized in the change of power — often those most implicated in stigmatized criminal activities — leave the formal sector, and many simply continue to exploit their criminal networks as a career move. Put simply: a government official or soldier who engaged in criminal activities to raise funds for purchasing sanctioned arms can continue in these activities unofficially after a change of power. This may perpetuate organized crime, or it may involve more creative political moves, like the formation of the mercenary organization Executive Outcomes by former members of the South African Defense Force . Either way, these people remain linked with international extra-state political and economic networks.

Second, most people in the country continue in their jobs. That includes those involved in money scams, illegal transfers of goods, biased legal rulings, and human rights violations. A new government may institute new policies, but most don't have the means to assign new people to all the legal, executive, and security jobs that carry these policies out. Put simply: a judge who condoned human rights violations during apartheid is unlikely to undergo a radical transformation of character after a change of government. This judge may be viewed by a new constituency as a neutral official, and left in place. Or a country may have so few trained judges that the choice is either this one or no one. Either way, old habits infuse new systems. This holds across government offices, security forces, educational institutions, and powerful business interests. Journalist Derek Rodney wrote that in post-apartheid South Africa,

> organized-crime syndicates are increasingly using apartheid-era covert structures to further their aims. State intelligence experts believe illegal privatized intelligence agencies are posing a threat to national security. The situation has deteriorated so much that National Intelligence Coordinating Committee (NICOC) coordinator Linda Mti has called for a comprehensive audit of the country's apartheid-era military, police and civilian covert structures.
>
> The aim is to root out rogue structures which are believed to be increasingly turning to criminal activities and furthering hidden political agendas. . . .
>
> The running costs of these front organizations were hidden in previous [apartheid-era] state budgets, although many are believed to have become self-sustaining. Some of these covert structures continue with their original briefs although they are no longer manipulated and controlled directly. They have become a driving force of a low-intensity conflict aimed at undermining [post-apartheid] government.[7]

Rodney's comment that many of these organizations have become self-sustaining is critical to understanding the difficulties of postwar transitions. As the TRC documented, apartheid-era forces participated in bank robberies, drug- and gunrunning, ivory smuggling, resource looting, and the like. The politics and the institutionalization of crime that shape a country aren't purely national phenomenon; they are deeply constituted through regional and international associations. South Africa's link to then Zaire (now Democratic Republic of Congo) is one example of many implicated in the fortunes of political instability.

Journalist June Bearzi wrote in South Africa's the *Star:*

> StarLine first learnt of the [Zaire–South Africa] smuggling networks in 1988 when it was investigating the organized "carnage" kings, who were having a field day decimating Africa's rhino and elephant population.
>
> South Africa was used as a pipeline to smuggle the horns and ivory to the Far East. StarLine also uncovered the smuggling of diamonds, cobalt and copper in concealed compartments in huge pantechnicons [moving vans] and trailers from Zaire through Zambia and Botswana to South Africa. . . . For many years, the operators have clandestinely sold their spoils [speaking here of diamonds only], valued at about 173 million Rand [USA$40 million] a month, in various countries, including South Africa and Belgium.[8]

Markets change moment by moment, and the fluid nature of non-legal networks allows them to adapt readily to new and expanding economic conditions. In 2000, four years after Bearzi's article, the metallic ore coltan (which is refined into tantalum and used in everything from cell phones and laptops to Sony PlayStations) became the commodity of the month, earning more than gold in the Democratic Republic of Congo. Mozambique and South Africa have become major drug transfer points, and illicit diamonds and non-transparent oil kickbacks have funded both war and peace in Angola. These, of course, are the media-sexy topics. But the meat and potatoes of extra-state systems remain further hidden from public scrutiny, as well as closer to everyday life. For example, Victor Dwyer investigated the issuance of false clearance certificates to car hijackers in South Africa that legally "prove" cars have not been stolen and render them legal for resale.[9]

These aren't small-change endeavors. South Africa's Moldenhauer Commission found that improperly and illegally issuing special licenses for family, friends, and those willing to pay bribes was a multimillion-rand business in the country's Mpumalanga area alone.[10] Derek Rodney found that for the country in general, "at least one in every ten consignment of goods which passes through South Africa's borders violates VAT [value added tax] export conditions, resulting in state tax revenue losses estimated at about R 17 billion [$3.9 billion] in the five years since 1992, when VAT was introduced."[11]

These realities have escalated in the twenty-first century. Peter Gastrow writes: "Most of the international focus on Southern African organized crime is on drug trafficking. This category of organized crime is regarded by regional police agencies as a significantly less serious threat than the theft of and trafficking in motor vehicles."[12] Gastrow explains:

> The reason why this form of criminal activity is regarded as such a threat isn't only because the theft of motor vehicles is widespread but, as mentioned before, this crime is closely intertwined with the trafficking of drugs, firearms, diamonds, and other illegally obtained goods. Stolen vehicles constitute a ready currency in exchange for a wide range of illicit goods. . . . The head of the Interpol's Subregional Bureau in Harare described their operations as follows: "All countries in the region have supplied intelligence that has been analysed by Interpol and by the countries themselves. There are very clear relationships and interlinking factors between crime syndicates operating in Southern Africa. It is not a secret to law enforcement agencies of the region that the criminals in the region have better co-operation links than the police officers. They seem to know who to contact at all times and budgetary constraints, foreign cur-

rency shortages, visa problems or governmental authority to travel did not control their movements."[13]

South Africa is now suffering one of the highest crime rates in the world, partly as a result of the degree to which crime was institutionalized in the years of apartheid and political violence. Mark Shaw observes: "There is a clear and crucial link between South Africa's transition and the growth in crime that has accompanied it. But it would be dangerously simplistic to argue that crime is purely a consequence of the transition. Indeed, strong evidence suggests that the roots of crime lie in the apartheid system that the transition sought to leave behind."[14]

Focusing on the issue of arms, sociologist Jacklyn Cock writes that the level of violent crime in post-apartheid South Africa is linked to the dangerous proliferation of light weapons and that this explosive combination can undermine the consolidation of what some have called the most important experiment in democracy since the end of the Second World War. Cock argues that solving this problem will require a holistic approach: "Discussions framed in narrow legal or technical terms are analytically deficient; the issue encompasses social relationships, values, beliefs, practices, and identities. The demand for light weapons is socially constructed; the supply is socially organized. Ultimately the proliferation problem in the region requires a social solution."[15]

INSTITUTIONALIZING VIOLENCE AND CRIME: A LOOK AT BRAZIL FROM SOUTH AFRICA

South Africa is emerging from minority rule and the associated political violence of apartheid-era governance. While clearly positive, this kind of transition brings its own problems. Comparing South Africa and Brazil, Brandon Hamber, who worked with the Center for the Study of Violence and Reconciliation in Johannesburg during the political transition in South Africa, argues that the high incidence of criminal violence and police brutality marking Brazil, and indeed much of Latin America, today is linked to the patterns of militarized abuse instituted during military dictatorships and political repression. "New forms of violence," he writes, "follow the move to democracy."[16]

Brazil's period of military rule extended from 1964 to 1985, and during this time thousands were tortured, 262 were murdered, and 144 were listed as missing. These figures, Hamber notes, aren't as high as the tens of thousands of "the disappeared" reported in countries like Argentina. But they are significant enough to have set into motion a system of police and military human rights abuses in Brazil that continues today. Part of the explanation, Hamber suggests, is the blanket amnesty granted in 1979, which ensured that no official truth about the political violence would be uncovered, and no public reckoning would take place. For Hamber, the power of this act is summed up in the following quote from the Brazilian Armed Forces on the 1979 amnesty: "We no longer talk about it, let us blot this page from history as if nothing has happened; once amnesty has been granted we can re-establish a state of constitutional normalcy."[17]

Hamber, following Coimbra,[18] argues that the philosophies and actions of the military police today stem from the military regime of the past. He points out that in 1992, for example, military police under state jurisdiction killed 1,470 people in São Paulo alone.[19] (By comparison, there were 27 similar deaths in New York City that year.) Hamber notes that torture is still practiced in the majority of police inquiries, and accusations of abuse are rarely investigated.[20] Perhaps the most shocking figure comes from a 1994 Americas Watch report quoted by Hamber that documents the deaths of 5,644 children and youths between the ages of five and seventeen between the years 1988 and 1991.

As elsewhere, the poor, marginalized, and powerless in Brazil suffer the most human rights abuses, writes Hamber. During Brazil's military regime, middle-class people such as academics, journalists, and labor organizers were targeted along with the poor, but the abuses against the middle classes largely ended with the regime, while those against the poor and powerless continue unabated. In a passage where he wittingly or unwittingly likens present circumstances to "war," Hamber writes:

> The result is a particularly heavy-handed approach to crime fighting and a broad range of human rights violations committed by the police and even the public. Coimbra (1996) argues that exterminations, lynchings, public justice are being encouraged (albeit covertly) and judges and perpetrators are being used to consummate the necessary social clearance. In Brazil, essentially built on a bedrock of structural violence and social inequality, a war against the poor prevails so as to maintain social order and economic elitism (cf. Pinheiro, 1994). All actions are justified as allegedly fighting rampant crime. However the methods violate human rights in the same way as in the past although the "cause" is significantly different.[21]

This institutionalization of militarized violence permeates many levels of the structures of authority. Ousted by a change of government, military officials can move directly into crime. But many don't have to move. Known military human rights violators frequently continue on in positions of power. Hamber cites a military torturer who was made Brazil's ambassador to the United Kingdom. In a final irony, many military human rights violators now head profitable and politically powerful private security firms, employing the same tactics as they did in their previous public roles. Hamber concludes that these realities are not limited to Brazil, but that many other Latin American countries, including Chile, Argentina, and Peru, show very similar problems. Countries coming out of an era of militarized governance, such as South Africa, can benefit from understanding, and correcting, this institutionalization of violence.

I have pointed out elsewhere that people don't simply kill or not kill, torture or not torture.[22] A vast and complicated set of beliefs and values must be in place to determine (and justify) who may and may not be killed, how they may be harmed, by whom, and under what conditions. These are all supported and sanctioned by strong appeals to ethics, morals, obligations, and duties. Hamber provides a statistic that gives pause for reflection in this context. In discussing the book *Brazil: Nunco Mais* (Brazil: Never More),[23] he notes that it includes descriptions of 283 types of torture used by the military during the 1964–1979 period. Arguments abound regarding the supposed utility of torture. Some hold on to the belief that torture is simply an expedient way to gain important information. Many recognize that torture has little to do with gaining information — many torturers don't even ask questions — and quite a bit to do with creating a culture of terror and repression.[24] Some argue that conceptual pathology lies at the heart of torture-based regimes, such as that during Argentina's "dirty war."[25] But can logic even embrace the idea of 283 different types of torture? This would seem to go beyond any notion of information gathering; beyond even a twisted logic of rule by terror and repression. Perhaps it goes beyond pathological, if such a thing is possible.

Important in all this is understanding the political and military philosophies, policies, and practices that make such actions possible, that justified them in the minds of those responsible for creating 283 different kinds of torture. How do philosophies and practices become institutionalized? What kinds of philosophies and practices do the people who performed and allowed these acts bring with them to work in the days *after* their regime gave way to a new one? What kind of political beliefs do they take away with them at the end of the day, into the streets, back to their communities and their homes? What exactly does peace mean to them?

PEACE IN THE MIDST OF WAR: PUBLIC WALL FRONTING PEACE'S HOME – A BARREN DIRT HILL IN THE CITY CENTER.

CHAPTER 11

THE AUTOBIOGRAPHY OF A MAN CALLED PEACE

I met Peace on the streets of Angola; the streets were his home. I have known him for several years, and each year he revealed a bit more of his life story to me. The last time I was in Angola, Peace was in his early twenties, and had already lived many lives: street child, soldier, thief, father, visionary. Peace has the gift all anthropologists look for: he could see beyond the obvious, through illusions, and into the heart of the indescribable — and he could put his observations in words. Peace and I had many conversations sitting on the curbs of Angolan streets. In his words, he wanted me to "understand the depth of the suffering of the street people of Angola."

The night before I was to leave Angola, Peace showed up at my residence unexpectedly. He said he had a present for me, something he knew I would love. He handed me his autobiography, handwritten in Portuguese, on a sheaf of papers.[1] It is the story of war, poverty, shadows, peace, and hope.

AUTOBIOGRAPHY

I was born in Benguela Province and came, with my mother, to Luanda in 1982. This was the same year in which I met my father who was living with another woman, a mulata.

After a year, I went to live with my father and soon thereafter I began to study in the first grade at Jungo School in Bairro Operário. For unknown reasons, we moved from the neighborhood of São Paulo to Barrio K where we lived with my stepmother and my half-brother (same father) because my father was not in Luanda at the time.

It was difficult to get used to my stepmother but as she wasn't one of those who are difficult, everything went well until she separated from my father in 1987.

In 1987, after that separation, my life began to become dangerous seeing as my father was frustrated. As I didn't have any adults to stay with I went to the 11 de Novembro Children's Home where I attended the 1987/88 and 1988/89 school years but from which I fled as I couldn't get used to the way of life there. As a consequence of this I didn't study for a year and I spent my afternoons riding a bicycle until I became very skilled—so much so that I earned the name "Peace."

I was so well known that wherever I went even the children called to me by name and I made lots of friends and then, for the first time, I started to like Arminda, who would become my first girlfriend. This was in 1991 and she was studying in the seventh grade at the Juventude e Luta [Youth and Struggle] School.

In 1992 I was arrested because of the bad company I kept and it was then that I started to smoke cigarettes, although I had already tried marijuana but I didn't smoke it. In prison I met many other young people who had committed a variety of crimes as well as others who, but for a lack of rigor in the treatment of their cases, would not have been there. At the time I was seventeen years old. At Christmas the prison didn't have any water or food. Visitations were daily and relatives had to bring food and water and bedsheets and mattresses as the beds were made of cement.

One of the things that struck me there was the fact that there in prison they sold everything from drinks to drugs.

Some [prisoners], because of hunger or addiction to smoking, traded their clothes for food or for cigarettes. The most disturbing was when a sixteen-year-old boy had anal sex for a bowl of food.

Confronted with such situations I asked myself: "My God, what country is this with no place to reeducate minors or to imprison them with decent conditions?"

I stopped having to face such sad and inhuman things after I was released.

Yes, I stopped seeing people dying of hunger.

Yes, I stopped seeing people being imprisoned without their families even knowing it . . . and then some days later when their relatives appeared they received the news that their son or nephew had died three days earlier.

It was very sad that as soon as I was released the confrontation between UNITA and the MPLA exploded and I entered the military. After the recruitment process, and nine months of basic training, I was placed in a brigade in the company that supplied the command. I participated in the liberation of Caxito and later graduated to sergeant second class.

In the month of June 1993 I asked my superior to let me go for a few days, seeing that I had just turned eighteen years old and needed to see my friends and family. So I left Funda [a municipality in Bengo Province] where my unit was located and went to Luanda to see my friends and family. Once in Luanda I was happy because more than a year had passed since we had all seen each other. During three days of vacation I could see Arminda, my girlfriend, and Dinho, my best childhood friend; with him I started to smoke marijuana in that same year, 1993. At the end of my vacation days I returned to my unit, where I remained until the liberation of Kwanza Norte, where I was hit by two enemy bullets in the lower region of my body and was soon evacuated to the military hospital.

As there were difficulties with medical assistance at the time, by the grace of God, they operated on my left femur and I recuperated for a couple months and then walked with crutches for another month.

Feeling hopeless, I didn't return to my unit but stayed at my father's house. He had already married another woman, a black woman, with whom I had problems for having dated her younger sister. This situation created big problems and family difficulties and as a result I left the house to live in a room, and it was from that date that I began to have very little contact with my father and the others at home.

In this period I already had bad habits: from cigarettes to women. Then I went back to study in 1994 in the eighth grade until, due to necessity, since my parents could no longer support me, I began to wash cars behind the Hotel Pacífico.

My dream was always to have a good position in society and even today I ask myself what I have done wrong in life to not have what others have.

In 1995, even as I was studying and innocent of what was going to happen to me, I began to smoke even more with my childhood friend. A year later I went to middle school at INE [National Institute of Education], where I was even well received by the sisters as the same building belongs to the priests of the Catholic church.

On March 3, 1996, drunk, I got into a fight with two guys in which one of them had a pocket knife. Defenseless, I ran off and hid by the Hotel Pacífico air conditioners, which are on the terrace of the first floor of the building next door. One of the security guards found me there and grabbed me and accused me of stealing one of the air conditioners.

So I was arrested on suspicion of theft and went to the Viana Penitentiary. There, dear reader, you better believe, I thought I was at the end of the world seeing malnourished young men and adults, imprisoned but with their sentence time already having expired some one or two years earlier, and not knowing how to resolve their situation. And if there is something I won't forget it is the number of deaths that occurred there, caused by everything from malnutrition to attempting to escape. It always pissed me off when I saw that when visitors were brought in they only showed the prisoners that were in good physical condition and they hid the "Biafrans," or malnourished.

Another situation that relates to common crimes—in the case of theft of a gas canister, a pair of pants, a cloth—in my opinion, these cases should not end up in prison and they take such a long time to resolve.

The funniest thing was when, in the hall, I would see some prisoners screaming, "Who has a cigarette to trade for farinha de musseque [ground dried cassava]?" So the one who needed farinha and had a cigarette shouted, "Here in cell 27!" and then they would trade. For me the break was always very interesting because of the sun and I would stay there watching the others tanning themselves like broiled fish.

Some were full of skin infections and other illnesses. When I was in prison, three or four people would die per day from hunger and from a variety of diseases.

Six months later I was released and I promised never to return to that damned place, to which I testified in church. It was a testimony that I based on the Bible and which affected many fellow sufferers who were also there in the Sunday service conducted by the Pentecostal Assembly of God.

Once free, I found a variety of difficulties due to the time I had spent between four walls. Sometimes I felt like the planet Earth was on top of me. On the other hand, I was also happy because I found that I had a son because before I went to prison I got a girlfriend pregnant. In that period Arminda had already died . . . a young woman that I had loved so much and who I remember even today . . . I have had many girlfriends, but not like her.

Since I couldn't find a job I returned to washing cars behind the Hotel Pacífico, where I met many young folks and even one guy considered the "king"—the "king" because he would beat up everyone and so they were all scared of him.

With my return the situation changed, given that I always opted for reason and he is one of those who whether or not he is right is always tough with his colleagues. At a certain point his reign was over when we fought because he had me put in the Second Squadron [police station].

As a result of this fight he ended up with a dislocated arm and totally embarrassed and he disappeared from the area only to reappear after a few months. Be that as it was, according to many of the other guys there, his days of exploiting people there were over. He would always make other people wash the client's car, and then, after the car was clean, he would pay each of them only 3 percent of the money he received. Sometimes he didn't pay at all, and those who complained were beaten up . . . and it was because of this that everyone hated him.

Summing up, with the "king's" fall, the weaker ones that didn't have clients felt relieved.

With time, the situation where we washed cars changed with the appearance of the police, who would spend the day charging us for each car that was washed. That's when I switched from day to night. I would spend the night as a "protector" for some friends and girlfriends that prostituted themselves. It wasn't easy for me to get used to but I finally managed and I made lots of friends, including foreigners, given that I speak a little English and was therefore able to translate for some guys who needed the girls for sexual relations.

My life was worsening because I spent the night awake and would only go to sleep at four or five in the morning to wake up at three or four in the afternoon.

I was always a nice person and some people even said they liked to hear me talk. Curious, I asked them why, and they said they liked to hear me talk because of my accent. This is good because I felt happy to know that everyone likes me.

As for my work colleagues behind the Pacífico, some were good and others bad and I, as always, knew how to choose friendships and the ones with whom I could best speak are J., Y., K., and N.—a boy who is sixteen who I liked so much and I even later went to live with him, seeing that he slept on the street.

As for romances I have to say that I have had many and the one that touched me most was Vanusa, a mixed-race girl.

It touched me most because it was good and I remember that on one Tuesday I was shirtless and shoeless on the roof of the small building that houses a generator behind the Hotel Pacífico. I looked to the right and saw a mulata with the body of a model, with long braids. So I called to her and she told me to climb down.

Climbing down, I gave her my hand and told her my name.

She asked me if I was Peace who studies at INE. I then answered "yes." Then she asked me if I was the Peace who sells weed? I said "yes" because at that time I sold weed, that is, marijuana, and I wasn't smoking. Continuing with the conversation, I tried to find out something about her. So she told me that she didn't have a boyfriend and that men are a pain. Seduced by her I said, look, they aren't all the same and that maybe she should try to find a different one.

I have never been so attracted by a woman—I could have kidnapped her!

Time went by and then we said goodbye to one another and she promised to appear the next day.

On Wednesday she showed up around 2 P.M. I was washing a car so I got a colleague to finish doing it for me and I went to attend to the slim girl with whom I dreamed of traveling to those lands where the deeper the better and that only I, only I, know.

The greatest coincidence was when I discovered that she had the same sign as I do and then she wanted to smoke so I took her to a place where it is safe to smoke pot [ngansa].

Feeling shy, I was without courage to say what I felt for her! "Hey man, why do you look at me like that?" she asked. I responded by saying, "You are very pretty." "Thanks," she said, taking a hit of the weed, and it was over. "I am waiting for the driver," she said. Surprised, I asked who her father was and she explained that her father was the boss of one of the sections of a nongovernmental business, or NGO, and that he was very mean. Then I got scared and suddenly the driver appeared and she took off without saying whether she would come by the next day.

One day later, on Friday, she showed up with a female cousin of hers saying that this girl wanted to start smoking weed.

Curious, I kissed her on the cheeks and we introduced ourselves and without avoiding the subject, I asked if it was true and she said yes and then we left to go to my room. When we arrived there I rolled a joint and Jessica was "baptized"—this is the term they use when someone starts smoking drugs. On the same day, without my knowing that she wanted to have an affair with me, Vanusa stayed in my room after Jessica left.

"Vanusa, I have to go work," I said, so that she would go. And she said, "I am going to stay because I don't have to go yet."

I went down to the Hotel Pacífico, where I washed cars. When I returned to my room I found Vanusa resting. At 7 P.M. I asked her if she wasn't going home. She answered, telling me not to worry, giving me more courage to confront her, and so I said, "Vanusa, given that we have known each other only a short time, how would you feel if I asked you out?" She then responded, "You fool! If I weren't interested in you, would I be here until now?"

Then I kissed her and she gave me a huge hug and took off my shirt. As she was also shirtless I began to kiss her earlobes and her nipples that were increasingly attracting me. With her voice very low I felt her groan, "Oh, Peace!" It was good, so good that we stayed together almost a week and it even seemed like a honeymoon.

It is sad because after six days we separated and we never saw each other again.

Today I am the father of a son and I do everything for him—suffering but bearing it.

THE END.

WOUNDED BOY RECEIVING THERAPY IN A MAKESHIFT CLINIC IN A SMALL BUDDHIST TEMPLE IN SRI LANKA. THE TEMPLE AND MONK WERE ATTACKED AFTER THIS PHOTO WAS TAKEN IN 1985.

CHAPTER 12

THE TIME OF NOT-WAR-NOT-PEACE

We stood at the military checkpoint to cross into the no-man's-lands. That isn't what they are formally called; in fact, I don't know if there is a formal name for these dangerous stretches of land and political irony. Our checkpoint was at the end of the MPLA government's zone of control. Ahead lay an ungoverned stretch of land, some kilometers across. Beyond it was another armed checkpoint, as you entered the zone of control of the rebel force UNITA.

> I will never get used to these, never feel comfortable, *said a man I was traveling with.* We are in the middle of nowhere, and we are in the middle of military control. These soldiers at this godforsaken outpost are law here. We have a joke, only it isn't a joke: they shoot and don't even bother to ask questions later. These borders are highly charged; people are not allowed free movement from government to UNITA areas, all movement is restricted and controlled.

This was 1996; it was "peacetime" Angola.

I was traveling with an agriculture team that had permission to help develop UNITA's crops. For government and UNITA alike, crop development was critical. The government and the NGOs considered over half the Angolan population to be suffering food deprivation. The croplands were largely under UNITA control, and political frictions or not, these lands produced food that the entire population needed. As the team explained their travel plans to the soldiers, I gazed out on the no-man's-lands. Under normal circumstances, they might be considered beautiful. Nothing but a single roadway marked this sweep of nature — no houses, no industries, no strip mining or logging, no pollution, no communications lines. High savanna stretched as far as eye could see. The UNITA territory was too far away to be visible.

But the land's natural beauty hid a deeper existential blemish. These checkpoints represented political domains: government control and UNITA control, peace or not-peace. The movement of people and goods across these domains was political, and therefore restricted. But of course movement was essential: UNITA's lands were the breadbasket of the country, and the government's infrastructure provided access to essential hard goods. Each group needed the resources of the other. While peace experts worldwide pointed out that separate political zones controlling the movement of people and goods didn't appear too "peaceful" and clearly inhibited development, the population carried on as best it could. For many, that meant braving the no-man's-lands to trade for life's essentials.

The no-man's-lands were unregulated. They belonged to no one, since the government's and UNITA's influence stopped at their checkpoints. Kilometers lay in between the two and ran for hundreds of kilometers along the lengths of political borders. But what, exactly, is a state? This question shows how strongly the idea is entrenched in popular thought that all land can be represented on a color-coded map with some sovereign group's name attached.

Yet here was a no-bodies'-land. It defied the ontologies of states. But it was not free of bodies. Unarmed traders stepped apprehensively across its natural beauty; in the folds of state-less-ness, soldiers hid from enemy soldiers in contests for control; roving bands of armed predators looked for easy prey; and land-locked pirates found it a haven. Millions of dollars worth of unregulated goods crossed these borders, exchanged hands, shaped power. Untold lives were lost. If it was a land of shadows, it was populated by ghosts: people without name or affiliation, for what trader, what soldier violating border laws would dare announce this? But the ghosts were also real. People say that a person left to die alone, without ceremony or burial, will wander the land, angry and tormented by sorrow. The no-man's-lands were filled with such ghosts.

. . .

There is a political reality we do not have a name for. In Angola, I have heard people call it a time of "not-war-not-peace." Essentially it is a time when military actions occur that in and of themselves would be called "war" or "low-intensity warfare," but are not so labeled because they are hidden by a peace process no one wants to admit is failing. Acts of war are called "police actions," "banditry," "accidents," or they are simply not called anything at all — they are silenced in public discussion. As one ex-soldier told me, "If we talk of this" — and he drew his finger across his neck in the universal throat-slitting sign — "we don't talk again."

A vast international machinery, a global bureaucracy, attends most peace processes. Diplomats from all points of the world host meeting after meeting. The United Nations sends everyone from high-level representatives to blue-helmeted ground troops — plus the massive infrastructures providing the goods and services to support them — in peacemaking efforts. The United Nations spent a million dollars *a day* in Mozambique and Angola preparing for the elections. Hundreds of INGOs are dedicated to the cause of peace, dispatching their personnel and their citizen's pennies to help. Lest people think that only a handful of INGOs operate in any given country at any given time, it is common to find upward of two hundred in locales in Africa, and three hundred in more accessible war-afflicted regions like the Balkans. In 1990, in the final years of the war, Mozambique hosted over 180 national and international NGOs providing services in-country.

Such people's lives, their careers, their reputations are staked on peace. These people work among a war-weary populace that often can't bear to think of yet another deadly round of war breaking out. *War* becomes a taboo word. Officially, the war dead, the refugees, the soldiers on the front lines, do not exist. "Illusion," as the street children in the following chapter say when talking of adults and their notions of power. Of course, policies cannot address war, for it isn't taking place. Peace is.

In 1996 the second United Nations peacekeeping effort in Angola was under way. The first had failed miserably when the 1992 democratic elections that the UN monitored as part of the peace process gave way to some of the most virulent fighting the country had seen since independence. Backed by several major world governments, the UN was invested in "doing it right" this time. They were overseeing the Lusaka Accords, and demobilization was under way.[1]

But it was a curious demobilization. UNITA continued to control over half the country, and populations were forcibly subjugated. No-man's-lands abounded. The UNITA "soldiers" showing up at the demobilization centers were often suspiciously young or old, suspiciously untrained, and carrying suspiciously old or broken weapons. People assumed that ordinary peasants were being "demobilized" while the true soldiers continued to operate in UNITA-held zones. Everyone was suspicious, yet no major changes or challenges were made. No one saw a way to address the situation without derailing the "peace" process. Or maybe it was just too big and complex a problem. "Peace," like war, becomes institutionalized, and institutions are notoriously difficult to challenge. Everyone did their job; no one knew how to do otherwise.

When I tried to return to Angola in 1997, the peace process was fully under way. UNITA had agreed to a government of unity, and the political resolution was being hailed as a diplomatic victory and a score for democracy. So why was I stalled for two whole months when I tried to get my visa? Laurent Kabila had just swept into Kinshasa, proclaiming that Zaire was now the Democratic Republic of Congo. Angolan government troops were dispatched to the Congo border "to control the Zairian refugees causing havoc in Angola," as the official word had it. What was not mentioned was that these troops had been dispatched to UNITA-controlled areas, areas where major diamond mines were located. UNITA, of course, claimed the government was waging war on them. No one mentioned that Zaire's Mobutu Sese Seko had supported UNITA and that Kabila maintained alliances with the MPLA government. With Kabila's success in Zaire/Congo, the MPLA could play a power card against UNITA and for the diamond-rich areas. Meanwhile, I had been waiting endless weeks for my visa, a visa that a parade of consular officers kept telling me would come "anydaynow." Finally, a sympathetic woman in an Angolan embassy in Africa said, "Give it up, Carolyn. It is too delicate to give visas now, with this war problem in Angola." "War problem": the "public secret," as Michael Taussig calls those truths everyone knows about but never speaks of publicly.[2]

I gave up trying in 1997. No visa—due to peace.

The next year, 1998, I was given a two-year multiple-entry visa to go to Angola. Peacetime, officially. But the headlines of Southern African newspapers read, "Angola Sinks Back into War." People in Luanda had begun stockpiling in preparation for escalated fighting, and all INGOs throughout the country were confined to provincial capitals the week I arrived: too many attacks and deaths had been taking place. I traveled to the province of Malange, where, everyone told me, tensions ran high. Attacks were taking place throughout the region with regularity—attacks formally called "banditry," a word the average townspeople sneered at: "Banditry, military, rogue troops, war — we have it all."

One of the local NGOs let me stay in a back room they had in their office, since accommodation (as well as electricity, fuel, cooking supplies, and just about everything else) was scarce. That evening several of the local Angolan staff returned to share a meal with me. Over food they relaxed into conversation different from the dialogues of the workaday world:

> "Can you feel it?" they asked me, looking out into the night sky.
>
> "Feel what?" I asked.
>
> "The war. It's here, you know. We aren't supposed to talk about it, but everyone knows."
>
> "Just a couple of years back, Malange was under siege and desperate. We had nothing, we ate grass—well, the lucky ones did; many did not live. And we can feel the same times again, coming. Food sources are drying up, we can't get petrol, medicines, the things we need.
>
> "And what happens? We are told that to try to do trade to get what we need is helping the enemy. 'What good reason do you have for being out here?' the soldiers ask—saying of course that there can be no good reason. The more we can't trade, the more desperate we become, the more we need to trade, the more it becomes a suspicious activity. People are shot for this.
>
> "But, look, in truth, the petrol is flowing, the food is moving, goods circulate. Trade is brisk. Excellent, some would say. But it is done by the soldiers. They shoot us for doing what they are making a fortune on. More goods than bullets go across the front lines."[3]

The same kind of violence was taking place all across Angola. When I arrived back in Luanda from Malange, I ran into a man trying to get his bags up the stairs to his room, just down the hall from me. The man was friendly, but he was shaking so badly he couldn't get his bags up the steps. I helped him with his things, and asked what had upset him so.

> "I work for the World Lutheran Council, and I was just evacuated from Moxico Province under horrible fire. We fled with gunfire and bombs going off over our heads. I had to crawl over dead bodies. The whole place erupted. I have lived there two years and have never seen anything like it. It was awful, I tell you, so many dead, so many bodies. The whole place occupied. We had to flee to DRCongo, and then up to Kinshasa, and I've just arrived back here. I'm from Cameroon, and I tell you, I've seen a lot in my

life, but I'm dreaming of going home now. I don't want to ever go through that again."

"What was the fighting about in the area where you were?" I asked.

"Fighting?" He looked at me and shook his head. "Fighting? In my area? This isn't fighting. This is the war. The whole damn province is in war. UNITA has occupied the whole place, the whole province and Cubango to the south, and just keep going from there. The government's on the offensive."

"War," I remarked. "No one here is using this word."

"Right. I wonder what all those dead bodies say they died of."

Everyone had stories of violence, of the deaths of people they knew. And everyone knew of someone who had been grabbed off the streets in military conscription sweeps, which had escalated dramatically in the recent weeks. Reports of fighting were coming in from all parts of the country, and the flow of internal refugees had turned into a river. And in the midst of all this, the country representative of Catholic Relief Services told me she had just received word from international headquarters that their hazard pay had been canceled. "Canceled?" I responded in surprise. "Yeah, we're at peace," she said. "They've declared the peace process a success."

This scenario helps to explain why countries undergo round after round of political violence; why war keeps "breaking out" time and again. In a very real sense, it is the same war, a war that never ended except on paper. I began this chapter by writing that a vast international machinery, a global bureaucracy, surrounds a peace process. People's lives, their careers, their raison d'être are staked on peace. The process of peace becomes bureaucratized. Globally bureaucratized. The diplomats and their governments, the United Nations, the INGOs, and the host countries become interwoven players in the peace process. This network can ultimately involve thousands of people and billions of dollars, and reputations on which a price can't be put. A habit emerges, and routinization—in the best Weberian tradition—sets in. Goals become defined in terms of these habits and bureaucracies. Values come to undergird this work. Media and policy herald these accomplishments. International trade agreements are forged on the declared stability. A political culture emerges, a political economy forms. With this vast peace-brokering network in place, how do you admit it isn't working?[4]

By 1998, even the UN special representative to Angola, Alioune Blondin Beye, of Mali, was saying "No, it simply is not normal in peace for nongovernmental armed forces to control over half the country." Casualties were mounting at an alarming rate. Nonetheless, the heavy habit of the peace process, the sham demobilization process, and the fact of war, remained entrenched. People watched the shadow of war move across the horizon to cloud their lives, their hands empty of the tools they needed to stop it.[5]

A CURIOUS INVERSION

The time of not-peace-not-war characterizing Angola isn't uncommon to politically troubled countries of the world.[6]

Sometimes, however, an island of peace forms in a country officially at war. It is peace that isn't recognized. Such has been the case in northwestern Somalia — the self-declared state of Somaliland — from the 1990s to this day. I was in Somalia in 1988 when President Siad Barre launched a military attack against Hargaisa and the surrounding areas in the north of the country. The attack was devastating to the citizenry, though at the time it was little reported in the international press. As the Barre regime gave way to factionalism and warlordism in the south, the north reconstituted itself along innovative traditional lines to form a stable self-governing nation. As Ken Menkhaus observes: "In Somaliland, President Mohammed Ibrahim Egal has not been able to gain international recognition for his secessionist state, but he has overseen the creation of a modest government structure, the rebuilding of part of the region's infrastructure, a revival of the school systems, the maintenance of a sage and lawful environment, and a revitalization of the commercial economy."[7]

The label "sovereign" might be applied to Somaliland, but, internationally, it is not, and this self-generated accomplishment receives little praise. In fact, Somaliland is a significant study site as an example, not of spontaneous self-destruction — which is so commonly studied — but of spontaneous *stability* in the midst of political chaos. Yet a curious quiet reigns. One seldom hears of diplomatic or political and military science studies that explore non-state sovereignty in the (post) modern era. This is likely due, in part, to the world's investment in states in the most ontological sense. Virtually all of the world's *formal* economic, political, and legal frameworks are predicated on the *necessity* of the state. If the state fails, and stateless "masses" create a stable political society — as is the case in northern Somalia — then the political philosophy of the state is thrown into a tailspin. The attitude toward Somaliland that I encountered at the United Nations provides a window into such worldviews. As Somalia collapsed and Somaliland emerged as a stable region, I spoke with several high-ranking UN officials operating in Somalia. They spoke with righteous anger:

> We can't believe it, but it is true: we can't get in. The people in this Somaliland have said they don't want the UN peacekeepers up there in the north. We can't believe how irresponsible this is, how dangerous. Don't they know what the reality is? How could they subject this place they apparently care so much for to such dangers? I mean, that's it for them; without us, they're lost. How could they make such a decision?

Uncertain about the source of their anger, I pointed out that Mogadishu, where they were operating, was a classic case of Westphalian-model anarchy, whereas Somaliland had achieved a stable peace. Why invite in outside forces to enforce a peace that already existed? In fact, I asked these officials, might not Somaliland be a model for surviving a state collapse? Couldn't it provide clues to achieving peace in other areas? Nobody listened. My questions might as well have been in an indecipherable language. The UN officials' response remained the same:

> The place is going to fall apart. What are those people thinking, how can they actually decide not to let us in? Without our help, the place is doomed.

Somalia had failed, and only states, and state-based international institutions, could "put it back together."

As we enter the third millennium, Somaliland—functioning and relatively stable—is still not recognized as a sovereign political actor by the world's nations or by the United Nations. The world insists on speaking of "Somalia" as if it were a state, and the battles for Mogadishu as battles for the control of Somalia. Somalia is a country defined by "war." Just as Angola was a country defined by "peace" at the turn of the century.

THE DEFINITION OF WAR

It would seem, then, that the definition of war is a political process. As a term, *war* isn't intended to match specific facts, but specific political goals. The goals change, and along with these the definitions of war and peace change apace. The dilemma is that diplomatic conventions and international organizations can't openly address real facts without causing grave insult to political sensibilities, and they can't assuage political sensibilities and address the actual facts of aggression and alliance. For many, surviving amidst the facts of peace and war, the definitions are empty words on meaningless pieces of paper.

WAR ORPHANS' AND STREET CHILDREN'S HOME INSIDE A STORM DRAIN UNDERNEATH CITY STREETS IN LUANDA, ANGOLA.

CHAPTER 13

PEACE

When I was doing fieldwork in Mozambique in 1990 a group of street children orphaned by the war lived near my residence in Quelimane. They would meet me every day when I returned home to talk about what had happened since I had seen them last and to see if I had any food for them. One of my strongest memories is their descriptions of how they looked after each other. These were predominately preteens, and they had developed sophisticated community structures. They formed family-like groupings, with older children looking after younger ones. New arrivals were taken in and looked after. They somehow managed to find the needy some bit of clothing, and they shared what little food they had. It was the same kind of remarkable community rebuilding I had seen among ordinary civilians who had lost everything on the front lines, albeit writ small. It is a story of optimism I have carried with me through the years.

This story was rekindled in a new way when I met a similar group of children in Luanda, Angola, in 1998. People in Luanda talked about children who lived in the storm drains under the city streets. They said how amazing it was to see kids pop up through the drains at the curb beside the roadways, but no one seemed to know about their lives. "These kids can be dangerous," people said, shaking their heads in both sympathy for and fear of the children. "They are violent."

One night I saw a group of children near the roundabout of a major city roadway. They were cooking something that looked like glue in a scavenged tin can over a small open fire. I stopped, squatted on the ground with them, and began a conversation. They had a piece of plastic that might once have been a chair, and they offered it to me. I declined, saying it was the chair of the chef. The "chef," a small child of about eight, looked up at me, took my hand, and asked if I would come visit his home. "Sure," I said, and he pulled me down the street, dodging cars and trucks. Then, at the side of the road, he scrambled down a storm drain. It was like a storm drain in any country, a small opening at a roadside. For street children, a drain is its own natural security system, since a full-size man would not fit into it. Without taking the time to think, I squeezed down the drain after the child. In my mind's eye, when I had heard about children living in the drains under the streets, I had visualized decaying, dirt-encrusted tunnels with children huddled in dismal conditions amid stagnant water and rats. Everyone I knew held the same idea. But when I entered the drain, I felt the world stop, existentially, for a moment — and my view of the human condition, in its most profound sense, expanded.

In this drain the children had created a home and a community. It was spotlessly clean. I remember being surprised that there was no smell. The children had lined the walls with pictures from magazines, no small feat for children with no money for food and clothing, much less glue. An old inner tube from a tire served as a chair. The children had somehow acquired scraps of fabric and rug and placed them on top of cardboard, lining the floors in home-style comfort. Some meters down the drain they had fashioned a wall, and at the end they had constructed shelves that held the few possessions they had managed to acquire. On one shelf stood a battered old vase that held a bouquet of paper flowers the children had made. Little bits of art, collected here and there from what the rest of humanity throws away, decorated the shelves and tiny tables. Holding my hand and leading me down to the end, the children sat me down next to an old powdered milk tin can connected to a strange assembly of wires and small bits of transistor boards connected by yet more wires. Delightedly, they turned on the radio. They had even fashioned a dial so they could tune in different stations. I followed the trail of wires to what looked like a pile of white Styrofoam, on which sat a small mountain of worn-out batteries the kids had patiently collected from the trash. No single battery had enough energy to power anything, but in a mass, they produced music. With a lump in my throat, I asked the children who had made this. They pointed to a boy of about eight, who grinned in recognition.

This is a community in the fullest sense. The children have instituted a strong code of conduct. They share everything they have with each other equally. Stealing isn't allowed, and if someone does steal, the children have a governing council where everyone sits down and finds a solution. They assign chores, with some of them washing clothes and bedding, others cooking, and yet others cleaning. They even instituted a security system for protection. If one is taken by the police, all the others go out to find odd jobs like washing cars or shining shoes, or maybe stealing, to scrape together the money to take to the jail and get their friend out.

I asked them if at night, when they were all comfortable in their "beds" before they went to sleep, they told stories about their ancestors and history. "Yes, of course," they answered. As I turned to leave the drain, they pulled me over to show me a sleeping boy wrapped up in a blanket, and began to gently pull the blanket from him. I whispered not to wake the boy, but that was not their intent. They lifted up the blanket to show me that wrapped up and sleeping with the boy were four plump, healthy and very happy puppies. Clearly, the children had shared what little food they could manage with the puppies' mother. They treated these puppies with a tenderness they themselves might never have known, and were obviously proud of their family-like community.

These children have come to Luanda from all over Angola, running from the war, from harsh conditions, or from impossible family situations. They are orphaned, abused, or the children of extreme poverty. They live in a world largely hostile to them: from Luanda to Manila to New York, most of the "civilized" world walks past them without seeing them. "Some people kick at us as they walk by," one child told me. Yet in extreme deprivation, they have created a community that is not only functioning, in the most adult sense, but also peaceful. They have fashioned family and support networks as best they can. In a world of violence, they have sought to create stability and accord.

As one youth told me,

> I carry a little bit of peace in my heart wherever I go, and I take it out at night and look at it.[1]

. . .

Where is the font of peace? Do we find it with the diplomats who drive unknowingly down the roads on top of these children's "home"? Or somewhere else?

If war starts long before the firing of the first bullet, peace is set into motion long before peace accords are engineered. In fact, peace starts at the epicenters of violence. This isn't a metaphorical comment, or a philosophical statement on the human condition. It's an observation born of fieldwork, an observation about the politics of power and change, and about how social transformations are effected.

Diplomacy and military science would have it that peace is brokered at the formal level, among those responsible for running countries and wars. This view perpetuates notions about the primacy of the state. In this popular lore-cum-wisdom, the masses are not sufficiently sophisticated to either run wars or realize peace. The "masses" — undifferentiated and unpredictable — are prone to unrestrained eruptions of violence (riots and vigilante lynchings) and to stunned inertia in the face of threat (troops protecting cowering civilians). They don't generate notions of higher law, justice, scientific breakthrough, diplomacy, or the advances of civilization — they are the beneficiaries. According to this popular lore, beating in all our breasts is the heart of a beast, a savage of Neanderthal proportions, that the thin veneer of civilization can keep in check only to a certain degree. It is the job of the visionaries and the gifted (of whom only a few in any given generation rise to the top of society as leaders) to fashion society in such a way as to keep the beast as tamed as possible. Without the guidance of these leaders and visionaries, civilization would give way to a lord-of-the-flies degeneracy.

If people can be convinced of this scenario, they can be convinced that the state, and those who rule in its stead, are essential to the survival of the human race. Any excesses and atrocities perpetuated in the name of the state may be forgiven with the observation that sometimes you have to burn the village to protect the nation. No matter how bad it is, this reasoning goes, without the state, existence would be unspeakably worse.

It isn't a simple matter to subject these notions to scientific inquiry: few would be inclined to dismantle the apparatus of the state to scientifically observe if what actually beats at the center of the unrestrained masses is a heart of darkness.

Yet observation of the human condition unrestrained by formal governing institutions is possible. In the massive destruction resulting from the lethal combination of modern technology and prolonged wars, the formal institutions of authority can essentially be bombed into rubble. Many wars of the twentieth and twenty-first centuries have been defined by sheer devastation, in which civilization is stripped of governing institutions, basic social services, croplands, trade and goods, and normalcy as people know it.

And how do average civilians act in these conditions? From my vantage point, those with weapons wreak the destruction of societies, and those without basically rebuild them — a reverse of the enlightened elite versus teeming masses scenario. It is only on the front lines, with those who have lost the most in a war they were never armed to fight, that the font of peacemaking and societal rebuilding is most visible. And it starts in the midst of war's worst — with average people. As a *deslocado* (an internally displaced person) told me one day during the war in Mozambique:

> There are people from all over here in these deslocado areas, many languages all being spoken at once. Some of these languages are those spoken by the men who attacked my home, killed my loved ones. But these people are deslocados too. We must not recreate the war here in our lives, no matter how bad they are.
>
> This war isn't about ethnicity. We lose if we accept this. If we are to survive we have to fight this. We have to fight the idea the war-makers devise that hate and vengeance and ethnicity and division matter. That this war is real. That it has some kind of meaning we all get wrapped up in. The only way to survive is for us to reject these ideas, ignore the divisions, refuse to accept fighting as the solution. We defeat violence by not fighting. We sit here in the dirt and hunger with our brothers and sisters who speak any language; we share what little we have.

What do people do when they have lost everything that defines home, hearth, and community? Few turn to armed vengeance, I have found. In my experience, most try to find safe farmlands, open trade paths with other needy communities, set up health care centers treating both physical and psychic wounds, and open schools for children. These schools often lack buildings, texts, and materials; they operate on the volition of teacher and student, and on writing in the smoothed earth. People find homes for children orphaned and dislocated by war, and they find places in their communities for refugees. They set up dispute resolution councils to deal with legal and social conflicts (often based on traditional authority structures, community groups, and councils of elders) and try to stop the avaricious from taking over the lands and industries of the poor and non-powerful. And they do this on their own — as individuals — without support from governing institutions, which in severe war conditions are largely under attack and functioning only in larger urban centers.

Some people engage in these acts for profit and power, and some commit serious abuses while doing so. But the key point is that most do not. People stop war by creating peace, not by fighting war better or harder or meaner. On the front lines, a philosopher who had never received any formal education told me:

> If you are exposed to violence, you become violent. It is a learned response. And this is a fact of life, not a fact solely of war. The war may come to a formal end, but all those people who have learned violence—learned to solve their problems, and conflicts, and confusions with violence—will continue to use it. They will be more violent with their families, with their friends, in their work. They will see violence as the appropriate response to any political contest.
>
> So is the war really over? Is the violence of war gone suddenly with declarations of peace? No, violence lives in the belly of the person and ruins society, unless peace is taught to the violent. And peace must be taught

> just like violence is, by subjecting people to it, by showing them peaceful ways to respond to life and living, to daily needs and necessities, to political and personal challenges.

So in the midst of finding food sources and health care centers and schools, people on the front lines tend to the larger issue of the human condition as well. They recognize that infrastructure means little if violence rules a society, and that infrastructure means nothing if there is no hope for a future. And hope for the future involves believing that the violence people have been subjected to will not remain the norm, that the world can be better than it is. This isn't an easy feat when your loved ones have been tortured or murdered, when everything you own has been destroyed, and no end to these cycles of violence is in sight.

Conventional wisdom posits that war must first be ended, and then the developments of peace can be attended to, as people are able to turn their energies to creating a future. But my data does not support this conclusion. It would seem peace begins — indeed must begin — in the thick of battle, among those least armed and often most violated.

This perception of peace isn't merely academic. As with the children in the storm drains of Luanda, such insights circulate in public places and conventions. I found the following writing on a piece of paper taped to a wall in London in 2001, the day after a bomb had exploded outside the BBC building as the tensions in Northern Ireland escalated. The anonymous poem is titled "True Peace":

> There once was a King who offered a prize to the artist
> who would paint the best picture of peace. Many
> artists tried. The King looked at all the
> pictures, but there were only two he really
> liked and he had to choose between them.
>
> One picture was of a calm lake. The lake was a perfect
> mirror, for peaceful towering mountains were all
> around it. Overhead was a blue sky with fluffy
> white clouds. All who saw this picture thought
> it was a perfect picture of peace.
>
> The other picture had mountains too. But these were
> rugged and bare. Above was an angry sky from
> which rain fell, and in which lightning played.
> Down the side of the mountain tumbled a
> foaming waterfall. This did not look peaceful
> at all. But when the King looked, he saw
> behind the waterfall a tiny bush growing in a
> crack in the rock. In the bush a mother bird had

> built her nest. There, in the midst of the rush of angry water, sat the mother bird on her nest.
>
> The King chose the second picture as the winner. "Because," explained the King, "peace does not mean to be in a place where there is no noise, trouble, or hard work. Peace means to be in the midst of all those things and still be calm in your heart.
> That is the real meaning of peace."[2]

War depends on fear of oppression, a belief in force, and a willingness to use violence. Soldiers fight wars and civilians support them because they fear losing what they have and hope to gain something they don't. War also depends on placing these fears and beliefs in a framework that specifies friend and foe, political alliance and alienation. When citizens hold these fears and support these beliefs, and when they are willing to use force in their name, war remains paramount.

So peace begins when people find violence the worst threat of all. With this, the fears and beliefs in force wane and support for violent solutions withers as a search for creative non-aggressive solutions waxes. This isn't merely a political process. It is forged in the center of daily life. It is carried through simple conversations and philosophical debates; crafted in art and reproduced in music; relayed in folktales and honed in literature. Even children—or maybe especially children—pick up this dialogue.

As Angola teetered on the brink of war yet again in 1998, the street children instituted a dialogue intended to remind everyone to share equally what few resources they had. When one child wants to keep more than the others, to lord over others, to control, the rest respond:

> Illusion. What you are saying is illusion. Like the big shots with their big cars and big guns. Like what got us into this mess in the first place. You want more than the rest of us? Don't be like that. That's just illusion.

When I discussed this with Lidia Borba, who works in UNICEF/Angola's Children in Difficult Conditions Bureau, she said:

> These children understand the politics of power thoroughly. Never would I have thought children so young would understand these complex issues. But they do, and they critique them. "Illusions."

In a curious happenstance I have found common to fieldwork but have never been able to explain, shortly after this conversation I picked up a book that began with the words:

> The illusion is performed out of doors, often in a dusty field. The magician works inside a circle surrounded by spectators, assisted by a young girl, his obedient daughter. Near the end of the show, the magician suddenly and unexpectedly takes hold of the girl, pulls a dagger from beneath his cloak and slits her throat.
>
> Blood spurts, spattering their smocks and sometimes the clothing of the spectators nearby.
>
> The magician stuffs the body of the girl into a bulb basket he has used throughout the show. Once she is inside, he covers the basket with a cloth, and mutters incantations.
>
> Removing the cloth he shows the audience that the basket is empty, the body of the girl gone.
>
> Just then the spectators hear a shout from beyond the circle. They turn to see the girl gaily running through the crowd into the magician's waiting arms.[3]

When I read this, I realized yet a further level of critique invoked by these child philosophers. For the war orphans living in drains under the road, the illusion refers to the very real, and very dangerous, politics of power. The purveyors of wars suddenly pull out daggers and slit throats, and then for the grand finale — peace — they attempt to show that no one really died, that no harm was really done, that no war-orphan street children exist.

I met another group of street children who lived in a part of Luanda where the drains ran open across a field. One night, the police burned them out. I arrived just after the attack and found the children devastated by their loss. Like the storm-drain communities, they had worked hard to create a home, putting up pictures, making furniture from scrounged makeshift items, even growing plants in battered tin cans. The police had rushed in at four in the morning, beating the children, even burning the little plants they had coaxed to life, and hauling several kids off to jail. "What do they expect you to do," I asked, "Disappear? Sprout wings and fly off?" One child looked at me sadly and said, "Yes. The rich don't want to look at us. We are not supposed to exist in their world."

Illusion. Peace, for some, is convincing the world that no war orphans, no sorrow, no lingering effects of brutal violence mar the (political) landscapes.

This "disappearing act" isn't restricted to war orphans and street children. I smoked cigarettes when I first began fieldwork in Mozambique in the late 1980s, and I used to buy them from war amputees who sold them in singles along the roadsides. I would buy a cigarette for the vendor and one for myself, and sit on the curb to listen to his stories of war and survival. In a land besieged with war, land mines, and a lack of medical facilities, amputee street vendors were a common part of the cityscapes. But when I returned to Mozambique in 1990, no amputee street vendors were visible anywhere. I asked after the acquaintances I had made the year before, and no one could tell me anything about where they had gone, or why. I became puzzled, and then suspicious. As I traveled out from the cities into the villages and countryside, I would ask if amputee war victims were returning home — had an influx arrived from the cities? No, people responded. The war was still being fought at this time, and in fact it was as bad as it had ever been — more, not fewer, amputee victims were being generated. For years I have asked after these war victims. No one has ever ventured an answer. Perhaps they were too much of a reminder of war's true realities. Perhaps, like the war orphans and street children, they were "encouraged" to leave the realm of the public eye. Illusions.

. . .

In chapter 6, I wrote that a profound irony underlay our understanding of power. Common wisdom holds that power, especially power embroiled in political and military matters, is wielded by the elite and transmitted down a chain of command to underlings. But as that chapter demonstrated, and as Nietzsche writes, "The doing is everything."[4] Personal actions embedded in local history, specific circumstances, and immediate biography determine a significant degree of power, however invisible this process is in top-down theories of power. There are power elites, loathe to admit they don't control ground actions — more loathe to admit this than to admit they are committing atrocities — who will act "as if" they intended actions generated at the ground level. They take authorship of action, and thus of the font of power, *after the fact* in such a way as to imply they had authored it before the fact. The classic "as if" ploy.

The same holds for the fonts of peace. Peace doesn't emerge unless a foundation exists upon which to build. War doesn't end and peace begin in a unilinear process: peace is constructed step by step until war becomes impossible. One might protest that this might be true of Mozambique, but it certainly does not hold true for the end of, by way of example, World War II, where the Allied forces and the detonation of nuclear weapons marked a decisive military victory. Cultural texts are infused with images of decisive victory. But most recognize today that Japan and Germany were running out of the material and cultural resources to wage war — supply routes were overextended, coffers were bankrupt, and civilian morale and support for the war effort were waning at home. Most conclude that the war was winding to an end at that time, and that bomb or no bomb, its conclusion was imminent.

Peace begins in the front-line actions of rebuilding the possibility of self (which violence has sought to undermine) and society (which massacres and destruction have sought to undermine).

Without the trade routes, schools, clinics, and family relocation programs, without the art and literature and media that set up belief systems of resolution over conflict, without a sense of a future, peace cannot emerge. No peace accords brokered at elite levels will work if these bases are not there to build upon. "The doing is everything."[5]

So the ironies of power reemerge here in peace as well. Elites broker accords "as if" they were the true font of peace, and thus of power. They take authorship of the institutions forged at the ground level by those who suffer the brutalities of the front lines the most—institutions forged in personal actions embedded in a context of local history, specific circumstances, and immediate biography.

I don't want to suggest that power is merely unidirectional, flowing from the ground up rather than from the top down. The "doing" of elites is as much of the story as the "doing" of average citizens. But elites can seek to make their actions appear more important in the rebuilding. The illusion of power, then, isn't the actual *process* of "doing," but of seeking to control the definitions of *authorship* of the "doing."

. . .

So where, in the final summation, does peace come from? Since it may well emerge from places mainstream theory tells us are unlikely, let us return to the ruminations of the children who live on the streets and in the storm drains of Angola. The children take great exception to the common statements that children born and bred in war are a "lost generation." This phrase is heard from Angola through Sudan, up to the Balkans, and over to Burma. It is intended to capture a generation of children who have grown up knowing severe political violence, and who have been deprived of settled communities, stable families, schooling, and the creative nurturance that peace imparts. But there is an underside to these comments. The jagged assumption is that these children are indeed "lost": that they will be prone to violence, instability, and aggressive poverty; that they will be limited in their ability to envision and create a better future. That they have looked into the eye of war and will reflect what they have seen.

> Illusion, *the children respond.* We know how we came to live this way. We can see who has and who doesn't, who gives and who takes. We know we take better care of each other here [on the streets] than any of us would find in the places we ran from. If you can tell us of a peaceful home that will

take us, we will go today. But the people with the nice cars and big homes are not asking us home. In the meantime, we create a life as best we can, and we do a pretty good job. You want to know what we need? We need to go to school. There is a school just down the street, and we watch the regular kids come and go, and when we ask if we can go we are turned away. We need a place to keep our things. If we get a book or some clothes, how can we keep them on the street? Someone just comes along and takes them. We need a chance, a job, people to believe in us.

Michael Comerford, an Irish priest and scholar working in Angola, responded to this story by asking,

Who is lost? The children, or those who drive by them without seeing?

Perhaps what is most distressing about the phrase "the lost generation of children" is that in the mere saying of this, the creative communities and peaceful traditions these children make are not recognized. The lost generation is a marker of deprivation and violence; not of creativity and peace-building. The designation of "lost generation" invokes *The Lord of the Flies* philosophies. And it conveys the impression that there is war, *or* there is peace: if children grow up in war, all they know is violence and suffering. But as Lidia Borba of UNICEF/Angola said when I was talking with her about where these children learn such peaceful strategies:

But it is natural they should know these things. Before they lost their homes, they grew up with daily kindnesses. They were loved and cared for; they saw people come to visit and treated with dignity and respect, they saw their family set up ways to support each other through good times and bad. Even walking the streets, the children see the goodness their cultures have to offer: the acts of helping, the community strength, the deeply held beliefs in the dignity of people.

Peace is everywhere in the midst of the war: in every act of daily caring. These children have seen this, they have thought on this, they have grown in this way, they have been nurtured in a culture that values these things, and they too have grown to value them. You know, it is how the children survive the streets, how we survive the war, by keeping these traditions of humanity alive in living day to day.

If war, as earlier chapters pointed out, starts long before the firing of the first bullet with the creation of divisions charged with aggression, then peace resides where non-aggression takes root in the fissures war has blown open. Like the bird who nests by a turbulent waterfall, peace makes its first tenuous handholds amidst the fiercest storms.

"THE FORTUNES OF WAR." WOMAN RUNNING A STORE ON THE FRONT LINES, HOLDING UP HER "CASH REGISTER" FULL OF MONEY. BIE PROVINCE, ANGOLA, 2001.

CHAPTER 14

THE PROBLEMS WITH PEACE

He made a fortune smuggling wheat during World War II. He was a boy from a poor family, a family with no means. Without the war, he would still be a poor boy, and his children would be poor. Now people call him "Mister" and they seek jobs from him. He has political power, and they vote for him. Now his family has joined the ranks of the landed.

They became rich selling looted art during World War II. Millions and millions of dollars exchanged hands on art looted from Jewish people, from the private collections of war's victims, from bombed museums and unguarded galleries.

Before the end of the apartheid government in South Africa, the unscrupulous used to come into Mozambique during the war there and collect war orphans to take back to South Africa and sell into sexual and domestic labor.

United Nations peacekeeping troops were making a fortune selling everything from cigarettes and alcohol to heroin and tanks in former Yugoslavia. Some estimated that upwards of half the economy was generated through these activities in the precarious times of war.

The gem profiteers found the political instabilities from Sri Lanka to Angola profitable – very profitable. Who paid attention to work permits, customs laws, border crossings, legal protocols? A world of peacetime marketeers made a "killing" on war.[1]

In 1998, when I was first making notes for this chapter, Sierra Leone made the papers again. I was in Angola at the time, and the stories of the two countries shared a glittering trail of teardrop diamonds. Sierra Leone's People's Party, headed by Tejan Kabbah, took up the reins of government in Freetown after Nigerian ECOMOG troops ousted Paul Koroma's junta-RUF rebels in February 1998. Swedish journalist Peter Strandberg described the process.[2]

As he visited the towns of Kailahun, Buedo, and Pendembu, among others, with the RUF troops in July 1998, he listened to the BBC reporting that Nigerian troops had taken those towns. The RUF soldiers he was with hooted with laughter. They had a firm hold on the eastern part of the country, and the Nigerians had incurred heavy losses — losses, Nigerian POWs told Strandberg, that were not being reported to the soldiers' families or to the press. The Nigerian soldiers' morale was low, they said. "Why fight for $150 a month?" But they continue to fight. Why? Duty, devotion, fear, obligation, and a lack of options are partial explanations for military duty. Especially military duty on foreign soil. The answer might more profitably be sought in a geological map: the Nigerians were trying to capture the diamond-rich area around the town of Koidu in RUF territory. The flow from Sierra Leone mines can add up to over half a billion dollars a year. Strandberg quotes Bockarie, one of the founders of the RUF guerrillas:

> We have fought many different enemies, troops from Nigeria and Guinea, mercenaries from Executive Outcomes [who have contracted for payment in diamonds here as well as in Angola] and Sandline and Nepalese Gurkhas, and after eight years they still haven't defeated us. What they want is our diamonds. The former Nigerian dictator Ibrahim Babangida owned mines here. Now it is [Sani] Abacha and the British mining companies who want to steal our country.[3]

New African editor Baffour Ankomah wrote at the time: "Forget the mercenaries, forget the Nigerians. All the indications point to a classic British/American job in Sierra Leone."[4]

Of course, it isn't only diamonds. Strandberg quotes civilian witnesses who describe how Nigerian troops looted banks and shops when they entered Freetown, and shot anyone who protested. They then packed up looted trucks and ships to ferry their booty back home. As Patrick Chabal and Jean-Pascal Daloz write: "The involvement of peacekeeping forces, in countries like Liberia and Sierra Leone, has led to claims that some foreign contingents, such as the Nigerian, have facilitated the internationalization of illicit trade or criminal activities."[5]

The irony, of course, is that actors from the Nigerians (a peacekeeping force) to international mining interests (based in peacetime locales) are in Sierra Leone ostensibly to promote peace and stability. Diamonds play havoc with human rights on all sides of the conflict, it would seem.

Militarization and profit can become even more complex and entangled, as was evident in another gem-rich locale. Given the nature of the quote, I leave the locale and speaker unnamed:

> Oh, we all know how the government troops mine on one side of the river, and the rebel forces on the other, and each has made a pact with the other about not attacking them or their transport lines. You do your business, and I'll do mine, and the war just goes along this way. Oh sure, there are intrigues and blowups: one side might see the chance to rout the other and gain a foothold on better mining land; might see a chance to extend their control over a region. But there is always the recognition that if they do this, they will leave themselves open for further attack, which will interfere with their ability to "get on with business."
>
> But one of my favorite stories involves routing one's own side. I've just seen this. Let's say a government commander holds Location A and is profiting from the minerals there. Another commander on the same side holds Location B and is controlling the mineral profits there. Location C is held by the rebel forces. So Commander A gets on the satellite phone and calls his buddy commander in the rebel forces—not his own side, but the "enemy side"—and says:
>
> "Hey, you go and attack Location B. The commander there will naturally call me for backup support, and we will come, but we will take our time and come slowly. You'll have time to get what you want. Then when we arrive, you fall back to Location C. We'll take over the mining then, and pay you a profit from this."
>
> So Commander A extends his area of control to cover Location B as well, including all the mining profits—extending it over a person from his own military. And his good buddy on the other side gets a kickback for his role in this.
>
> Of course, the tragedy in this is that each time one of the troops takes Location B, all the citizens flee the region, and a river of internally displaced people stream out with only the clothes on their backs. About one-third of the population in the country is internally displaced, and aid is getting to about a third of them. So these people's lives are ruined, for what? For these games of the militaries. Nothing more than games.

This reminds me of losing my academic innocence about war and aid in wartime Mozambique. Not surprisingly, it involved precious stones. Hundreds of battles dotted the landscapes and cityscapes of Mozambique, hundreds of thousands of lives were being lost. To an unpracticed eye, it isn't obvious why battles erupt on one particular patch of dusty savanna and not another. My question was laid to rest in part when I found a mineral resource map of the region. When I laid it on top of a map marking the battle sites, the mines and sites lined up. But the same question continued to rankle about international NGO aid: why does an emergency plane loaded with food and goods for starving war-afflicted populations brave one embattled site and not another one a hundred kilometers down the road? There are many answers to this question, and most of them are based on calculations of need, land mines, fighting, and available runways. Many I have seen are based on what we would call true heroism. But this doesn't tell the entire story.

In the thick of the Mozambique war, I visited a region as decimated by war as any I had seen: one set of troops, and then another, took and retook this town over the space of years. I had hitched a ride with an emergency aid cargo plane, and hearing it return, was preparing to head for the runway to get a ride home. A group of women I had been talking with came up to me and asked if I wanted *pedras* now. In Portuguese, the national language, *pedras* means stones (or, as we might say in English, "rocks"). The first image that popped into my mind was me lugging a bunch of river rocks back home on the plane, perhaps for a garden. Pretty naïve. The women pressed me. "You don't want *pedras*? The other people who come through here all carry off bags of them." I realized then that they were using the slang word for gems — diamonds. "No thanks, I'm not interested in stones," I responded. "But you mean to tell me other foreign-aid people come here and carry off gems?" It had never occurred to me that there were NGOs profiting from the gem/war equation. "Yes," the women I was speaking with smiled, "bags of them." The end of innocence.[6]

. . .

By 2000 Sierra Leone and Mozambique had achieved a more enduring peace, but resource-rich, war-weary Angola continued to suffer rounds of military battles. In October 2001, the UN Security Council released its report stating that UNITA's illicit diamond business was continuing to fuel the war effort, and despite UN sanctions, was bringing in between $1 and $1.2 million in revenues a day. The contentious relationship between peace and profiteering is visible to most Angolans. When I returned to Angola in the fall of 2001 after being away for several months, I was greeted with similar versions of this comment:

> You ask how is it here now? Not good. The war, you know, just goes on. The rich get richer and the poor don't just get poorer, they starve and die. The money exchanging hands in this war is beyond belief; who in control is going

> to pass this up for peace? The powerful can get what they want because we live not in peacetime conditions where we have a rule of law, but in conditions where the law of force rules.

And the subtexts, voiced quietly over a beer in informal settings:

> Ah, you know, that guy with the IO [International Organization], he's running diamonds under cover of relief work.

One of the most interesting observations on this came from a man who as a youth had lost some of his family and was forced to live on the streets of Luanda, Angola. He was conscripted as a soldier and fought for some years before he was shot and released from the military. Unable to find work or housing, he returned to live on the streets, was arrested for stealing at the age of sixteen (already a war veteran), and served a jail sentence. He now does odd jobs on the streets (some perhaps less than legal; the security forces stopped me one day and asked why I was talking with a street thief). He is one of the more intelligent and deeply thoughtful people in my interviews. One day, when we were talking over a cup of coffee, he said:

> Peace? Forget it. There's too much money to be made here. Money like you can't believe. Look, all us soldiers saw it. I was sent to the eastern provinces and part of my "war effort" was to help with mining diamonds. We worked hard in this war all right, getting and carrying riches for the commanders and the political elites. You see all these things moving in and out of the place, and you realize, it isn't a small stream of goods and profits, it's a real river.

He gestured toward the street:

> Look out there, look at the cars driving by, the latest Mercedes and loaded 4 × 4s, driving down the road avoiding the rubbish and potholes from broken water pipes and the kids washing in them. Look at the way the people are dressed, look at where they are going, look at the kind of power they have. It's only the war that makes this possible. And don't think they don't know it. You think they could drive these cars and dress like this and wield this kind of power if peace were to come to Angola?
>
> Peace? If peace came the money would run, it would disappear over the horizon, you would need binoculars to see any money around, it would be so small and far away.

. . .

Through the course of this research, the term *war* has for me come to be associated not only with military actions, but with questionable if not illegal industry, land takeovers, and international wildcatting. This view intersects with Paul Collier's observation:

> This discourse of grievance is how most people understand the causes of conflict. A thorough analysis of the causes of a conflict then becomes a matter of tracing back the grievances and counter-grievances in the history of protest.
>
> An economist views conflict rather differently. Economists who have studied rebellions tend to think of them not as the ultimate protest movements, but as the ultimate manifestation of organized crime. . . . Rebellion is a large-scale predation of productive economic activity.[7]

Wildcatting, as I use the term here, is based in international business concerns that can be legal, indeterminately legal, or downright illegal — but that yield quick, and often vast, profits, commonly in the context of political instability. As Tony Hodges writes, resource-rich countries suffer four times as much political instability and violence than states with fewer resources. Lack of governmental control, weak enforcement, loose laws and regulations, corruption, and desperation have fueled these business coups.[8]

While we are busy charting the flow of diamonds and drugs the less charted commodities of daily life like food, clothing, soap, and pharmaceuticals circle the globe in the shadows — and generate just as much profit. Christian Dietrich, who has written on the diamond trade in war-troubled zones of Southern Africa, said in a conversation with me in Antwerp, Belgium:

> War perpetuates closed societies. In emergency situations, militaries and governments control air and transport routes, import and export sites. They oversee, and often control financially, the products that enter and are consumed in the areas under their jurisdiction. The militaries' view is, "We have to close airports for security reasons, and only our planes can get in and out [of course, with the caveat that our planes carry the essentials of trade]. . . . We don't need to build hospitals because we have a war—and wouldn't you rather have us military around than the murderous enemy?"
>
> These aren't wars over resources, per se. Instead, war facilitates the looting of resources. And it isn't just about controlling the diamond trade, for example, it's about controlling the whole closed economy that supports and sustains the economy: soap, petrol, food, and so on.
>
> This is "organized scarcity." In war, the controlling factions don't like it that average people grow crops—it means people are self-sufficient. They can't control the delivery of essentials. Question: in the final tally, are you really making profits from diamonds or from all the soap and petrol and food and essentials that people need?

Dietrich noted Tony Hodges's work on Angola, which shows that the political and military elite — a very small and closed circle of acquaintances of considerable power—controls the majority of all resource and business access in the country. Dietrich said:

> Speaking of formalizing the economy, take the example of diamond-rich countries. There are thousands of informal miners prospecting for gems. Governments want to formalize these informal workers, bringing all gems through registered government corporations.
>
> Do you really want a predatory state corporation regulating the informal diamond industry? There are dirty people behind formal regulatory agencies with world-wide links . . . links with cartels, with money launderers, with questionable intelligence agencies, and with repressive militaries around the world. Are these the people to regulate the diamond industry? I'd rather see a vibrant informal economy than a highly regulated formal economy with a few profiteers.

There are any number of unscrupulous international enterprises happy to aid and abet political conflicts in order to turn a profit or enjoy the gains of power sharing. Wildcatting guns and drugs networks, "security companies," and influence peddlers are common examples. Classical economics states that business, speaking generally, flourishes in ordered, organized, and stable environments, and thus will naturally gravitate toward regions of stability. While this is true of many, and perhaps even most, businesses, there are numerous industries that find the frontier mentality and impaired legal systems of warzones their best medium for profit.

But more traditional and established multinationals can also be the beneficiaries of political disorder. In the words of a person who asked to remain unnamed:

> We got the energy concessions in a straightforward way, so straightforward I still have to have a drink to talk about it. The war caused massive floods of refugees fleeing the fighting, which of course took place in resource-rich areas. The political and military bigwigs then laid claim to the land. When the war ended and the refugees returned, they returned to find their homes and lands and businesses taken over by the powerful of the country.
>
> And gee, the government records office was burned during the war's fighting. "You say, 'Mr. Refugee, was this your land? Do you have any records that prove this? No?'"
>
> But that's not the end of it. For this whole thing to work, they need us foreigners to come in and develop the industries. So we partner with the business leaders to get access to these resources. We come in and set up the business and we hire these poor refugees whose land it was to begin with for fifty cents a day. And dammit, we make a fortune.
>
> Hey, we're heralding in peace and development.

Global Witness and the research staff at the Institute for Security Studies in Pretoria have written of the oil profits fueling the war in Angola.[9] Angola has some of the richest offshore deep-water oil sites in the world. The sites are largely secure from the threat of war and are home to some of the largest oil companies, especially those with the resources to develop deep-water sites. Oil is the Angolan government's main revenue source, and the money raised was instrumental in the war effort. Though never explicitly expressed, the implication hung over business negotiations that the government might not be as quick to sell off important blocks if the war, and thus if the need for foreign currency, were not so drastic. Angola has received some of the highest signature bonuses in the world for site bids (some $900 million for three blocks in 2000). But not all the oil companies bidding for sites are major international petroleum players. Some are smaller, and they linked with larger companies, sometimes seemingly at the government's behest. Global Witness suggests that in some cases these companies also trade in weapons, and the oil bids for weapons deals are central to negotiations. The fact that some of these companies sold their oil leases shortly after gaining them, and seem to have supplied the government with important weapons systems, supports these contentions.

Global Witness asks that petroleum firms become more involved in developing the integrity of the industry in relation to governments, corruption, and the perpetuation of war. I spoke with six members of Global Witness in the fall of 2001 in London. Their goal is to induce businesses to make transparency central to their basic practices. With a simple set of guidelines that call for more responsible business/government deals and anticorruption practices, Global Witness has shown that war-related profiteering and corruption can be significantly reduced. Their campaign against corrupt timber practices in Burma stands as one of their first successes.

My 2001 interview with Martin Eldon, the head of Texaco in Angola, shows the complex global realities faced by the world's larger industrial concerns. Eldon sat on the top floor of a wood-and-glass Luanda office above a beehive of international activity that runs some of the more productive petroleum sites in the world. From this bird's-eye perspective, the Texaco chief reminded me of everything petroleum runs in the world, its place in twenty-first century society. Little that graces our everyday lives doesn't involve oil in some way. In this view, oil indeed is the grease running the world as we know it today.

> We care, of course, we care. But we don't do anything here we don't do anywhere. Everywhere in the world businesses offer the equivalent of sig-

> nature bonuses to get and seal the deals they want. There is nothing illegal in this. The same thing happens in the U.K.: monies are paid to the government to secure certain business rights. And what business in the U.K. monitors where their signature bonuses go, how they are handled, if the queen secrets some of it for herself, or spends it on the military? Can you imagine a company in the U.K. or USA telling the government they wanted to monitor how these monies were recorded, invested, channeled, spent? If any was diverted for untoward purposes? It's just unthinkable. And yet people seem to think that is what we should do with the government here. Why ask in one place and not in another? It is the same thing. Business just isn't set up to monitor and control how governments deal with the money they take in.

When I asked Eldon if the war in Angola and the government's desperate need for foreign currency was a boon to conducting business here, he just looked at me blankly, then handed me some coffee in a beautiful china cup, without answering. He seemed truly perplexed: whether by my question, that should by corporate protocol remain unvoiced, or by his reluctance to formulate an answer, I don't know.

> But you know, Carolyn, with your interest in non-formal economies and unregulated trade—oil is one of the most monitored and legal industries there is. We record every transaction, every drop of oil, every step of the way. It is virtually impossible to circumvent the extensive monitoring process we have put in place. This isn't a commodity that easily lends itself to smuggling, diversion, or unrecorded traffic. In many ways oil is the hallmark of the sophistication of a formalized economy.

Compared to diamonds, human labor, seafood, and timber, this is true, but I reminded him that oil smuggling in China was a multi-billion-dollar-a-year activity. To an executive concerned with production, though, these postproduction activities were another realm of "business." Six months after this interview, I spoke with another petroleum executive in Angola who estimated that easily 10 percent — and perhaps much more — of all oil moves outside of legal boundaries.

These imbroglios of business profiteering don't apply only to war contexts. The postwar period finds a country with war-damaged infrastructure, industry, and trade. Many postwar countries are beset by high unemployment and inflation, low productivity, a shortage of essential goods, and few ways to quickly rectify the situation. They are vulnerable to international businesses that demand highly profitable in-country concessions and to national elites who can benefit from granting them. Even when these are detrimental to the country and to its population in general, powerful international interests often win out. One-sided tax breaks, lopsided development, and a product and profit base that is channeled out of the country are common to postwar nations. In a vulnerable country, the world's power elites are more able to influence political process, economic law, and foreign relations policy — and a number do so to their advantage. For some, provoking political instability isn't only good business, it is good politics.

Political scientist Will Reno has shown how a governing group will undermine their country's infrastructure and resource base so that their opposition can't use these to gain power — power that could oust those currently in privileged positions.[10] In these cases, resources are used as political currency: providing political patronage, alliances, and power bases. If leaders are willing to cannibalize their own countries, is it unlikely that sprawling foreign and international interests are willing to cannibalize other people's countries?

HOW DOES THIS AFFECT THE PEOPLE AT GROUND ZERO? (OR, WHY PEOPLE STILL CAN'T FIND ENOUGH TO EAT AFTER THE WAR HAS ENDED)

An African economist said to me that many African countries coming out of war suffer the same cycles of postwar stagnation:

> For most civilians, life is so miserable during wartime that peace becomes a beacon of hope: with peace, the horrors will cease. For many, these horrors include hunger, deprivation, joblessness, homelessness, a lack of social services, and social dislocation as well as fear, violence, and assaults. Peace promises answers to all these dilemmas. But it is an elusive answer. Worse, after independence, many countries' economies take a serious downturn after about twelve to fifteen years.

Why, he wondered, don't countries today learn from these patterns and institute different policies rather than continuing to implement policies sure to follow these cycles of economic problems?

> I asked him: "If, at the end of the colonial or apartheid era your government asked you to recommend an economic development plan, what would you recommend?"
>
> He responded: "My first inclination is to say that the countries must ask their people to continue working in the same way for several years while economic policy is carefully revised to meet new standards."
>
> "But, how could you ask your community, your friends, your own family

to work on under *chibalo* (forced labor), to continue to suffer a lack of medical care and education while the elite few enjoy these privileges?"

"Ah, herein lies the problem."

Peace is rooted in the legacies of war. I have written about the necessity of developing inter/national trade and supply routes for obtaining military supplies in wartime. Networks such as these don't disappear—become de-militarized—with the mere signing of a peace accord. These militarized networks are critical to understanding postwar transformation and development, and for answering painful questions such as, "Why can't people find security from violence or enough food to eat *after* a war has ended?"

At the start of militarization, people employ preexisting exchange routes and retool them for military needs as well as developing new ones to meet war demands. For example, as one group becomes estranged from another—be they the Karen people in Burma or the Croatians and Bosnians in Yugoslavia in the period just preceding 1991—they find that survival strategies depend on developing their own supply routes for daily subsistence requirements from food to energy. Age-old informal trade routes are adapted to move contemporary necessities: gasoline into Croatia, medicines into Karen areas, rice into northern Sri Lanka.

Subsistence, informal, and gray-market trade routes are particularly amenable to being rediverted to war supplies: they are simultaneously well established and flexible, they move through the everyday markets of a community without relying on government-controlled institutions; and they are strongly linked with international economies.

This is equally true for governments, which often need to move military supplies around sanctions and may employ extra-state methods of procurement and payment. Consider the fact that in Africa, unrecorded trade between countries in sub-Saharan Africa roughly matches that of recorded trade. As an example, Stephen O'Connell writes:

A non-trivial share of this trade involves arbitrage between different national price structures for goods traded with common external partners. This pattern is as old as the underlying tax differentials: Hopkins (1973) cites the diversion of French-area groundnuts through British Gambia to avoid Senegal's export duty before 1855. More recently, Tanzania and Ugandan coffee has fetched a higher price if smuggled across the Kenyan border, Ghanaian cocoa has for extended periods been worth much more if sold to the marketing authority in Cote d'Ivoire, and subsidized Nigerian oil, meant for the domestic market, has been sold profitably in neighboring Togo. The point applies to manufactured goods as well (see, for example, Deardorff and Stolper, 1990; Berg, 1985; and Azam, 1991): Togo's relatively low tariff on automobile imports generates a stream of imports destined for the higher-tariff, higher-priced Nigerian market, and Nigeria's ban on cigarette imports generates high profits for smuggling of cigarettes from Niger.[11]

Or, as Chabal and Daloz write: "We would argue that in Africa the unofficial has always been more significant than the official."[12]

These networks of exchange and profit extend across Africa, linking with continents both east and west. The simple act of smuggling cigarettes from Niger to Nigeria involves a complex and sophisticated international network of actors and actions. Guns and advanced computer equipment can also be sent along the same route as cigarettes and the latest pirated DVDs. This is the militarization of non-formal trade. The ante is upped.

Before the outbreak of formal hostilities, informal trade routes dealing with subsistence supplies seldom become targets of state or military intervention: in fact, governments and militaries often benefit from informal economies. Prewar Yugoslavia was unlikely to work to suppress gasoline movement in Croatia, the Burmese government to stop the flow of medicines into Karen areas, or the Sinhalese-majority military to stamp out rice shipments to the Tamil in the north. Indeed, informal trade may be considered critical to the very viability of the state:

Yet government policies [in Nigeria and Benin] in the areas of tariffs, banking laws, currency values, and import regulations confound official trade between the two countries. Meanwhile the border is the site of rampant smuggling, where unregistered markets provide a livelihood for many of the people living between Lagos and Cotonou/Porto Novo. The illicit exchange is crucial to the economies of both countries. Officials are forced to turn a blind eye or risk further undermining the region's precarious infrastructures. Such illicit activities further impede effective governance and economic development but, for the moment, they set up an informal regional economic integration by default — one that official multilateral arrangements between states (e.g., ECOWAS or SADC) have repeatedly failed to achieve.[13]

But when gasoline powers tanks and troop transports, when medicines save soldiers, and when guns travel with rice shipments, subsistence trade routes become militarized. The vehicles, for example, that brought gas to prewar Croatia and the ships that landed needed rice in the Tamil north of prewar Sri Lanka — once the vehicles of petty informal traders, nonaligned mafias, or legitimate enterprises — became viewed as real or potential military supply routes with the outbreak of war. They became targets. This targeting disrupts the flow of basic necessities into civil society and can have a devastating impact on people's ability to survive. As people develop new routes for obtaining life's necessities, these too become militarized, both as supply routes for local forces and as targets of attack by opposing troops seeking to cripple civil society altogether.

. . .

The middle-aged man sat down to rest and talk on the veranda of the shop. He chewed a matchstick and periodically gestured with it when he wanted to make a point. He was the quintessential trader-family man: plain shirt and slacks, a ready and kindly smile, a keen business sense honed to support his community and family, that which he valued most.

> We've always run goods and people across these borders. We do it, our fathers did it, our grandfathers did it, back to the time when these stupid senseless borders didn't divide us all.
>
> Honestly, how would we survive otherwise? It's not like the government is knocking on our door with baskets of plenty. And this trade keeps us linked into larger communities—with our people in other locations, with other regional groups, with international goods and markets. Food, clothing, electronics, petrol, machinery, you name it.
>
> So, you know, when the war heats up, we are tapped to carry arms as well. And now we have to navigate all kinds of political divisions and threats. And it gets deeper: the commanders begin to control areas of trade, and to get permits, transport, permission, a person has to grease the palms of the commanders. Now it's like we are working for them in a way. And the damn war now sits on our doorstep. . . .

The man continued:

> Yes, the war has come to our doorstep, and how are we going to get this thing off our doorsteps? Those commanders who control "business," who rake profits off all the "trade" in the area, who control the traffic and transport in and out of the region, who grab up the best land in the extremes of war. Are they going to let go of this with the end of the war? I doubt it. And all those soldiers who have been "deployed" to get and transport natural resources—what jobs will they do at the end of the war?

Such men, whose trade networks extend back generations, face competition and co-optation not only from military and political elite of their own country, but from those of other countries. When I was in Namibia in 1997, the news was full of stories about a decorated Namibian air force officer who had been flying military planes filled with clothing, medicines, food, books, industrial components, electronic goods, and other commodities into Angola and flying out with diamonds. As Mark Chingono writes of Mozambique: "It was the 'big fish,' the professional racketeers in their fancy suits and posh cars, not only from Mozambique but from other countries as far north as Zaire, Nigeria, and Sierra Leone and Germany who really benefited from this business."[14]

These aren't isolated exchanges. By the turn of the twenty-first century, this region was recognized as a transit point for Latin American and Southeast Asian drugs, counterfeit money, financial fraud, money laundering, and cosmopolitan goods. Networks of Lebanese traders, Nigerian gangs, Russian mafia, Asian interest groups, and western cartels meet and transact business across these terrains, linking them with worldwide interests in a classic globalizing strategy.

The problem then exists: how do communities reestablish normal, viable trade routes? This is true for both the formal and the non-formal economy. Even in peaceful times, a significant part of a society relies on informal exchange to survive. In the aftermath of war — in whose wake economic and regulatory infrastructure has been decimated — informal systems are often central to subsistence and rebuilding. As the head of World Bank in Mozambique told me several years ago:

> We can't really talk about it, but it is right there in the center of everything. The informal economy. It isn't what we do as development and financial specialists: talk about the informal sector, support its financial basis, even recognize its true scope. But good God, look at the indices for this country. It has some of the lowest standard of living indices in the world. Yet if you look at the country, look at the people, they are doing better than the indices suggest, across the board. Mozambique is the success story of Africa: it has maintained peace, it is developing at a significant rate, the economy is expanding in exciting ways, people are really beginning to make it. And we can't explain it, because we don't deal in the informal sector formally. Of course, these boons are set in informal development—something done completely by the people themselves, something done without the help of INGOs or GOs. Mozambique is essentially succeeding, in part, because of its vibrant informal economy.

Unfortunately, the tentacles of militarization don't evaporate spontaneously with the signing of a peace accord.[15] One of the problems is that people who have access to international contacts and goods, the vehicles and passes to transfer them, and the means to negotiate these profits into power are often involved in some way with politico-military institutions. These associations are the very networks of access. The formal sectors of politics and economy are interlaced with informal exchange.

Wartime economic relationships follow markets into peace. Wartime profiteers emerge as peacetime economic and political leaders. Markets aren't as free as democratic ideals would have them. In Mark Chingono's words: "While, as Thucydides, Hobbes, and Rimmer speculated, war destroyed markets and commerce, it must be stressed that it also *created* others where none existed before, and *more* rewards for those prepared to take the risk."[16] The end of war often finds rich resource and land concessions, industrial locales, patronage systems, and control of key aspects of trade consolidated into the hands of an exclusive elite — political, business, and military leaders who have extended domains of personal control during the war. Once such gains have been consolidated in the frontier-like conditions of war, the owners may now find that the stability of peace allows them better profits. But the fact remains that the systems were honed in exploitative conditions, some of which continue during peacetime in the form of unfair hiring, work, and pay practices, and restricted legal recourse. In these conditions, access to political, economic, and military power continues to rest in the hands of a few.

Yet even the people dedicated to business ethics can find that postwar conditions hinder their best attempts to formalize their enterprises. Consider the conditions many postwar societies face: in addition to militarized and decimated infrastructure, old currencies may have collapsed, and with them, banking systems. On the international market, new currencies may be no more valuable than the paper they are printed on. Currency exchange rates often fluctuate wildly.[17] National production is likely to be severely curtailed, resulting in a heavy reliance on import goods that requires foreign currency. Antiquated and militarized laws, corruption, and onerous taxes, levies, and tariffs can plague all levels of business endeavor. Even the most legal of companies may find they have to exchange monies, goods, and services on the black market. As one successful businessman, a man noted for integrity in business, noted: "If I followed the letter of the law in every case, I'd be out of business. Period."

While national economic and political systems may remain militarized, the military and political leaders aren't the only profiteers. Militarization benefits global vendors. It benefits international wildcatters. It benefits legitimate vendors of information, services, and technology in the urban centers of the world who sell their goods for the hard currency that oil, drugs, and precious gems buy. An extensive network of people have grown wealthy on these extra-state exchanges; they aren't easily convinced to give them up for less lucrative pursuits.

PROFITS, OR JUST INTERNATIONAL BUREAUCRATIC HABIT?

Sometimes profits are difficult to pinpoint. Take the example of United Nations peacekeeping. As noted earlier, the UN was spending a million dollars a day preparing Mozambique for peaceful and democratic elections in 1994. Who, exactly, this money benefited was a question I seldom heard raised. Nor did I wonder about it until I volunteered to be an election monitor and was attending a group briefing in Maputo some days before the elections.

I sat with my election roommate, a Kenyan journalist. The room was filled with hundreds of monitors, and this was just one of a number of groups being briefed over the space of several days. As the journalist and I casually talked about the group during breaks, we noticed that most were European; my roommate was one of the few Africans present. As a journalist, she began to do a studied survey: most in fact had come in from Europe. Both of us had volunteered to monitor elections, but most in the room were being paid by the UN — an airline ticket, a per diem of $100–$200, in-country travel, lodging, and full rations. As the briefing went on, the election kits (from booths to ballots) were demonstrated — technological pre-formed in-box wonders that netted millions for the urban industrialists who landed that contract. These election booths folded into compact boxes, and, once delivered to the polling stations, popped out into a lightweight urban-style metal frame and reinforced cloth single-person booth designed to ensure voting privacy and symbolize democratic process. They were delivered countrywide on UN planes from first world factories flown by European pilots and serviced by western mechanics and then moved to the polling stations by Mercedes trucks. Even the ration packs and the bottled water were from urban industrial centers, and of a level of sophistication that seemed both excessive and unnecessary for monitoring an election. Each box was an engineering feat of reinforced paper, Styrofoam, and plastic. A "nutritious" (in a very western cosmology) selection of food groups was offered: sandwiches, biscuits, fruit, sweets — each food group individually wrapped in plastic and nestled into its own little compartment in the colorful box. Again, this netted millions for some lucky contractor in an urban locale far from Mozambique, and more millions for the allied industries that subcontracted to these firms, to the shippers that sent the goods, and to the transport companies that ferried them internationally. The million dollars a day spent on the elections in Mozambique bought few local goods or services. Most made a loop back to western industries and personnel — passing through Mozambique without stopping.

This was a lesson brought home to me time and again. When I was in war-ravaged Kuito, Angola, in 1996, I was still capable of being surprised by UN extravagances. The example that sums this up for me involves exclusive imported beer. The Brazilian blue helmets I met there not only had Brazilian food, but even Brazilian beer, flown in to Angola. "How else would we get these people to stay here, in these conditions, and do this?" a leading UN official said to me when I asked about this. Here I was, sleeping on the floor of Africare's office, eating what could be scrounged in the local markets, and drinking warm local beer. I briefly pondered leaving anthropology for the cushy world of UN peacekeeping.

Apart from that, my appreciation of the international financial and personnel flows that mark UN work became more sharp. The transport, supplies, service technology, communications and information equipment, and security hardware were advanced industrial. A world, literally an industrial world, of "necessities" underlay these sophisticated systems: soap and blankets and rations; uniforms and arms and recreation supplies. The United Nations is good business, for some.

PART FIVE

DANGEROUS PROFITS

The illegal has to exist for the legal to make sense. Anarchy provides the borders that bring the state into focus.

Popular conception would have it that a simple line divides two separate spheres: state distinct from non-state; the legal controlling the disruptive Hobbesian beasts waiting to dismantle civilization as we know it. Simple, but inaccurate. The state is infused with the non-state; with both the legal and the illegal. Power and politics, whether in the modern or the post-modern state, require wealth. Certainly, contenders for state power use the power of economics in all its guises in their pursuit of sovereignty. Unregulated monies can make and break nations. The shadows allow *untold* wealth, literally.

Trillions of dollars move across the world along non-state and nonlegal lines. If criminals and terrorists are hard to catch, it is perhaps because some within the state structure have made use of these same channels under cover of the shadows. Power covers its trails. Who, then, controls the profits attending to these trillions of dollars; and how are they being used? Today, wealth flows across national and conceptual borders with ease; who manages this flow will be one of the core questions defining the twenty-first century.

"VISIBLE" INDUSTRIES IN RUINS; BEHIND THIS, DEVELOPMENT TAKES PLACE IN THE SHADOWS. BIE PROVINCE, ANGOLA, 2000.

CHAPTER 15

IRONIES IN THE SHADOWS

(LITERALLY) UNTOLD PROFITS AND A KEY SOURCE OF DEVELOPMENT

In 1995, after attending a conference in Croatia, fellow anthropologist Linda Green and I traveled through Hungary to Romania. I hadn't been to Hungary since the 1970s, and the country, painted in shades of gray and green, had impressed me as quiet and somber. But what I remember most was the storytelling abilities of the people I met. One day, standing on one of Budapest's bridges over the Danube, an acquaintance told me about the Russian massacre of 1956. He described how people feared walking across this bridge because it was hard to avoid seeing the bodies of friends and strangers floating downstream. "The river ran red then," he said. "We called it the river of red tears." This man, and others like him, brought Budapest to life for me those decades ago: the Danube, not blue but red; the bars and restaurants tucked quietly off main streets where, over warm food, cool discussions of politics flowed with an eye to the door; where wine ran more freely than the buses.

The Budapest I encountered twenty years later was bustling, colorful, cosmopolitan, and at times frenetic; the city was a free-for-all. But in fact, Budapest wasn't free for all; it was only free for some. Vast markets, both informal and formal, moved western goods into Eastern Europe, and eastern goods to the west. From sewing machines to prostitutes, industrial equipment to drugs, Hungary stands at a powerful set of crossroads traveled by businesspeople of all kinds. Vast wealth marks some of its citizens and their enterprises, while many other average citizens quietly suffer hunger or illnesses, toiling in jobs that sometimes continue to pay socialist wages in capitalist markets. Watching the Budapest of the 1990s,

I thought of the American western frontier: wide-open economies where many options and fewer controls make millionaires of some and paupers of others; where new infrastructures pop up before state controls catch up in monitoring them; where "melting pot" means the blend of formal, gray, and black markets and the international players who stir these pots of gold, deprivation, and danger.

When I think of the central role informal markets play as they coalesce around the demands of war and peace, Janine Wedel's research on refrigerators in Poland comes to mind. In the 1980s, when Janine and I were both graduate students at the University of California, Berkeley, she was researching the in/formal economies of Eastern Europe. She worked in Poland, studying the flows of everyday supplies as they were produced formally in Soviet industries (seldom reaching the masses of civilians who needed them), and were procured informally across political, economic, and state borders, making their way to working-class kitchens. Wedel followed refrigerators as they were made and then lost to bureaucratese, skim-offs, poor workmanship and materials, transport difficulties, and the vastness of Soviet need compared to the realities of its production. What emerged from her analysis was how central informal markets are to daily life. Wedel pointed out that these networks were as vast as the formal markets, perhaps even more organized and efficient, and certainly critical to the survival of a society and its economy.[1]

Wedel's refrigerators enter into a broad sweep of historical exchange and contemporary practice that have been honed over centuries of trade through the vicissitudes of politics and the cycles of plenty and poverty. These systems of exchange are often constructed as carefully as formal markets; and they don't disappear with changing governments or economic philosophies. These informal systems operated in Eastern Europe in World War II and during the Cold War. They operated in Sarajevo when formal governmental institutions collapsed during the war in the early 1990s. They brought in food and supplies for desperate civilians; moved allies in and refugees out; brought in alcohol, cigarettes, prostitutes, and drugs, in part through UN peacekeeping networks (which even transferred tanks from Russia to Serbia and armaments from Europe and Asia to Bosnia).[2] And in the postwar years, they continue to operate.

When formal governmental frameworks are in flux or decimated by political transition, these non-formal networks may be the only supply networks functioning.

When the former Soviet Union broke into sovereign states, its economy broke into new patterns, too. As one formal economic reign ends, and before another formal one emerges to replace it, there is a void of formal structures. Ukraine or Tajikistan can't retool their entire economies overnight, moving from satellite states dependent on a Soviet government to sovereign states responsible for their own infrastructures. In the same way, as Sarajevo or Mozambique move out of war, they meet a similar flux of formal intervention and infrastructure. The mafias of Russia that have been central to news stories since the collapse of the Soviet Union; the use of Southern Africa ports for smuggling gems, drugs, and weapons; the vast monetary empires that run through Southeast Asia behind formal sectors are all, in this analysis, expected results of postwar change and political transitions. They should be expected by the negotiators of peace settlements and political transitions, rather than taking them by surprise.

There is a profound irony in the observations I have made concerning shadow realities. The realm of the unregulated is a realm of possibility and danger, where great fortunes and great cruelty are possible. But it is also where the average person turns for survival in an unsure world. The arena of the shadows is a place where power regimes are contested, where new forms of capital, access, and authority arise — some crumbling before they master any real influence in global affairs, others supplanting old regimes with new.

If shadow networks were merely illicit systems bent on rapid and potentially immense gain, they would not provide the challenge they do to legal regimes. It is this very irony — the fact that extra-state systems provide not only dangerous wildcatting of resources outside of legal controls, but also offer a means of development to people with few alternate means of survival — that makes shadow regimes a serious source of power in the contemporary world.

I want to advance several hypotheses on the relationships among shadow economies, power, and development. But first, let me put this topic in the context of a common, everyday occurrence. The story involves the extra-state commerce in drugs. The mere mention of the word *drugs* tends to evoke dangerous, exotic images of illicit drug empires, broken addicts, and untold fortunes. But it is not cocaine, mandrax, marijuana, or heroin that interests me here — they're too obvious. Instead, I want to talk about pharmaceutical drugs. Relatively few people use illegal drugs, but virtually everyone needs medicines, and many can't afford them. Vast numbers of pharmaceuticals move across the divides of il/legality, often many times, in global flows that address the most core concerns of life, death, and illness.

PAISINHO'S WOUND

A new boy had joined the street children who had staked out a home on a bit of pavement in the block where I stayed in Angola. I had known this group of boys for several years: their claim to this stretch of street extended back at least a half a decade. The new boy said his name was Paisinho. He was hard to talk to; he hung at the back of the group, seemingly trying to fold into himself. Manush, at twelve the oldest of the group and therefore responsible for its well-being, explained: "Paisinho has a wound, and we think it needs medical attention. We could use your help; it is just getting worse and worse." I asked Paisinho if I could see his wound, and he reluctantly agreed. It was as if in showing it he became even more vulnerable – strength is valued on the streets. Paisinho raised his pant leg to show me a wound on his calf so severely infected I feared he might lose his leg. Thus began an odyssey into the world of pharmaceuticals.

Paisinho and I went to a clinic, where the nurse did what she could with the limited medicines she had available, but they didn't make a dent in the infection. The nurse then suggested if I could pay in U.S. dollars, she would take me to a pharmacy that had the five or six items she deemed necessary to treat the wound. I agreed. Given the war, the attendant problems of importing most necessities, and the high tariff policies of the country, pharmacies carried a limited, and very expensive, line of drugs. By the time I left the pharmacy with the items needed, I had paid a king's ransom – an amount of money beyond the means of all but the most affluent people in the country. It was more than what I would have spent for the same items in the USA or Europe.

Paisinho's wound took a long time to heal, and the medicines quickly ran out. I went to buy more. But this time the children themselves told me it was stupid to buy at the pharmacy. Informal markets in pharmaceuticals are not hidden: the streets are lined with vendors who put an extensive range of pharmaceuticals on cardboard boxes on the sidewalks and whose tables brim with bottles and capsules. In the provinces, some markets seem to have more pharmaceuticals than food. The drugs available run the gamut of famous and not-so-famous drug companies from all over the world; and they offer treatments for just about any known illness or condition. The children knew all the street vendors in the area and took me to their favorite. We looked at his wares and began to discuss what we needed. When I mentioned something that was not on display, he and his friends opened duffel bags filled with merchandise, and in each case produced exactly what I asked for. The children, the street vendors, and I had a detailed discussion of the various brands. Even children of ten knew the positive and negative aspects of major brands and types of medicine. The street vendors gave directions on taking the drugs, much like pharmacists. In a matter of minutes (my transactions in the pharmacy had taken considerably longer), I left with everything I needed. The cost was *ten times less* than what I had paid in the pharmacy. The drug that cost me $50 in the formal market was available on the streets for $2. The children had said it was stupid of me to buy at the pharmacy; for most of the country's citizens, it is simply impossible.

As the children continued to get sick and need various medicines, from antibiotics to anti-malarials, and as I casually struck up conversations with "street pharmacists," the breadth and scope of the trade began to emerge. Four major distribution systems link a poor street child with a wound to a multi-billion-dollar global market in "drugs" . . . these perhaps as profitable as the trade in cocaine, marijuana, and heroin, but produced—if not distributed—legally. Each of the four is explained in the following quotes from people in Paisinho's town.

1. CONTAINER DRUGS

> We just go directly to the containers [off-loaded at the ports] and the warehouses and buy the drugs. You do your business right there. We specialize in drugs, because that's what we are known for, that's what we do. But you can get anything at the containers and warehouses. Anything from anywhere in the world. We go with friends who specialize in everything from western furniture to weapons. If you stop by my place here for medicines, and mention you want, say, anything from light bulbs to a "hot" deal on the latest 4 × 4 Jeep, I can tell you where to go and how to get it.
>
> These people who bring in the containers from all over the world, they are big. They have connections all over the world, and connections all over the government and military here. They can "get things," and get things done. This country develops around them. If you know them, anything is possible.

In researching this, I have found no single model that explains these businesspeople. Some of the warehouse owners are leading figures of the society and are working hard to develop the country as transparently as possible. Others follow profits along blurry lines of il/legality. Some actively broker in the shadows and specialize in non-legal goods and services. They all help keep the system running.

Import and export taxes, levies, tariffs, fees, and fines sustain governments worldwide, cutting into the profits of businesses. Given the fact that even in the most legally stringent ports in the world, for example, in the USA, EU, and Hong Kong, only between 1 and 5 percent of all shipping is monitored. A remarkable 95 to 99 percent of all containers and ships come into any given port without a search or hands-on evaluation. If people can buy pharmaceuticals on the streets for $2 that cost $50 in the formal shops, it's pretty clear that these commodities didn't enter the markets along purely formal channels. Magnify that by all the commodities one can get in "street markets." Paisinho's drugs came in a container with a host of supplies that keeps the country operating, for good and bad.

2. MILITARY DRUGS

The drugs? They fell off the military truck.

This simple explanation by a street vendor points to a "wealth" of information. In the words of a development specialist:[3]

> The place is pretty much awash with military drugs. Military stores come in, and the commanders take control of these, and then sell them off and pocket the proceeds. It's quite a business. And it's not like they are restricted to selling only the normal consignment of drugs. By creating alliances with requisitions, they can order larger shipments, special supplies, expensive brand names.
>
> The ramifications of this "business" are extensive. This is not just someone pocketing a little extra. The proceeds the commander gets from this he can turn around and invest in shops, pharmacies, enterprises — you name it. But he is investing not with his own money, but with money he has gotten entirely for free. He does not have the same sense of responsibility with this money as people do with capital they, and their livelihoods, depend on. And he doesn't have the same taxes, interest rates, and bureaucratic red tape that people do who go through legal channels. Add to that the fact that this commander's merchandise cost him nothing. He can sell at ten times below the market rate and still make a profit. No businessperson working along traditional legal lines could ever hope to compete with this pricing. So the commander can end up with a veritable monopoly.

In a perfect world, no one would see such a system as a viable solution to development. Even in war, development specialists can see that unfair business practices aren't a solid foundation on which to rebuild the socio-economic structures of a society. But while these practices are unfair and extra-legal, they do bring medicines to a desperate population, most of whom can't afford to pay formal prices for the drugs they need to save their lives. So people like Paisinho can find antibiotics for $2 on the streets that in the pharmacy cost $50. In no way do I justify or condone these practices in saying this. My intent is to point out the difficult realities people face in seeking to survive.

3. COUNTERFEIT DRUGS

> There are factories all over the region [Southern Africa] making counterfeit pharmaceuticals. They run across all the countries around here, I'm guessing they run all over the world. They can make just about any drug, counterfeiting just about any brand. They are good, they look just like the real thing. We, of course, deal in the real brands. I mean, what would happen if we sell an auntie from the neighborhood with twelve kids counterfeit birth control pills that aren't as good as the real brand, and she comes huffing up to us, pregnant? What does that do for our business? We can tell the difference between the real and counterfeit merchandise if we look carefully at the trademarks and packaging materials.
>
> We get a lot of pharmaceuticals from factories in Asia that we are sure are counterfeit. Truth is, some of this stuff is respected in its own right: factories that provide low-cost drugs that work as well as the high-priced brand names.

4. BANNED DRUGS

> The drug you took to treat your malaria in Angola last month is banned here in Europe, *said the tropical medical specialist in London who was treating me for yet another malaria attack.* In fact, it has been sanctioned by the World Health Organization: it can cause heart attacks. When it was banned, the pharmaceutical companies did not stop making it. They just exported it to Africa. It is widely sold there: and this "dumping" is a cost-cutting measure, so you find it out-competing safer drugs.

As a WHO official told me later when I followed up this story:

> This isn't uncommon at all. Pharmaceutical companies can put a lot of time, effort, and money into researching and developing a new drug. Then, when they decide to run with it, they have to tool production for this particular drug. It's a huge investment, as far as they are concerned. To find out down the

road that the drug is dangerous—even that it is banned—is more a financial than an ethical hardship for some. To toss this out and begin again from scratch researching and developing a whole new drug—which, like its predecessor, may ultimately be banned—to invest all that time and effort and money long before any gains are realized . . . well, that is more than some are willing to do. So they continue to make and sell the drug. Hey, it treats the disease, they tell themselves, and all drugs have side effects, don't they? They make a decent profit selling them in non-western countries. It's the same thing with drugs past their expiration dates. Where do you think those end up?

There are few things as sure in life as health and illness, so it isn't surprising that a huge extra-state industry has developed around pharmaceutical drugs. What is surprising is that with all the global attention on illegal drugs, little is said about the illicit production, trade, and dumping of pharmaceuticals and the role these actions play in global economies.

Pharmaceuticals are interesting in that they present a set of ethical complexities that don't adhere to illegal drugs. Illegal drugs are not generally considered health care products — they are luxury or recreation items. But pharmaceuticals are essential to health. Drugs that are adulterated, banned because of serious and even fatal side effects, expired, or poorly counterfeited can maim and kill.

Extra-state and development ethics take on their pressing and potentially explosive character at this intersection of a poor street child suffering a life-threatening wound and a global multi-billion-dollar industry with political, economic, and military elite interests worldwide. Of course, these conundrums also arise with many other extra-state commodities and services, from those central to industrial development through water and agricultural systems to developing and maintaining critical trade networks. Everything from educational supplies to information technology moves into cash- and development-poor regions in ways that are simultaneously exploitative and beneficial.

. . .

Having set this stage, I turn now to advance several hypotheses in exploring the relationships among shadow economies, power, and development.

1. Extra-State Trade Is Centrally Linked to Development. A complex system must be in place for Paisinho to get street medicines: production sites that can be tapped for extra-state consumption; distribution networks that require shipping, handling, and transport; trade alliances that make this complex system of shipments viable; and revenues that fuel further investments. Resources that do not exist in the formal sector flow in and out of countries, and these flows require infrastructure.

Development is in part jump-started along non-formal economic lines. Here we can see that the traditional categories of "informal economy" and "high-tech gray- or black-market networks" are both theoretically and practically misleading. The war orphan selling Marlboro cigarettes and the old women carrying tomatoes into food-impoverished communities along informal routes are linked into the same system as the man who is carrying out $20 million worth of gems. In this way, for good and bad, people gain the means to plant crops, start up industries, and develop trade routes.

Perhaps it isn't surprising that development should be so centrally linked to the extra-state and the informal. Maria Faria of the World Food Program in Angola captures this dynamic:

> I have never understood how people survive here, but they have learned to live with the war. They do all kinds of business, all kinds of trading, all kinds of work. I think that it is people's mentality that is the key to their survival: they know they are on their own. They know things don't work, that the government can't provide for them, that no one is giving them what they need. So if no one is providing the essentials, they have to find their own solutions—they will go around the problem of survival one way or another, until they find a way.
>
> This is *their* survival. It is not the government's or the foreigner's or the INGO's or any formal organization's. The people have created a system to survive. They have made their own lines of survival, and their own lives of survival.
>
> And this survival is not an individual matter: people survive linked in broad extended families and communities. They set up networks of kin relations countrywide and internationally. A person in Lubango has a family member—maybe a cousin's husband's daughter—in Malange: they will send whatever they have to each other, and to others in their extensive net of relations all over. And they survive.
>
> This is development.[4]

My intention is not to idealize the non-formal. It is to show that as dangerous, illegal, and exploitative as this trade can be, it is often the means by which citizens gain the currency to buy industrial necessities, agricultural supplies, and development goods. Such illicit goods purchase hard currency, they broker power, they allow investments into land, legal industries, and political partnerships. They spawn and support subsidiary industries, both legal and illicit. And of course, daily necessities like clothing, textbooks, and medicines follow these same trading trajectories. If development is to take place without relying on illicit trade in dangerous goods, viable ways of making goods, services, and payments available in these difficult circumstances need to be created.

Ironically, in many resource-rich and war-torn countries, the non-formal may provide more in-state resources than the formal economy. I have heard the following words almost verbatim in numerous countries:

> The money flowing into the state often disappears into a black hole of corruption, personal gain, party patronage, and mismanagement. The tremendous wealth elites can command is seldom put back into the economy and the development of the nation and its population as a whole. It is channeled out of the country, to the North; or to in-country luxury development that benefits only the most exclusive. The state and civil society collapse around this.

Instead, foundational in-country development appears to take place mostly with businesspeople like the ones I have quoted in the previous chapters: from the man who said he comes from generations of cross-border traders who are strongly invested in their families' and communities' well-being to the person who brought television sets, Mercedes Benzes, and industrial equipment to the front to develop his region. Maria Faria continued her observations:

> We are starting to see normalcy in the thick of things, people begin organizing themselves as a means of surviving, and this shapes the development of the country as a whole. But it is the middle class and the poor who are the source of this. They don't make fortunes in an international way and then move these fortunes out of the country. They are invested in their relations, in their country. They truly love their land, no matter how much hope they have lost in the war, they love their country, and are unwilling to leave. So what they do, they do here, and they invest back here. People start helping one another and the country; they start development at the middle and low economic levels. And Angola will make it. My mother told me when I was young: if you can survive here, you can survive anywhere.

These people, who are the most invested in their communities, are at the same time the most invisible actors in formal state-level and international economics and development concerns.

2. Extra-State Networks Are International in Character and Link Local Economies with Transnational and Cosmopolitan Production Sites. There are no formal national pharmaceutical companies in Paisinho's country. All drugs are imported. The government imports a restricted selection, which may or may not meet the needs of the population. Yet the poorest, least educated street child knows the brand names of pharmaceutical companies worldwide — and a wide range of their drugs are available. Conversely, on the more exploitative side, the large multinational pharmaceutical companies depend, in a way they would prefer to remain invisible, on the illnesses of all the Paisinhos globally. In a basic economic sense, the street vendor is a vendor for the pharmaceutical company, and Paisinho a client. It is not a simple linear matter of core production and periphery consumption: it is a powerful interrelated set of dependent associations.

Classical economic theory posits that economic activity follows a continuum from local through national and regional to international. If these linear typologies ever explained the dynamics of economic activity, they do little to explain the contemporary world. The twenty-first century finds no contradictions in a child soldier in tattered shorts on a distant front linking globally on a sat-linked computer communications system; in China pirating 97 percent of all software; in Asian drug cartels transmitting shipments through Africa to link with illicit resource trade heading to Europe; in the desperate and the poor who buy "street pharmaceuticals" shaping global multinational performance. It is nothing more than a quaint idea to think that the people of any region in the contemporary world, no matter how remote or poor, don't know the latest cosmopolitan brand names, international work flows, hit videos, and political dreams and nightmares.

Even in this international context, profitable extra-state trade remains intricately tied to informal trade.[5]

Rich transnational extra-state associations require the hunger of average people — the hunger for food, jobs, recognition, daily necessities, survival. Informal networks may be said to be, in some ways, the sites of production for the shadows globally.

3. Governments and INGOs Don't Always Define Extra-State Practices as Negative. Quite simply, most governments would rather have non-formal economy pharmaceuticals on the streets than have all the Paisinhos with life-threatening illnesses die from lack of access to medicines.

If people bring industrial, agricultural, health care, educational, and transport supplies into the country along unregulated lines in ways that stimulate the economy, higher human development index standards will ensue. If there are no other ways to meet the challenges of development, a government may find that these benefits outweigh the risks of the political instability a more debilitated economy might unleash.

These realities are belied in development programs: virtually every aid, development, and economic enhancement organization deals directly, and generally exclusively, through the formal sector. These deal little with the vast majority of people in countries like Angola. Most of the (development) monies coming into the country are flowing through the formal sector and then out of the country, either via foreign goods-and-services purchases, or via corruption.

The last issue is critical: the corruption that is currently a prime topic of concern in development circles has its main font in the formal sector — the sector that intergovernmental loans and aid monies are channeled through. At the same time, aid may well be routed into the very structures that are most likely to foment continuing conflicts.

4. Extra-State Transaction and Its Connection to Development Link with Political Power. The street vendor of drugs is unlikely to become a high-powered businessperson; and little Paisinho has even less chance for such a career. But the street vendor is "cannon fodder; the front line soldier," says Detective Richard Flynn of Scotland Yard. Such a vendor is dependent on people with the kind of political, economic, and social connections and sources of wealth who are able to negotiate the blurry lines of il/legality in moving pharmaceuticals from cosmopolitan sites of production through international shipping routes and borders to local populations. The powerhouses behind moving street pharmaceuticals have wide-ranging business interests, international contacts, and wealth, all of which can be "bartered" into political stature. Successful businesspeople not only have the ear of government and international organizations, they most commonly *are* the government and international organizations.

People adept at manipulating the junctures of il/licit markets often invest in legal enterprises and political careers, both nationally and internationally.[6] Money is useless, obviously, unless it can be used, and currency — from the cleanest to the dirtiest — has little value until it can enter the legal economy. Gains from extra-state transactions allow investments into land, legal industries, and political partnerships.

5. Clear Distinctions between Legal and Illegal, State and Non-State, or Local and International, Are Often Impossible to Make, Which Raises Ethical Questions about the Positive and Negative Qualities of Extra-State Phenomena. To hearken back to Susan Strange's insight: "The fact is that while financial crime has grown enormously . . . it remains, legally and morally, an indeterminate gray area. The dividing line is seldom clear and is nowhere the same between transactions which are widely practiced but ethically questionable and those which are downright criminal."[7] One of the most interesting and morally ambiguous issues in this gray area is money laundering. The degree to which money laundering is il/legal is not as clear as popular debate would have it. The USA introduced money laundering laws only in 1986, for example, and many countries have no such laws at all, or only toothless ones. In fact, it is difficult for banks to even know it is taking place. American banks often have hundreds of associations with banks worldwide for the transfer of monies, and some of those banks may not even have an office, much less a home country: "Several U.S. banks were unaware that they were serving foreign banks that had no office in any locations, were operating in a jurisdiction where the bank had no license to operate, had never undergone a bank examination by a regulator, or were using U.S. correspondent accounts to facilitate crime."[8] There is no doubt that money laundering can be detrimental to a country's financial and political health. As John McDowell and Gary Novis write: "Unchecked, money laundering can erode the integrity of a nation's financial institutions. Due to the high integration of capital markets, money laundering can also adversely affect currencies and interest rates. Ultimately, laundered money flows into global financial systems, where it can undermine national economies and currencies."[9]

At the same time, money laundering brings millions or billions of dollars into a country—money that must then move into legitimate enterprises. As such, it becomes a major economic force. By way of example: Mozambique, with peace and an increasingly stable development trajectory, has increasingly become a favored site for money laundering. One of the more common means is the tourism industry. For good or bad, the money laundered into the tourism industry builds infrastructure, provides jobs, and brings in tourist dollars—which may provide stability to attract legitimate foreign business investors. If money is increasingly being laundered into non-western locales, both negative impacts and developmental forces are magnified. "In some emerging market countries, these illicit proceeds may dwarf government budgets, resulting in a loss of control of economic policy by governments. Indeed, in some cases, the sheer magnitude of the accumulated asset base of laundered proceeds can be used to corner markets — or even small economies."[10]

A country's success is built job by job, business by business. Infrastructure gains coherence only through each new communication link, transport route, and educational facility. Like legal gains, laundered money flows into the formal sector, into government coffers as taxes, into jobs and infrastructural developments. Charles Goredema, the leading researcher on money laundering at South Africa's Institute for Security Studies in Cape Town, told me that some people in western countries did not want to see money laundering leave western countries for emerging markets like Mozambique because, however illicit, it still represented such enormous cash flows.

6. The Junctures of Licit and Illicit Economies Shape Formal Global Markets. Paisinho is one poor street child living in the midst of a war. The drugs he buys are invisible in global economies. But "economy" is not a singular noun, and "transaction" doesn't consist of a single individual. The 6 billion people in the world will all face illness at some time in their lives, and most will seek medicines of some kind. Economies don't care whether the Paisinhos of the world buy their medicines in legal pharmacies or from unregistered street vendors. A pill sold is a pill sold — profit is profit. Magnify this by the global rate of illness. Illegal drugs, by UN estimates, bring in some half a trillion dollars a year. Medicinal drugs easily trump this figure. Magnify this discussion across all the il/licit flows of global commodities and services, and the impact on global financial markets becomes more visible.

All the goods that, in the cycle of production and consumption, move outside of formal state channels ultimately constitute profits for legitimate businesses. All $500 billion worth of illicit weapons sold annually, for example, constitute a profit for legal arms industries in the industrial centers of the world. When the gems and oil of Angola or Burma buy computers and armaments (or clothing, medicines, and VCRs) from cosmopolitan centers, the money helps define the financial realities of these centers, regardless of whether it arrives through formal or shadow means. "The flexible connection of these criminal networks in international networks," writes Castells, "constitutes an essential feature of the new global economy."[11]

All these financial realities factor into corporate sales, bank (laundered) revenues, cost-of-living indices, the viability of gross national product to national economic health, and so on. As Mark Chingono observes: "The informal economy seems here to stay, and may even become the mainstay of the economy."[12]

AMOR MATA PESSOA: LOVE KILLS (LITERALLY, LOVE KILL PERSON) – GRAFFITI ON A BOMBED BUILDING AT THE WAR'S FRONT IN MOZAMBIQUE, 1991.

CHAPTER 16

WHY DON'T WE STUDY THE SHADOWS?

John Kenneth Galbraith must have been smiling when he delivered the line, "Finally, a large corporation can conduct its own foreign policy." An economist known for his wit, Galbraith was speaking with coauthor Nicole Salinger for their 1978 book, *Almost Everyone's Guide to Economics*.

Galbraith: The big multinational oil companies have their own policy in dealing with the Middle Eastern governments. Sometimes it differs from that of the State Department. If it is the same, it is partly because these firms have a good deal of influence on the State Department. The Lockheed Corporation, in conducting its foreign policy in Japan, Holland, Italy, and elsewhere, has had more success in destabilizing governments than has the CIA, with the difference that Lockheed operated only against friendly governments. Japanese cabinet ministers and Dutch princes aren't vulnerable to the influence or financial resources of the average retail grocer.

Salinger: In France we think of the large corporation as having power from its ability to offer or withdraw employment. If it threatens a shutdown, the government quickly pays attention.

Galbraith: This, too, is a source of influence. It's what saves the firm that is in financial trouble. With us it is also very important where weapons orders are concerned. A firm that might otherwise close down has special leverage in getting orders from the Pentagon. And with the Congress.

You asked me earlier about how political economy became economics. You can see how the big corporations are now putting a significant political element back into economics.

Salinger: Does that mean that the textbooks should have a section on corporate political influence? Or corporate bribery?

> *Galbraith:* In the advanced courses it would be called econometric aspects of extra-legal functions. It is partly because economics cannot digest the political operations of the corporation in such a refined way that these things are ignored in the textbooks. Not many economists live so far out of the world that they would deny the political power of the modern corporation, its importance in real life. But there is no elegant theory of corporate thimble-rigging and political subornation which lends itself to university instruction. So it has to be ignored.[1]

Perhaps as important as uncovering the dynamics of extra-state networks is the question of why so little data or discussion of the non-formal exists. Most people assume this data is available. But such assumptions are easy to challenge: How many university courses and texts address extra-state economies and their impact on global economies and politics? How can you calculate the impact of illicit gem flows on European stock markets? What economic indices are available to predict—based on the intersections of formal and extra-legal transactions—where economic crashes such as that faced in Asia in the late 1990s and in the West after the September 11 attacks will occur? How can one calculate the entire economy of a country—in full—and how this shapes a country's relations with other states?

Let me begin with an example. In 1998, I stopped by the United Nations Development Program (UNDP) and the World Bank in Luanda to obtain data on the 90 percent of the Angolan economy that was at that time non-formal, and its relationship to the 10 percent of the economy that was formal—figures I had gotten from the UN itself. No data were available. I made appointments with the senior economists of both institutions to ask how viable policy could be implemented when the indices they used bore little resemblance to the economic realities defining the country. "How," I asked, "could development programs to help the entire country be effective if they were based on data that represented only 10 percent of the economy?" The head of the World Bank in Angola responded: "We simply don't deal with those things, they aren't issues we are concerned with." End of discussion.

Alexander Aboagye, the senior economist of the UNDP office, gave a more robust answer. A Ghanaian trained both in classical economic theory and the realities of on-the-ground programs, he appreciated the ironies of the situation:

> We have a serious interest in figuring out how people actually survive in these seemingly impossible conditions; how the informal markets affect the economic realities of the country; and where the true bases of development potential are in the economy. . . . But like most formal agencies, we are bound,

> by mandate, to dealing with formal economic arenas. Such mandates are generated at the highest levels of the organization.
>
> To compound matters, classical economic theory simply does not have the capacity to deal with these questions.

Individual people do undertake studies of extra-legal activities, but if these studies don't generate new economic theory and global indices capable of representing non/formal economies as a whole — as they affect both national and global nodes of decision-making power — institutions remain unchanged. As an example, in 1999 I was speaking with Emmanuel Dierckx de Casterlé, the UNDP resident representative in Mozambique. When I asked him about non-formal economies and their relationship to development, he immediately grew interested:

> "Many here believe that the postwar economic successes Mozambique has had are intrinsically tied to the informal economy and its interpenetrations with formal development," he said.
>
> "Why, then," I asked, "don't you study this in greater depth?"
>
> He seemed truly perplexed: "But we are interested in this, as I have been saying."
>
> "Why then," I persisted, "don't you publish this work?"
>
> "But we do!" he exclaimed. "Our UNDP reports discuss these issues."

I picked up the several-hundred-page UNDP country report on Mozambique that had just been published in Geneva and asked him to show me where these topics were discussed. He opened the book and leafed through it. Then he picked up some of the other UN reports lining the shelves of his office and studied them. Finally, he looked at me with a grin and said:

> "This is really interesting, there really isn't much in our reports, and little in our conferences either."

In point of fact, the massive UNDP country report on Mozambique for that year mentions the non-formal only in passing, in just a handful of paragraphs. Though central to economic viability in the day-to-day development work on the ground, the non-formal and the extra-state don't seem to translate into formal organizational structures or knowledge. How does one research the relationship of formal and non-formal in shaping the development trajectories of Mozambique, or any other country? There is no answer to date: it is not possible to get solid empirical answers from formal UN, IMF, or World Bank country or international reports.

I find it fascinating that major international bodies that are formally assigned the guardianship of transnational economic accounting focus on the formal economy in country reports — including countries like Mozambique, where, by these organizations' own words, over half the economy takes place along non-formal lines — and then say this reckoning represents "the economy."

. . .

Why does a vast sweep of international economic work ignore a vast sweep of international economic reality? My anthropological curiosity piqued, I decided to do an ethnographic study of the populations that produce the cultural norms of what is deemed "economic" — with economists and development professionals constituting my "field site."

Even asking questions posed a problem, I found, because there is no clear term to refer to what I call here "shadow economies." Informal markets are taken to be small-scale domestic or cottage industry, usually revolving around agriculture. People don't tend to think of international extra-state multi-million/billion-dollar mining or information technology transactions as "informal trade." Research is done on illegal activities — mafias, trafficking in drugs and luxury goods like ivory, and weapons — but generally a sharp division is drawn between formal and illegal enterprises, and little is provided on how these illegal economies configure global economic and political practices.

If terminology is threadbare, empirical methodologies for researching extra-state phenomena are even thinner. Try finding a book to give a graduate student who wants to go to the field to study extra-legal activities, a book that outlines research methodologies, details empirical analyses, provides economic equations for calculating extra/state GNP and its insertion into the global economy, or theorizes about these complex undertakings. Try finding the resources to teach your students or discuss with your colleagues how to formally chart non-formal activities and demonstrate the interpenetrations between state, formal, and non-formal economic realities. Brendan Geary, a student at the University of Notre Dame, conducted research for me in London looking into how many economics books and texts contained any information on extra-legal economies, and if they did, what information was available. He looked at the bookstores of major universities and at the largest bookshops in urban London. He found that many major texts on economics included virtually no discussion of extra-legal economic matters of any kind. If they did, they provided a maximum of several pages of generalities. None contained methodologies for collecting data, conducting research, and empirically analyzing data with a rigor demanded for formal economic analyses. Geary's conclusion:

> Within the academic circles of one of the world's largest cities, shadow economies mustered no more than a passing glance. The shadows not only exist outside of the world of (neo)classical economics, but also, and more importantly—(neo)classical economics functions defiantly in the face of these faceless economies.

I put this question of terminology to several economists before the end of the war in Angola when UNITA's Jonas Savimbi was still alive:

> Let's take the example of Savimbi, *I said,* the leader of the UNITA forces in Angola. He controls upwards of half a billion in gem proceeds a year. This is not properly illegal, for while he is not a government, he can be said to have been fighting a war and controlling land and resources as a political contender. It is not properly legal, either, as he is not a government, pays no state-recognized taxes, and adheres to no formal international treatises on trade as a rebel force. Some of these revenues go to the outfitting of his troops and political activities. These supplies come in through a vast array of international connections, variously legal, extra-legal, gray market, and black market. And, as is so usual in war-affected societies, the majority of civilians are suffering deprivations in everything from food through clothes and schoolbooks to medicines, and they are themselves trading across cultures and borders for these essentials. Standing between these two arenas are civilians who make considerable profit in the interstices between the gems, weapons, and daily goods trade, variously running or trading goods from VCRs to stolen Mercedes and the energy to power them. What, then, do you call this?

The answer I most often received from economist to economist, country to country, was "informal economy."

But, I reminded them, in their own publications they used the groundbreaking International Labour Organization definition of *informal sector* from the 1972 ILO study in Kenya: "ease of entry, reliance on indigenous resources, family ownership, small scale of operation, labour intensive and adapted technology, skills acquired outside the formal school system, and unregulated and competitive markets."[2] I spoke with Dirk Hansohm, one of the leading economists at the Namibian Economic Policy Research Unit (NEPRU), about his definition of *informal economies.* By his definition, some 4 percent of the GNP in Namibia is generated through the informal economy: the small agricultural and cottage industries that impoverished people develop to survive.[3] But, I said, this definition, and the 4 percent figure, didn't account for the very profitable and complex markets that were trading gems for weapons, for medicines, and for the Mercedes crossing Angola's and Namibia's borders. The day before, a senior UN economist had told me that Namibia, given its political stability and developed infrastructure, was a major crossroads for cosmopolitan trade routes of the East and West for considerable contraband. Namibia had also recently been recognized in media and INGOs alike as a way station in a very lucrative international illegal drug network stretching from Latin American and Asia through Africa to Europe. "If this is part of the informal sector," I asked, "how can one say the informal economy comprises only 4 percent of the county's GNP?"

From academics to UNDP economists, I have found this question does not rankle, but causes curiosity and animated speculation. Many, including Hansohm, responded to this question with the same reply: "Classical and textbook economics does not deal with this, we have no methodologies for studying this, no one has mapped the empirical complexities of these economies . . . but it is fascinating." And, when I ask if major conferences and development specialists deal with this vast sweep of interrelated shadow economies and the politics that girds them, the answer is always the same: "Seldom, but it appears to be changing for the better."

. . .

In trying to answer why "we don't talk about these things," three levels of explanations emerge: the practical, the cultural, and the political. These combine in a discussion of the larger issue of power.

To begin with the *practical* answer. Clement Jackson, an economist with the UNDP in Windhoek, Namibia, cited several primary reasons why little economically useful data existed on economies outside of formal sectors:

> First, subterranean markets aren't easily quantifiable. Our tools as economists aren't adapted well to this kind of analysis. Researchers would have to go directly to the field, we would have to do the footwork ourselves, counting and cataloging this market as it unfolded in everyday economics. This would be a formidable challenge.

I pointed out that, as an anthropologist, I saw field research as neither unreasonable nor formidable, especially if it results in a more accurate economic index. Jackson shot me a look as if to imply that anthropology was a quaint if unrealistic discipline, little adaptable to the world of economists. After assuring me that fieldwork is indeed a formidable barrier to the people populating his profession, he continued:

> Second, nonformal markets are defined by flux and shifting patterns of exchange, making observations, generalizations, and quantification difficult. Economic theory has little in the way of methodologies to meet the demands of this flux. And third, a serious impediment is nonformal markets' relationships with criminal activities.

NEPRU economist Dirk Hansohm added another significant factor, echoing Clement Jackson, as to why so little data was generated on nonformal economies. Hansohm smoothed his tie and brushed off the sleeve of his tailored suit, leaned back in his ergonomically engineered chair, sipped some coffee from a china cup, and smiled:

> You have to go out and collect this data. You have to do fieldwork. And quite simply, most people don't like to do fieldwork. Data in this case is a matter of convenience. It is uncomfortable and hot or cold and dusty to go out and do fieldwork. You get sweaty and sore. You have to deal with people and all their foibles; God, you'd have to deal with petty traders and criminals and the endless confusing buzz of people doing business.
>
> It is far better to sit in one's office and relate to documents. And these documents deal with formal economies exclusively: they come straight from the government's statistics office. We are trained that way, to think that going to the government's statistics office is economic investigation. And by convenience, we allow ourselves to believe this: it is much more comfortable than having to go out and do—ugh!—fieldwork.
>
> A tradition of education backs this. The whole educational system teaches young scholars that "research" is going to the library. And slowly we come to accept that we don't form our own opinions, but learn from others; we don't start at the ground level, but with secondhand data and theory that others have published. It is what we in Germany call "pale theory"—that what you think in your head as an intellectual is what counts, not what takes place in the world.

This leads us to the second reason why it has been so easy to dismiss non-formal sectors from formal study: the *cultural* or epistemological. Economists have by tradition focused on formal markets. Tradition defines epistemology; scientific *habitus,* if you will.[4]

It's taboo to question why formal indices don't consider the untold trillions that configure global economies outside of what economists have defined as worthy of study.

It's taboo to suggest that development policies fail because they have been constructed on the basis of faulty assumptions and data. Instead, the popular cultural answer is that development policies fail because of the realities of underdevelopment, corruption, poor infrastructure, hegemony of western elitism, sociopolitical resistance, and the difficulties of implementation — both in the development organizations and in the host countries. The difficulties extend to asking why these realities aren't factored in to the basic policy and development equations to begin with, or how far that corruption extends. For example, in one country where I was collecting data, USAID was paying for essential supplies and infrastructural development in a war-affected region. I assume USAID was unaware of the fact that the resources they were providing and paying for were also being used for considerable gray- and black-market exchanges, and even in the transport of stolen cars and luxury items. I am sure USAID was unaware of the fact that the manager of the western company they contracted with was skimming off money and using it in various other nefarious wartime economic enterprises. But, returning to the larger issue of cultural habits, the question remains: How is it that formal agencies can actually remain unaware of these realities? How is it that the "taboos against knowing" can be so strong?

The *political* answer raises a deeper set of concerns. A senior UN economist (whose name I have removed from this quote for "humanitarian reasons") I spoke with from the organization's European headquarters identified a further powerful factor, one that takes us into the realm of power and profit as well as the sphere of the practical and the conceptual:

> We at the UN have to follow the mandates set out for us, and as important as studying economies outside the formal sector may be, as crucial to policy as this is, these issues fall outside the realm of our mandate. And as such, we simply can't study them. Period.
>
> And why? Look where the mandates came from: the leaders forging UN policy. All that seafood illegally harvested off the coasts of Africa, for example, and sold around the world. Who do you think is doing that harvesting? Who do you think is selling and eating all that seafood? The citizens of the countries forging our mandates. Multiply these considerations when it comes to the mined resources of Southern Africa. Then extend that equation out to other "nonformal" goods and services worldwide.

This answer sheds light on the response I most notoriously receive when I ask economists why there is a dearth of empirical studies of extra-state realities: *such work is dangerous.*

The implication is that it is dangerous because it can be linked to criminal networks and they are, by definition, dangerous. If you study gem smugglers or gunrunners — not to mention corrupt security forces — you might end up as one of the statistics you were collecting.

But the more telling question is, "dangerous to whom?" As I've suggested in previous chapters, these networks of power, services, and goods rival formal state structures in important ways; non-formal economies aren't merely monetary concerns, but sociopolitical powerhouses. Considerable fortunes are made and lost, and these fortunes intersect with formal states and economies in myriad ways. In truth, the divisions between non/formal and extra/state are far less distinct than classical theory and popular discourse would claim. The danger might thus be to our very conceptions of power and economy; to our carefully crafted theories about the nature of the relationship between state, individual, and authority.

POWER

All three answers — the practical, the cultural, and the political — join in more overarching considerations of *power*. If studies of war are ultimately studies of the human condition, then research into the shadows is, in the final analysis, research into power. Here I would like to return to the theme of the chapter on power: that power lies in controlling definitions of power, and in the profound irony that power rests in part on the very illusions that power exists.

So why don't we study the shadows to the same degree we study the formal institutions of the world? As a starting point, I return to Charles Tilly's classic analysis "War Making and State Making as Organized Crime."[5] The licit and the illicit link arms in both war making and state making, and herein lies their power, a power fundamentally linked with control over resource extraction, capital accumulation, and the control of violence. Europe's consolidation of the modern state in the 1600s, its very political and economic successes, were in part due to recognizing that sovereignty extended across territory and into the seas; across legitimate enterprise into piracy; across into the excesses defining colonialism — however carefully these relationships had to be erased in formal speech and reckoning.

Yet the state wasn't the natural or privileged culmination of progress; of the Reformation and Enlightenment; of the evolution from kingly rule; or any other of a host of explanations that place the state at the pinnacle of human toil and reason. In fact, the state was not the only regime of social, economic, and political alliances seeking to maximize resource extraction, capital accumulation, and control over violence. It was just, says Tilly, the most successful.

Common wisdom holds that two things can't exist in one place, and this myth is central to making the processes and profits of the shadows invisible. This "wisdom" supports the convictions that the state is the predominate form of sociopolitical and economic relations defining the modern world. If the state reigns, it reigns supreme; if it falls, it will be replaced by something else (anarchy, to most theorists). Any other competing set of economic and political associations are by definition marginal.

In fact, multiple competing regimes of power and accumulation exist, variously hindering and assisting one another. The vast network of shadow alliances represents not merely an "outlaw" offshoot of the state, but a competing set of regimes of accumulation, control, and action. These regimes may at times benefit state structures and authorities; they may at times out-compete them. Should these non-state networks become more adept at controlling resource extraction, capital accumulation, and a justification of violence than the state, they will supplant the latter in primary authority; if they prove less adept, they will wither and be supplanted by new and emergent forms of political and economic relations.[6]

Yet something is still missing: why are the constructed invisibilities discussed in this book so complex? One more piece of the puzzle rests with the discussion in the chapter on power. Of course, people and regimes concerned with maintaining power construct rationalities in their favor; of course they seek to improve their own hold on the control of resources and violence; of course they seek to define "true" govern-ment(ality). It is in this equation that another core factor emerges. Governments, like militaries, exist not by the raw brute fact of power — but because people *believe* in this power. Ten thousand soldiers can't control a million people unless those people accept the right of the militaries to control the means of violence and the rights to power. Thus, a great deal is invested in maintaining the illusion that governments and their militaries not only have the right to power, but indeed *have* power. If their millions of citizens simply refuse to recognize their right, and turn to other means of governance, a particular government simply ceases to have authority. It ceases to be. Regimes likewise fade, the way kingly rule was eclipsed by the modern state.

A great deal of effort has gone into producing the idea that the state is the fulcrum of power and authority in the modern world.[7] Yet the state too is just another invention, to echo Margaret Mead's classic words on warfare. Just a more successful invention at a given point in history. The state is not without its contenders. The trillions of dollars generated in the shadows, and the millions of people involved in this work, represent a system that in some ways can be deemed sovereign.[8] So while crafting invisibilities around the shadows hides some of the immense profits that people, industries, social groups, and states make from extra-state means, the invisibilities also hide the fact that the state is *not* the ultimate, the supreme, the unchallenged governing authority in the modern world. The sheer power carried in extra-state systems — the power to shape global economic and political realities — demonstrates the partial nature of state authority. And this demonstrates that the state's power is not preeminent, but a carefully crafted illusion that exists only because a population chooses to grant it believability.

No single system of power reigns supreme, no ultimate hegemony prevails in the world. We have known since Foucault that resistance to any single or supreme form of authority appears the moment authority is wielded, bringing into play multiple forms of social, economic, and political relations. As the modern (Enlightenment) state is reconfigured by the realities of twenty-first-century globalization, the nodes of sociopolitical and economic power shift as well. In the same way that the international networks of traders during the time of kingdoms helped preconfigure the modern state, and their market tribunals presaged contemporary international law — the shadow networks of today could foreshadow emergent power formulations on the horizons of political and economic possibility. I do not imply here that this is positive change: power is not by definition a teleological process.[9]

It may be convenient to think that globalism emanates from and most powerfully affects the cosmopolitan centers of the world. But perhaps, as Ngũgĩ wa Thiong'o implies in *Moving the Centre,* Mozambique and Angola, Africa and Asia, are the sites where new configurations of power shaping the world are most visible.[10] For it is here that flexibility, the breakdown of entrenched institutionalization, the politics of survival, and the creativity of development meet in very dynamic ways.

And herein rests one of the key aspects of the intersections of il/licit power. Angolans, for example, are familiar with the paths regulated and unregulated commodities take around the world. They have seen international wildcatters amass considerable fortunes from the ashes of war and political turmoil. Fortunes are made on these illegal sales, and political power stems from these fortunes. Industries are forged on these profits, and industries merge into transnational corporations with the power to influence world markets and international law.

Yet these relationships aren't as highlighted — or even apparent in many cases — in Western political and economic theories. The "politics of invisibility" is no accident: it is created, and it is created for a reason. It would appear the modern state is as dependent on shadow economies and warzone profits as it is on keeping these dependencies invisible to formal reckoning. Jean-François Bayart captures these complexities when he writes, "The matrices of disorder are frequently the same as those for order."[11]

Contemporary scholarship has been strongly influenced by theories that have divided power relationships into "core" and "periphery," reproduced in more current analyses that divide the "Global North and the Global South" as developed/developing or (successfully) globalized/need-to-globalize to survive.[12] These theories provide interesting fodder for analysis, but they assume (often with an air of arrogance) that the "core" is geographically located in cosmopolitan centers of the world. Indeed, the theories are generally produced in the "core."[13]

In terms of the topic at hand, the resource wealth of Angola, the Democratic Republic of Congo, Burma, and a host of war-afflicted countries is not merely "useful" to cosmopolitan centers; it is critical. It is not the periphery of the economic system: it is central to it. The combination of formal and extra-state economies in these countries is, in fact, the "breadbasket" of cosmopolitan industrial centers.

So from the cosmopolitan urban industrial centers of the world flow high-tech weapons, communications systems, medical supplies, clothing, cigarettes, and jeans into the Angolas of the world along extra-state lines. Precious stones, valuable resources, and human labor flow back to the cosmopolitan urban industrial centers illicitly. At the same time, formal revenues, such as oil, fuel a country's wars, its development, and global industry. These war-torn locales, it would seem, aren't backwaters on the global map. They, and their wars, are essential to cosmopolitan business.

This is a dirty little secret. People tend to point out that, for example, Angola's "economy" plays a small role in global affairs. This is one of the greatest sleights of hand that exist in current economic analysis. When people say "economy," they're actually referring to "formally state-recognized economies" — the 10 percent of Angola's state-regulated economy. None of the world's transnational corporations or international organizations that monitor global economies publicly record the profits they make through extra-state means. If we were discussing Colombia instead of Angola, the extra-legal flowchart would certainly include the country's multi-billion-dollar-a-year illegal drug industry. For Congo it would include gold, zinc, col-tan, and other precious minerals. For Burma it would include the proposed transnational oil pipeline, timber, and the Thai cross-border sex industry. It is precisely the "Angolas" that are creatively kept in the analytical shadows by "core" analysts and those who benefit from this lucrative set of relationships.

The profit trail is extensive, and equally non-transparent. Vehicles — produced in industrial centers — transport non-legal goods from production to consumption, fueled by petroleum products and piloted by professionals. Handlers transport the commodities, experts test them, accommodating financial institutions lend and launder money, and less-than-legitimate security forces take a cut, ignoring the law while pretending to uphold it. Each step in the myriad set of transfers that moves any commodity across time, space, international borders, and the boundaries of the law employs a host of people, generates considerable profits for the "top management," and carries these non-transparent earnings into the markets of the everyday life of global realities. In a nutshell, pilots, mechanics, custom agents, and the legal experts who specialize in extra-state strategic planning get rich along with industrial front-point producers.

In any scientific investigation, it would be unthinkable to render analyses and policies on the basis of a data set that was missing a significant portion of its data. But that is precisely what is taking place when classical economics disregards non-legal and non-transparent economic activity and the political power it encompasses.

Maybe, in the final summation, the illegal and the illicit are too important to discuss. Wars, shadows, governments, and enterprises remain intertwined. As multinational corporations and transnational companies overflow not only national borders but also sovereign laws, so too do extra-state networks globalize and render new legal and political arrangements.

If it seems the profiteers hold the trump cards, there is a dangerous side, one hidden by the constructions of invisibility surrounding il/licit gain and influence. If only formal economic and political instruments are used to assess a world of formal and extra-state power, it isn't possible to understand either the true nature of economic and political reality as it affects our lives and world or the impetus to war and the potentialities for peace. Power tends to forge its own legitimacy; states evolved before their justifications. Sovereignty is a product of this process, not a natural attribute of an inviolate need.

The links of war making, banditry, extraction, and state making continue. Who will be most effective at mobilizing economies and the force to protect them in the future as yet remains an unanswered question.[14] It will remain opaque to analysis as long as we lack accurate and adequate data on global economies as a whole. It would be foolhardy to assume extra-state activities don't affect the most basic aspects of national and world economy: equities viability, currency strength, market health, and standard of living. It is perhaps as foolhardy as rendering these processes invisible so the impact of extra-state forces on global markets can't be assessed — so that crises can't be successfully avoided, development accurately implemented, and the profits of political violence challenged.

"NO-MAN'S-LAND": BRIDGE MARKING THE FRONT LINES. ANGOLA, 2001.

CHAPTER 17

EPILOGUE

TWO SIDES OF THE SAME COIN

> "Nada é permanente neste mundo, excepto a morte!" — disse ele, de sobrolho franzido.
>
> Se soubesse que naquele momento a sua vida fazia a mais curta contagem regressive por ele nunca imaginada, talvez proferisse todos versos e verbos; os existentes e os inexistentes. Mas pode ser que talvez não.
>
> *"Nothing in this world is permanent, except death!" — he said, with furrowed brow.*
>
> *If I knew in that moment that his life would make the shortest telling he could ever have imagined, maybe I would have offered all the verses and verbs, all those existing and those not existing. But maybe not.*
>
> Zezo Baptista[1]

SIDE ONE

A few days ago, I heard that Charlie died. I had just returned from Kuito, and had gone to a birthday party held at in Luanda. At the party, I ran into the head of Halo Trust, the de-mining organization working in Angola. We struck up a conversation, and I mentioned that I had made my first trip to the central provinces of Angola five years before, and that the Halo Trust group there had taken me out to show me the basics of de-mining. Laughingly referring to the popular wisdom that de-miners are both rigorously professional and socially wild, I mentioned I had been at a birthday party after the de-mining lesson, where Charlie . . . — and before I could finish my sentence, the head of Halo Trust said, "Threw himself face first into the birthday cake." "Yeah!" I said, "How did you know?" "It's a story of infamous proportions now," he replied. "Did you know Charlie died last year?"

I didn't know. As wars rumble across the global terrain, chased by profiteers brokering deals and diplomats brokering peace, an unknown number of people live and die outside of the public eye in Kuito, and all the Kuitos of the world. This was the same region where "Blades" — as the pilot was fondly called — was shot down while making a humanitarian flight to besieged civilians. When I was in Mozambique, Blades always let me hitch rides on his humanitarian flights to do my research. Blades's story was doubly tragic: his son flew out to the site of the crash two days later to see what he could learn about his father, and he too was shot down. Neither survived.

Kuito is a haunting place, and one I have grown to love. A provincial capital without city electricity or piped water, it stood at the epicenter of the violence in Angola. In 1993, Kuito was the scene of devastating battles: the government and rebel forces literally fought house to house and in some cases room to room in a city where the lines dividing the two contending forces ran down the main streets of the town. When I visited in November of 2001, the town had little changed since my first visit in 1996. People live and work amid bombed-out buildings, sell their products and produce in several blocks of muddy city streets, and scramble for food, water, and energy. Soldiers, police, and internally displaced people are omnipresent.

Kuito would by normal estimates be a city of tens of thousands. But at the end of 2001, in severe fighting just months before the war's end, some 150,000 *deslocados* had come in from more rural areas. Many were forcefully resettled by government forces seeking to remove, as Mao Tse-tung first put it, any water the rebel fish might find to swim in. Others fled increasing violence against civilians by both sides. Those who reached Kuito were the lucky ones. People spoke of the trauma of seeing deslocados arriving in smaller towns outside Kuito and dropping dead in the streets from starvation. Others braved heavily mined areas, too often unsuccessfully, to search for a bit of food to feed their families.

Kuito hosts a limited number of international and national nongovernmental organizations providing humanitarian assistance. During the war, it was not an easy place to work. Most of the NGOs deal only with humanitarian crises; there are few resources to do more. The INGO

Concern, which opened its house and kitchen to me while I was in Kuito in 2001, runs a program for female survivors of land-mine explosions as well as general health and agricultural programs for the vast population of deslocados. Médecins Sans Frontières (MSF) provides medical assistance: outside of MSF, in 2001, there was only one resident doctor in the entire province, and she was away attending an extended training course. The MSF doctor performed about twenty major surgeries a day. Demining teams from Halo Trust and Care work in one of the most heavily land-mined regions of the world. The UN, UNICEF, and World Food Program struggle to assist hundreds of thousands of war-afflicted in a province where travel is restricted to a few routes and the most desperate are often in isolated regions. Local NGOs seek to provide crucial social services with scarce, and often nonexistent, resources. All of these people work six and often seven days a week, generally for meager salaries. Most work exceptionally hard, and care deeply. They work with local populations who exponentially magnify that equation of long work hours, pitifully limited resources, and poor or nonexistent salaries. All face malaria, debilitating parasites, the ubiquitous land mines, and (until the end of the war) the threat of finding themselves on the front lines any given morning when they wake up.

These are not the people we hear about. They tend to be as invisible as those who smuggle diamonds or launder money throughout the warzones that span the globe. Yet, in the people living and working in Kuito — in the Kuitos of the world — rests the heartbeat of human survival. As I wrote in chapter 6, without the grunt soldier on the front lines pulling the trigger, there is no war. And in the global flow of trillions in aid dollars, for both positive and negative ends, the unpaid deslocado who helps rebuild a community, the local nurse working for a few dollars a month to try and stanch the flow of war as well as the blood of its wounds, and the poorly paid INGO staff putting in seven-day weeks are the front lines of peaceful solutions.

It is here we find a counterreality to global urban political and INGO dialogues about "donor fatigue," the amorality of populations that have become aid dependent, and the hopelessness of ingrained cultures of violence. This emerged when I talked with Maria Faria of the World Food Program in Angola:

Maria: What can you say of hope? For most of us it is fleeting, a hard thing to believe in. Most of us in the country, if we have salaries at all, have salaries that taken alone can't feed our families. We have been promised peace and seen war shatter these promises time and again, and we become fearful to even hope.

Carolyn: But people can't live without believing in something. What is it that people hold on to here, that makes it OK to get out of bed in the morning?

Maria: Dignity. We hold on to dignity. Underneath everything, we keep our networks of family and friends and associates alive and we always nurture these networks, for it is how we survive. We lend dignity to these loves and friendships and associations; we still believe in people, and in making communities. We have faith in people. It is believing in dignity—in our own and in that of those around us—that keeps us going.[2]

In a final curious irony: in crafting the parables of power that are "just so" and "as if" stories, in silencing the truths of violence, and in deleting indices of the vast profiteering that emerges from war and the suffering it exacts — the stories of hope, human dignity, and peace are deleted from formal accounting as well.

SIDE TWO

As I pass through Johannesburg from Angola on my way home in 2002, the "war against terrorism" rages, fought across mountainous terrains and dinner tables worldwide. I find it hard to recognize how difficult it is to predict acts of aggression and to "find terrorists." After twenty months of traveling, following the tentacles of war and its shadows across people's lives and countries' borders, I have forgotten how *not* to see the shadows.

Whether people are working in or against a state system, they need weapons, food, medicines, and texts; they need vehicles, gasoline, and spare parts; they need electronic equipment and communications systems. Most also want cigarettes, alcohol, or drugs. They need hard currency to buy these things, and they need the products that translate into hard currency. They need banking systems and the means to transfer funds, however informal or unregulated. They need the shipping routes to get the objects of their desires.

These are hard facts that leave objective traces — clear footprints — along the world's economic, political, and social pathways. These systems are not invisible because of any intrinsic nature of their own, but because of an unwillingness to see them. Do we really want to understand them?

asks Mattijs Van de Port. "Do we really want an academic text that is disturbing?"[3]

This unwillingness to see into the shadows may in part be due to the degree to which the extra-state and the extra-legal are woven into the fabric of everyday life and formal institutions. Virtually all of the trillions of dollars that move across the boundaries of legality each year ultimately pass through formal economies — unlaundered money is merely a piece of paper or a group of computer pixels until it gains financial recognition, and that recognition is conferred by the world economy. These intersections are powerful zones of profit and power. To see them, to understand the dynamics shaping war and peace, to "win wars against terrorism," and to develop accurate analytical tools for understanding these intersections, is to see both along the margins of human existence and into the heart of where societies live their lives.

GLOBALIZED SYMBOLS IN GLOBAL WARS.

POSTSCRIPT

THE WAR OF THE MONTH CLUB—IRAQ

As I put the final touches on this book the war in Iraq heated up, turned violent, and forced a regime change. The Democratic Republic of Congo, with nearly two and a half million deaths on the hands of the current provocateurs, has faded into the media background. So too have wars from Colombia to Burma. North Korea is a blip on the radar screen of militarized response. Perhaps it will emerge into the war that accompanies the final touches I do on the page proofs of the book. If not, there will be another.

When I sat down to write each chapter for this book, I traveled back in my mind's eye to revisit the people and places I wrote about. It is the only way I know how to write about war: being there. In some ways this kind of writing takes its toll: I cannot abstract the suffering of war nor delete the people from the front lines; but in this I hope people reading my work can, in some sense, visit places and meet people they otherwise might not. It is in this meeting that war comes to take definition. But Iraq is different. I have been asked to give interviews by the media, to speak at public venues, and to write on the Iraqi war. I find myself resisting, and I realize it is because I cannot enter the war in my mind's eye to speak of it. I am not there; I am in a comfortable office experiential light years away.

But silence, as I have so often written, is not the best option either. So I have become curious as to what I can know about Iraq, not being there. The question is pressing: I have long said that while all wars have a unique set of characteristics—a compendium of the intersections of history, people, and institutions in the flux of action—they are also shaped within a larger milieu of war created through constant international exchanges of people, commodities, ideologies, politics, and configurations of power. The USA-declared war in Iraq ushers in a new era. What exactly this era will be can only be gleaned from a complex analysis of the way these military actions play out across the political, economic, and social terrains of the global present, and the way it becomes inscribed into people's — and here I mean people of all countries — understanding of power.

The question is also interesting to me as this is the first time since the Vietnam War I have been in the USA while the country was engaged in an overseas war or military action. I am used to listening to public discussions of war by people who know war firsthand. I experienced the 1991 Gulf War from the vantage point of northern Mozambique. I was in the Province of Lichinga when the war began. Mozambique's war was at a fever pitch at the time, and Lichinga is at the end of the world in most people's conceptions. It is the most remote part of Mozambique. Lichinga did not have electricity, running water, or public transport services, much less globally linked media, due to the war's destruction. Yet I remember well sitting with a group of people in the rough equivalent of a coffee shop (no coffee, no shop) as they explained to me what was taking place in the Gulf War. If a person has not experienced the sophistication of information one can find in war-depleted remote locales of the world, it is hard to imagine. But it is nonetheless true: extra-state systems carry information as well as people and commodities. Survival for many depends on this. The descriptions and explanations I received at the time were remarkably accurate and erudite. When I traveled some time later to Beira, one of the country's main towns, and had the opportunity to watch global news services like BBC, CNN, and South African News on satellite dish, I became aware of how rich the news I'd encountered in Lichinga was. I knew as much as, and in some cases more than, the world's major news services were reporting. CNN focused predominately on military tactics and hardware. I had information both on this and on the more human elements of the war: the core dynamics of the war; the way soldiers, civilians, and power brokers were responding worldwide; and the likely alliances, frictions, aggressions, and outcomes emerging from the war. I heard stories of how soldiers acted on the front lines, and why. And I could feel the plight of a parent trying to find food or stanch the flow of blood from a family member's wound. The war came alive as a reality in people's lives. And given the complex analyses I encountered, I had a good sense of where the war would lead, not just that day, that year, and that country, but across alliances, antipathies, nations, and years.

But something different transpired for me during the spring 2003 war in Iraq. Being in the USA and trying to understand the war was perplexing: I could not find the war. I don't mean the constant barrage of news coverage on "the war," the political mud-slinging among people of opposing views, or the video clips of military advancements. I mean the way war smells, feels, tastes, looks, and acts. I found myself wondering why there was no comprehensive coverage of the global weapons/commodities/resources trade that links the world's continents and countries, when novice students in my classes could map how these flows affected everything from war outcomes to civilians' ability to gain survival necessities. I wondered why, in all the focus on Jessica Lynch, no one spoke about how she experienced war; how violence and rescue insinuated themselves into her beliefs and dreams for life. How did people in Iraq feed their families, find care for the critically ill, think of freedom during bombing raids? What old vendettas were settled that no one reported on? How did power remap through city streets and conflicting loyalties? How did it remap internationally? Not just the public words, but the deals done behind closed doors.

Most of these events will never be analyzed; most war stories, from soldiers to civilians, will never be told to the public. Women, having dodged bullets, will turn to the patient rebuilding of their lives and communities without ever uttering a word to CNN. War orphans craft innovative communities far from the eyes of political analysts. Fathers bounce a child on their knees, wondering what set of laws they will have to plan around the next day. Smugglers grow rich.

The justifications that fanned the flames of war will grow cold, charcoal to etch lines in dry textbooks. They are now history. Today new stories capture the public eye; new networks of power move through underground channels. New wars are already in progress. Few discuss where or what they will be; many do not know, having been taught that a war doesn't exist until a weapon is discharged, until a declaration is made that this is not mayhem, but war.[1]

Somewhere in all this, the thread of the story of Al Qaeda unraveled. This speaks to a new era of war. Al Qaeda is a network, not a nation-state. As such, it has no geographical home to attack. It is, by definition, extra-state. It acquires commodities, from currency to weapons, through extra-legal channels; it fights along unconventional lines. It manages power through non-state means. This is an anathema to states, which are set up to operate in a logical political science universe of other states. How does one war against shadows? Iraq, in this instance, became the solution. But

Al Qaeda is not equivalent to Iraq, not in geography, not in political affiliation, not in religious conviction, not in power structure. In sheer objective fact, Saddam Hussein's downfall little affects the dynamics of networks like Al Qaeda. In some ways, ironically, the attack on Iraq may help them. It is easier for a state to attack another state. The ability of guerrilla, paramilitary, and terror-based movements to topple colonial rule worldwide has long shown that states are vulnerable to aggressions from extra-state networks. There are many results to any war. But one that I do not see discussed much in the USA is that extra-state networks fare better against superpowers than do nation-states.

If it is hard for me to find the war in Iraq — ontologically speaking — from the USA, it is even more challenging to find Al Qaeda from the USA. I can glean from the media that in fact a regime change did occur in Iraq. In the vacuum of power rogues looted the defenseless, religious leaders emerged to provide structure, and average people struggled with collapsed governing systems. From my own research in warzones, I know what the media does not address: a collapsed government cannot provide any services, so the citizenry struggle with shortages of food, medicines, energy, and fuel that can be lethal. Those who survive will do so by using international extra-state networks to get necessities; a few will become rich. In this, world alliances are redefined. In the aftermath of war, people are forging new global loyalties and alliances, thinking about flows of weapons/commodities/resources in new ways, and preparing for new wars. No one I've spoken to outside the USA felt they could be neutral. A war involving a superpower involved the world, and everyone had to forge a place from which to survive it. September 11, the military actions in Afghanistan, and Iraq have solidified these movements to new, twenty-first-century, global political formations. Much is still formally invisible.

Our understanding of non-state networks is far less developed than our understanding of states. At present, we have few reliable resources capable of explaining the fundamental character and impact of a group such as Al Qaeda on the power equations defining political and economic change. Even the most basic questions exceed our theoretical grasp: How does a highly organized extra-state network function? How does capturing or killing a top leader in the group affect its overall power structure? How do new recruits fill vacuums in power? How do the networks collapse? If an extra-state network is indeed a social, economic, and political extra-state system, it is based in the kinds of enduring, complex market and financial organizations I have described throughout this book. These networks link people and countries internationally. The data from my research shows that these networks do not collapse easily. Nor are they easily eradicated. New commodities, new people, new regimes of authority, and new ideologies shape extra-state realities continuously. Such systems tend to adapt, not disappear. To effectively combat those who seek to effect regime change through targeting noncombatants, as with the September 11 attack, it is essential to understand how extra-state networks operate in contrast to states. As I have asked throughout this book: How is authority managed? What shape does power take? What determines belonging, recruitment, loyalty? How are commodities, monies, and people moved and managed? These are not idle questions aimed at a disappearing Al Qaeda. A new era of power contestations is forming in the twenty-first century. Looking at the history of extra-state groups defeating the colonial world, people have learned that the extra-state is the most powerful way of challenging the state and of combating a superpower. Yet our understanding is embryonic: much of the workings of the extra-state remain in the shadows. To leave these in the shadows is to allow them to retain, quite literally, untold power.

NOTES

1. PROLOGUE

1. Patricia Pinnock, *Skyline* (Johannesburg: David Philip Publishers, 2000), 15.

2. The riots reflected larger and more enduring religious, ethnic, and political fissures in Sri Lanka. The population of the country is 80 percent Sinhalese (Sinhala speaking) Buddhists, and approximately 12 percent Tamil (Tamil speaking) Hindu. Government and military positions are predominately held by Sinhalese Buddhists. The Tamils, a majority of whom live in the North of the country, have long sought better representation in government and policy — either by democratic process or by the creation of a separate state. In 1983, an armed Tamil faction retaliated against government repression of Tamils by a guerrilla attack that killed thirteen soldiers. The riots were ostensibly sparked by this: some Sinhalese (including civilians, soldiers, religious figures, and government employees) formed into mobs and attacked Tamils. Tamils did not riot against the Sinhalese in return. The violence spread nationwide and lasted a full week, during which time thousands of Tamils lost their lives and one-sixth of the country's infrastructure was destroyed.

3. *Wildcatting*, as I use the term here, is based in international business concerns that can be legal, indeterminately legal, or downright illegal — but yield quick, and often vast, profits, commonly in the context of political instability.

4. War so little matches classic accounts of war that a truism has emerged for me through the years I have studied violence at its epicenters: if you want to prepare yourself for studying violence and peace, assume that what popular wisdom in society — the prefabricated configurations of "truth" that ripple across the fluid bodies of social talk and text — tells you is exactly the opposite.

5. Mattijs van de Port, *Gypsies, Wars, and Other Instances of the Wild: Civilization and Its Discontents in a Serbian Town* (Amsterdam: Amsterdam University Press, 1998), 30.

6. Barbara Ehrenreich, *Blood Rites* (London: Virago, 1997), 1–2.

7. Avner Greif, "Contracting, Enforcement, and Efficiency: Economics beyond the Law," in *Annual World Bank Conference on Development Economics 1996,* ed. Michael Bruno and Boris Pleskovic (Washington, D.C.: World Bank, 1996), 239–65. These shadows are not peripheral to a country's economic and political systems, but deeply enmeshed in them, as the following quote addresses: "How has this happened? How has the Cosa Nostra come to play such an important role in the core economy of New York City? . . . It is an astonishing and lamentable chapter in the history of American law enforcement that almost until the end of a half century as Director of the FBI, J. Edgar Hoover denied the existence of "mafia" or "Cosa Nostra" and refused to devote any special intelligence or law enforcement resources to this species of American criminal. . . . It is not only law enforcement that has failed to come to grips with organized crime. The American political system has not set itself against organized crime, in part no doubt because organized crime is active in politics." Ronald Goldstock et al., *Corruption and Racketeering in the New York City Construction Industry: The Final Report of the N.Y. State Organized Crime Task Force* (New York: New York University Press, 1990), xxvi–xxvii.

8. The work presented here is not traditional ethnography, though it may well become traditional along the course of a continuously interconnected twenty-first century. It addresses questions that flow across borders and neat distinctions. "Ethnography is predicated upon attention to the everyday, on intimate knowledge of face-to-face communication and groups. The idea that ethnography might expand from its committed localism to represent a system much better apprehended by abstract models and aggregate statistics seems antithetical to its very nature and thus beyond its limits. Although multi-sited ethnography is an exercise in mapping terrain, its goal is not holistic representation and ethnographic portrayal of the world system as a totality. Rather, it claims that an ethnography of a cultural formation in the world system is also an ethnography of the system, and therefore can't be understood only in terms of the conventional single-site mise-en-scène of ethnographic research. . . . For ethnography, then, there is no global in the local-global contrast now so frequently evoked. The global is an emergent dimension of arguing about the connection among sites in a multi-sited ethnography." George Marcus, *Ethnography through Thick and Thin* (Princeton: Princeton University Press, 1998), 83.

9. We can no longer separate images of Vietnam from rock'n'roll era music, stories of the rebels in Sierra Leone from the movie *Rambo: First Blood,* Bosnia from the feature-length films set in the war, Afghanistan from CNN.

3. MAKING THINGS ~~INVISIBLE~~

1. Mattijs van de Port, *Gypsies, Wars, and Other Instances of the Wild: Civilization and Its Discontents in a Serbian Town* (Amsterdam: Amsterdam University Press, 1998), 27.

2. Ibid., 28.

3. Ibid., 102–3.

4. Arthur Redding, *Raids on Human Consciousness: Writing, Anarchism, and Violence* (Columbia: University of South Carolina Press, 1998), 14.

5. Ibid., 34.

6. P. Gasparini Alves and D. Cipollone, *Curbing Illicit Trafficking in Small Arms and Sensitive Technologies: An Action-Oriented Agenda* (Geneva: United Nations Institute for Disarmament Research, 1998).

7. Karl Maier, *Angola: Promises and Lies* (Rivonia, U.K.: William Waterman, 1996), 59.

8. For an excellent study of war economies and the politics of the invisible, see Mark Chingono, *The State, Violence, and Development: The Political Economy of War in Mozambique, 1975–1992* (Aldershot, U.K.: Avebury, 1996), 127.

9. Charles Tilly, "War Making and State Making as Organized Crime," in *Bringing the State Back In,* ed. Peter B. Evans et al. (Cambridge: Cambridge University Press, 1985), 169–91.

10. Michel de Certeau, *Heterologies: Discourse on the Other* (Minneapolis: University of Minnesota Press, 1986).

11. Marc Augé, *Non-Places: Introduction to an Anthropology of Supermodernity,* trans. John Howe (London: Verso, 1995), 35–36.

12. Ibid., 32–33.

13. This creation of recognition lies at the heart of in/visibility. In *Non-Places,* Augé continues with an observation that for me applies to the cosmopolitan notion of place that permeates modern(ist) politics and professional thought: "The indigenous fantasy is that of a closed world founded once and for all long ago: one which, strictly speaking, does not have to be understood. Everything there is to know about it is already known: land, forest, springs, notable features, religious places, medicinal plants, not forgetting the temporal dimensions of an inventory of these places whose legitimacy is postulated, and whose stability is supposed to be assured, by narrations about origins and by the ritual calendar. All the inhabitants have to do is *recognize* themselves in it when the occasion arises. Every unexpected event, even one that is wholly predictable and recurrent from the ritual point of view (like birth, illness or death), demands to be interpreted not, really, in order to be known, but in order to be recognized: to be made accessible to a discourse, a diagnosis, in terms that are already established, whose announcement will not be liable to shock the guardians of cultural orthodoxy and social syntax. It is hardly surprising that the terms of this discourse should tend to be spatial, once it has become clear that it is the spatial arrangements that express the group's identity" (44–45).

14. Stanley Cohen, *States of Denial: Knowing about Atrocities and Suffering* (Cambridge: Polity, 2001), 10–11.

15. Ibid., 141.

16. Ibid., 105.

17. Ibid., 108.

18. David Hecht and Maliqalim Simone, *Invisible Governance: The Art of African Micropolitics* (Brooklyn, N.Y.: Autonomedia, 1994), 91–92.

4. FINDING THE FRONT LINES

1. Patrick Chabal and Jean-Pascal Daloz, *Africa Works: Disorder as Political Instrument* (Oxford: James Currey, 1999), 1.

2. Ibid., 83.

3. Alfred Vagts, *History of Militarism* (New York: Meridian Books, 1959).

4. Some of Joel Chiziane's photographs can be seen in my previous publications: Carolyn Nordstrom and Jo-Ann Martin, eds., *The Paths to Domination, Resistance, and Terror* (Berkeley and Los Angeles: University of California Press, 1992); Carolyn Nordstrom and Antonius C. G. M. Robben, eds., *Fieldwork under Fire: Contemporary Studies of Violence and Survival* (Berkeley and Los Angeles: University of California Press, 1995); Carolyn Nordstrom, *A Different Kind of War Story* (Philadelphia: University of Pennsylvania Press, 1997); Carolyn Nordstrom, "A War Dossier," *Public Culture* 10(2) (Winter 1998).

5. Patricia Pinnock, *Skyline* (Johannesburg: David Philip Publishers, 2000), 34.

6. Zeno's paradox states that to get from one point to another, one must first reach the midpoint between the two; and then the next ensuing midpoint, and so on. As there are an infinite number of midpoints between any two given points, a clear movement from one point to another is not possible. R. M. Sainsbury, *Paradoxes,* 2nd ed. (Cambridge: Cambridge University Press, 2000).

7. John Keane, *Reflections on Violence* (London: Verso, 1996), 4.

8. Valentine Daniel, *Charred Lullabies: Chapters in an Anthropography of Violence* (Princeton: Princeton University Press, 1996), 7.

9. Cynthia Enloe, *Maneuvers: The International Politics of Militarizing Women's Lives* (Berkeley and Los Angeles: University of California Press, 2000).

5. VIOLENCE

1. John Keane, *Reflections on Violence* (London: Verso, 1996), 6–7.

2. Some of these photos can be seen in the following sources: Carolyn Nordstrom, "A War Dossier," *Public Culture* 10(2) (Winter 1998); Carolyn Nordstrom and Antonius C. G. M. Robben, eds., *Fieldwork under Fire: Contemporary Studies of Violence and Survival* (Berkeley and Los Angeles: University of California Press, 1995); Carolyn Nordstrom, *Girls and Warzones — Troubling Questions* (Uppsala, Sweden: Life and Peace Institute Press, 1997).

3. Patricia Pinnock, *Skyline* (Johannesburg: David Philip Publishers, 2000), 10.

4. Tim O'Brien, *The Things They Carried* (Boston: Houghton Mifflin/Seymour Lawrence, 1990), 70.

5. Ibid., 80.

6. Bao Ninh, *The Sorrow of War: A Novel of North Vietnam* (New York: Riverhead Books, 1996), 48–50.

7. United Nations Security Council, *Compendium of Presidential Statements and Resolutions, Security Council* (Geneva: UN Publications, 2000).

8. Allen Feldman, *Formations of Violence: The Narrative of the Body and Polit-*

ical Terror in Northern Ireland (Chicago: University of Chicago Press, 1991); Valentine Daniel, *Charred Lullabies: Chapters in an Anthropography of Violence* (Princeton: Princeton University Press, 1996); Linda Green, *Fear as a Way of Life: Mayan Widows in Rural Guatemala* (New York: Columbia University Press, 2000); Carolyn Nordstrom, "Requiem for the Rational War," in *Deadly Developments: Capitalism, States, and War,* ed. S. Reyna (Amsterdam: Gordon and Breach, 1999), 153–76; Carolyn Nordstrom, "Deadly Myths of Aggression," *Journal of Aggressive Behavior* 24(2) (1998): 147–59.

9. Elaine Scarry, *The Body in Pain: The Making and Unmaking of the World* (New York: Oxford University Press, 1985).

10. Carolyn Nordstrom, *A Different Kind of War Story* (Philadelphia: University of Pennsylvania Press, 1997).

11. Paul Richards, *Fighting for the Rainforest: War, Youth and Resources in Sierra Leone* (Oxford: James Currey, 1996).

12. Marcelo Suarez-Orozco, "A Grammar of Terror: Psychocultural Responses to State Terrorism in Dirty War and Post–Dirty War Argentina," in *The Paths to Domination, Resistance, and Terror,* ed. Carolyn Nordstrom and JoAnn Martin (Berkeley and Los Angeles: University of California Press, 1992), 227–46.

13. Ninh, *Sorrow,* 89.

14. Ibid., 36–37.

15. Antonio Carlos Macieira, "Os Falsos Profetas de Paz," *Jornal de Angola* (16 November 2001), 3.

16. Michael Taussig, *Shamanism, Colonialism, and the Wild Man: A Study in Terror and Healing* (Chicago: University of Chicago Press, 1987).

6. POWER

1. Steven Lukes, *Power: A Radical View* (London: Macmillan Press, 1974).

2. Michel Foucault, *Power/Knowledge,* trans. Colin Gordon et al. (New York: Pantheon Books, 1972); Michel Foucault, *Discipline and Punish: The Birth of the Prison,* trans. Alan Sheridan (New York: Vintage Books, 1979); Michel Foucault, *The History of Sexuality, Volume 1: An Introduction,* trans. Robert Hurley (New York: Vintage Books, 1980); Michel Foucault, "The Subject of Power," in *Michel Foucault: Beyond Structuralism and Hermeneutics,* ed. H. Dreyfus and P. Rabinow (Chicago: University of Chicago Press, 1982), 208–26. Antonio Gramsci, *The Modern Prince and Other Writings* (New York: International Publishers, 1968); Antonio Gramsci, *Selections from the Prison Notebooks* (London: Lawrence and Wishart, 1971). For a dynamic set of examples in a globalizing and African context, see Ngũgĩ wa Thiong'o, *Moving the Centre: The Struggle for Cultural Freedoms* (London: James Currey, 1993).

3. Foucault has written a tremendous amount on the topic of power. One of his most concise explanations concerning the decentered study of power states: "The important thing isn't to attempt some kind of deduction of power starting from its center and aimed at the discovery of the extent to which it permeates into

the base, of the degree to which it reproduces itself down to and including the most molecular elements of society. One must rather conduct an *ascending* analysis of power, starting, that is, from its infinitesimal mechanisms, which each have their own history, their own trajectory, their own techniques and tactics, and then see how these mechanisms of power have been — and continue to be — invested, colonized, utilized, involuted, transformed, displaced, extended etc., by ever more general mechanisms and by forms of global domination." Foucault, *Power/Knowledge*, 99.

4. Friedrich Nietzsche, "The Genealogy of Morals," in *The Birth of Tragedy/ The Genealogy of Morals* (New York: Doubleday, 1956), 1–132; Friedrich Nietzsche, *The Will to Power* (Garden City: Doubleday, 1968). This theme has been updated in sophisticated ways for the contemporary era in, for example, Judith Butler, Ernesto Laclau, and Slavoj Žižhek, *Contingency, Hegemony, Universality* (London: Verso, 2000).

5. Nietzsche, "The Genealogy of Morals," 179.

6. Pierre Bourdieu, *Outline of a Theory of Practice* (Cambridge: Cambridge University Press, 1977); and Pierre Bourdieu, *Pascalian Meditations*, trans. Richard Nice (Cambridge: Polity Press, 2000).

7. Veena Das, "Our Work to Cry: Your Work to Listen," in *Mirrors of Violence: Communities, Riots, and Survivors in South Asia*, ed. Veena Das (Oxford: Oxford University Press, 1990), 345–98.

8. As I have noted previously, soldiers range from formal allies through hired mercenaries to largely uncontrolled militias and profiteers fighting alongside national troops or guerrilla and rebel forces.

9. UNICEF, *The State of the World's Children* (Oxford: Oxford University Press, 1996); UNICEF, *The State of the World's Children 2003* (Oxford: Oxford University Press, 2003); UNICEF, *Adult Wars, Child Soldiers* (Geneva: UNICEF, 2002); Carolyn Nordstrom, *Girls and Warzones — Troubling Questions* (Uppsala, Sweden: Life and Peace Institute Press, 1997).

10. In authorizing negative events after the fact *as if* they had been intended (rather than risk exposing the illusion of natural power), the idea emerges that to be a bad leader is preferable to being no leader at all. Thus further lore is generated: that somehow excessive violence is an act of power, that unrestrained force marks a powerful military, that presiding over chaos is a sign of control.

7. ENTERING THE SHADOWS

1. In 2002, a number of years after these flights and conversations with Joe and his group, I was sitting at a BBQ with another group of humanitarian pilots in another war and another country. As the evening progressed, I mentioned the topic of "midnight runs." The pilots looked at me blankly. This tactic of (pilots) guarding and (anthropologists) getting information was something I had learned long ago with Joe and his friends. I mentioned Joe (the world of humanitarian pilots is something akin to a large extended family) and the flights I had made with his group. Everyone relaxed: I had gone from outsider to adopted family in

a sentence. One pilot had just returned from Afghanistan, and launched into a full hour's explanation of the same kinds of seemingly impossible alliances and cross-group exchanges Joe had described for a war half a world away. How he had flown critical goods from one side to another; people to opposing camps, leaders and military officials — local and foreign alike — to the least likely places. His fellow pilots, there were some ten at the BBQ, chimed in with similar stories. Afghanistan, the main speaker continued, was as wild as any place he had seen: politics and power in the making. Such conversations among humanitarian pilots can be found at "BBQs" worldwide — wherever violence and profit meet.

2. Some of the ways of procuring revenues were not only legally, but morally, questionable. The article continues by discussing the "gangsterization" of Turkish politics, exploring the kickbacks Justice Minister Agar received from drug traffic, and then moves on to say that it is the actions of "Yesil (Green) that exemplify the gangsterization of Turkish politics. Born in 1953, he began to work for Turkish intelligence in the early seventies. By 1985 he was the lead executioner of the Intelligence and Anti-Terror Team of the Gendarmeria, known as JITEM, which began implementing a program of executing leading Kurds such as lawyers, businessmen, and journalists who were 'suspected' of supporting the Kurdish guerrillas. This killing program was similar to the Phoenix program that the American CIA implemented in South Vietnam against suspected Vietcong sympathizers and may very well have been inspired by it. . . . One of the usual practices that characterized Yesil's executions was to seek and obtain ransom money from relatives of already executed victims, falsely promising their release. Yesil shared the money with army and security officials as well as his protectors in the high echelons of the security mechanisms of the Turkish state." Institute Diethone Scheseone, "The Gangsterization of Turkish Politics" (Athens: Panteiro Panepistimio Kiononikon and Politicon Epistimon, 1998), 1–4.

3. Susan Strange, *The Retreat of the State: The Diffusions of Power in the World Economy* (Cambridge: Cambridge University Press, 1996), 117–18.

4. Manuel Castells, *End of Millennium,* vol. 3 of *The Information Age: Economy, Society, and Culture* (Malden: Blackwell Publishers, 1998), 178.

5. Ibid., 167.

6. Richard Norton-Taylor, "Trade in Torture Weapons Rises," *Guardian* (Manchester, U.K.), 27 February 2001, 17.

7. For example, all but two of the Fortune 500 companies in the USA are involved in some form of armament production. The USA is responsible for 49 percent of the weapons sales globally. Even if these companies are in full agreement with national and international weapons sanctions, the $500 billion a year in illegal weapons sales is cash in the tills of the producers and distributors. At the legal level, these represent a significant tax base for the government.

8. George Lopez and David Cortright, "Making Targets 'Smart' from Sanctions," paper delivered at the International Studies Association meetings, Minneapolis, 18–22 March 1998.

9. Meenakshi Ganguly, "A Banking System Built for Terrorism," *Time World,* 5 October 2001, 21.

10. Patrick Jost and Harjit Singh Sandhu, "The Hawala Alternative Remittance System and Its Role in Money Laundering" (Lyon: Interpol General Secretariat, January 2000): 2. http://www.interpol.int/Public/FinanceCrime/Money Laundering/hawala/default.asp [10 November 2002].

11. Ibid., 5.

12. Castells, *End of Millennium.*

13. Strange, *The Retreat of the State,* 111–12.

8. A FIRST EXPLORATORY DEFINITION OF THE SHADOWS

1. Angola gained independence from Portugal in 1975, and civil war erupted within a year. The main contenders for power have been the government (MPLA: Movimento Popular de Libertação de Angola — Popular Movement for the Liberation of Angola — headed by José Eduardo dos Santos) and the rebels (UNITA: União Nacional para Independencia Total de Angola — National Union for the Total Independence of Angola — headed by Jonas Savimbi). While several peace accords were developed and broken by renewed fighting in the twenty-five years since independence, the peace accord that went into effect when Savimbi was killed in 2002 has, to date, held.

2. Manuel Castells, *End of Millennium,* vol. 3 of *The Information Age: Economy, Society, and Culture* (Malden: Blackwell Publishers, 1998), 178.

3. Arjun Appadurai, *Modernity at Large: Cultural Dimensions of Globalization* (St. Paul: University of Minnesota Press, 1996).

4. William Reno's analysis of "shadow states" — nation-based systems of power and patronage paralleling state power — is a helpful starting point for understanding how such systems operate on a larger scale. William Reno, *Corruption and State Politics in Sierra Leone* (Cambridge: Cambridge University Press, 1995); William Reno, *Warlord Politics and African States* (Boulder, CO: Lynne Rienner, 1998).

5. These "extra-state" behaviors (outside of states' and international law's formally defined and recognized institutions) comprise sprawling international realities that remain largely undocumented. To use the word *extra-state* doesn't mean that these actions take place outside of all state structure — they often partake of state infrastructure in significant ways — but that they represent different power configurations from the state: organic states intersected by fluid international networks.

6. I do use the term *non-formal* in defining the shadows. The distinction I use in this analysis for non/formal is precise: *formal,* as applied to the state, refers to *formally* recognized state-based institutions and the activities they support. *Non-formal* applies to institutions and activities that exist *apart* from formal state structures and processes. This isn't to say that formal and non-formal are physically separate loci of power and action. A businessperson or government official who uses legal oil sales to buy weapons in Angola is acting in the formal market, but when those same people sell oil or diamonds for military supplies or personal gain outside of the state's public channels, they are adding to the non-formal economy.

My use of a slash (non/formal, il/legal, il/licit, extra/state) designates both meanings in the term: non/formal signifies *both* formal and non-formal.

7. Mark Chingono, *The State, Violence, and Development: The Political Economy of War in Mozambique, 1975–1992* (Aldershot, U.K: Avebury, 1996), 101. Chingono quotes from the International Labour Organization, *Employment in Africa: Some Critical Issues* (Geneva: ILO, 1973).

8. George Lopez and David Cortright, "Making Targets 'Smart' from Sanctions," paper delivered at the International Studies Association meetings, Minneapolis, 18–22 March 1998; Bureau for International Narcotics and Law Enforcement Affairs, *International Narcotics Control Strategy Report 1996* (Washington, D.C.: U.S. Department of State, March 1997).

9. United Nations Research Institute, *States of Disarray: The Social Effects of Globalization* (London: UNRISD, 1995).

10. Susan Strange, *The Retreat of the State: The Diffusions of Power in the World Economy* (Cambridge: Cambridge University Press, 1996), 115.

11. Gary Slapper and Steve Tombs, *Corporate Crime* (Essex: Addison Wesley Longman, 1999).

12. Suraj B. Gupta, *Black Income in India* (New Delhi: Sage, 1992).

13. Avner Greif, "Contracting, Enforcement, and Efficiency: Economics beyond the Law," in *Annual World Bank Conference on Development Economics 1996,* ed. Michael Bruno and Boris Pleskovic (Washington, D.C.: World Bank, 1996), 239–65.

14. Clement Jackson, UNDP economist, personal communication, Windhoek, Namibia, 1997.

15. National Geographic, *Diamonds of War,* National Geographic/PBS documentary, 11 February 2002; Alex Yearsley, of Global Witness, personal communication, 2002.

16. Xinhua News Agency, "The Story behind China's Biggest Smuggling Case," http://www.China.org.CN/English/2001/Jul/16632.htm [26 July 2001].

17. John Sevigny, "Mexican, U.S. Officials Discuss Measures to Combat Freon Smuggling," Environmental News Network, http://www.enn.com/News/2003–02–07/S_2548.asp [7 February 2003].

18. Michel Camdessus cited in John McDowell and Gary Nevis, "The Consequences of Money Laundering and Financial Crime," *Economic Perspectives* 6(2) (May 2001): 4–6.

19. Hendrik Neto, *O Roque: Romance de um mercado* (Luanda, Angola: Fundação Eshivo, 2001), 20–21. Translated from the Portuguese by the author.

20. Castells, *Millennium,* 167.

21. David Hecht and Maliqalim Simone, *Invisible Governance: The Art of African Micropolitics* (Brooklyn, N.Y.: Autonomedia 1994), 77–79.

22. Clement Jackson, personal communication, Windhoek, Namibia, 1997.

23. William Shawcross, *The Quality of Mercy: Cambodia, Holocaust, and Modern Conscience* (New York: Simon and Schuster, 1984), 236–37.

24. Owen Lippert and Michael Walker, eds., *The Underground Economy: Global Evidence of Its Size and Impact* (Vancouver, B.C.: Fraser Institute, 1997);

R. T. Naylor, *Wages of Crime: Black Markets, Illegal Finance, and the Underworld Economy* (Ithaca: Cornell University Press, 2002).

25. For Italy, see Donald Rutherford, *Dictionary of Economies* (New York: Routledge, 1992), 42. For the USA, see Susan Pozo, *Price Behavior in Illegal Markets* (Aldershot, U.K.: Avebury, 1996); and Greif, "Contracting, Enforcement, and Efficiency." The Internal Revenue Service places it more conservatively at 10 to 20 percent of GNP.

26. Ed Ayers, "The Expanding Shadow Economy," *World Watch* 9(4) (1996): 11–23.

27. Ibid.

28. Charles Tilly, "War Making and State Making as Organized Crime," in *Bringing the State Back In*, ed. Peter B. Evans et al. (Cambridge: Cambridge University Press, 1985), 169.

29. Ibid., 170. See also Thomas Gallant, "Brigandage, Piracy, Capitalism, and State-Formation: Transnational Crime from a Historical World-Systems Perspective," in *States and Illegal Practices*, ed. Josiah Heyman (Oxford: Berg, 1999), 25–61.

30. Tilly, "War Making and State Making as Organized Crime," 173.

31. Ibid., 186.

32. Reno, *Corruption and State Politics in Sierra Leone;* Reno, *Warlord Politics and African States;* Jean-François Bayart, *The State in Africa: The Politics of the Belly* (London: Longman, 1993); Béatrice Hibou, "The 'Social Capital' of the State as an Agent of Deception," in *The Criminalization of the State in Africa*, trans. Stephen Ellis (Oxford: James Currey, 1999), 69–113; Janet Roitman, "The Garrison-Entrepôt," *Cahiers d'Etudes Africaines* 140 (1998): 297–329.

33. Both Strange, *Retreat of the State,* and Castells, *Millennium,* see the ultimate authority of the state being undermined by transnational associations and organized crime. In the ironies of complex theory, this may be as true as the observation that states, and their cosmopolitan centers, depend in some crucial ways on non-state power systems of resource extraction, exchange, and profiteering.

34. Hecht and Simone, *Invisible Governance,* 83.

35. John Comaroff and Jean Comaroff, eds., *Civil Society and the Political Imagination in Africa: Critical Perspectives* (Chicago: University of Chicago Press, 1999); Judith Butler, Ernesto Laclau, and Slavoj Žižek, *Contingency, Hegemony, Universality* (London: Verso, 2000); Michael Hardt and Antonio Negri, *Empire* (Cambridge: Harvard University Press, 2000); Joan Vincent, ed., *The Anthropology of Politics* (Oxford: Blackwell, 2002); James Ferguson, *The Anti-Politics Machine: "Development," Depoliticization, and Bureaucratic Power in Lesotho* (Cambridge: Cambridge University Press, 1990); Stanley Tambiah, *Leveling Crowds* (Berkeley and Los Angeles: University of California Press, 1996); Homi Bhabha, *The Location of Culture* (New York: Routledge, 1994); Johannes Fabian, *Power and Performance: Ethnographic Explorations through Proverbial Wisdom and Theater in Shaba, Zaire* (Madison: University of Wisconsin Press, 1990).

36. Ngũgĩ wa Thiong'o, *Moving the Centre: The Struggle for Cultural Freedoms* (London: James Currey, 1993).

9. THE CULTURES OF THE SHADOWS

1. The October 2001 UN report on Angolan conflict diamonds confirmed this: a major routing for conflict gems at the time passed through Portugal.

2. For an excellent companion story focusing on a Congolese woman working in Angola's diamond areas, see Filip De Boeck: "Dogs Breaking Their Leash: Globalization and Shifting Gender Categories in the Diamond Traffic between Angola and DRCongo (1984–1997)," in *Changements au Femenin en Afrique Noire,* ed. Danielle deLame and Chantal Zabus (Paris: L'Harmattan, 2000), 87–114.

3. Paul Richards, *Fighting for the Rain Forest: War, Youth, and Resources in Sierra Leone* (Portsmouth, N.H.: Heinemann, 1996): 101–2. See also De Boeck, "Domesticating Diamonds and Dollars: Identity, Expenditure and Sharing in Southwestern Zaire (1984–1997)," in *Globalization and Identity: Dialectics of Flow and Closure,* ed. B. Meyers and P. Geschiere (Oxford: Blackwell, 1999).

4. Global Witness, *A Rough Trade: The Role of Companies and Governments in the Angolan Conflict* (London: Global Witness, December 1998): 11.

5. Ibid.

6. Suraj Gupta, *Black Income in India* (New Delhi: Sage, 1992).

7. Hendrik Neto, *O Roque: Romance de um mercado* (Luanda, Angola: Fundação Eshivo, 2001), 64–65. Translated from Portuguese by the author.

8. These collections of people intersect with larger and legitimate political collectivities. A few examples suffice. There are no illegal non-state aircraft or truck manufacturers, no illicit way to produce petroleum. But goods, smuggled or otherwise, require them. And, on the personal level: how many diamonds gracing the engagement and wedding rings on our fingers, purchased in a perfectly legitimate store in one's hometown, have not had a checkered history? Over half of the gems leaving Angola, for example, do so outside of legal state means. In this sense, from the Boeing plant to the jewelry store, shadow powers dip into the normal and the mundane of state-life. Another example is less widely recognized but equally influential in shaping ground-level politics. UN peacekeepers have been praised for providing solutions to intractable wars, and their work has at times been exemplary. But the story is of course more complex than that. Sarajevo provides an apt example. During the worst of the war, when UN peacekeeping troops were stationed there, a large percentage of Sarajevo's economy was diverted into black marketeering through UN troops. A. B. Fetherston and Carolyn Nordstrom, "Overcoming Habitus in Conflict Management: UN Peacekeeping and Warzone Ethnography," *Peace and Change* 20(1) (1995): 94–119; Maggie O'Kane, "The Soldiers Are out of Control: They Are Feasting on a Dying City," *Guardian Weekly* (5 September 1993), 1.

9. I have done interviews with United Nations officials and lawyers, asking what actual data they have on what rules of conduct define these systems and how they are "enforced." Each one — from the UNDP officers (Dr. Aboagye, Dr. Clements, Dierckx de Casterle) to the academic economists (Professors Dutt and Melber) — said that the question is fascinating, but the data sparse. Theory can't emerge without primary data.

10. Diego Gambetta, ed., *Trust: Making and Breaking Cooperative Relations* (New York: Basil Blackwell, 1988). Trust implies interpersonal and, in these complex international networks, cultural and cross-cultural, definitions.

11. Diego Gambetta, "Can We Trust?" in *Trust: Making and Breaking Cooperative Relations,* ed. Diego Gambetta (New York: Basil Blackwell, 1988), 59.

12. Ibid., 230.

13. Ernest Gellner, "Trust, Cohesion, and Social Order," in *Trust: Making and Breaking Cooperative Relations,* ed. Diego Gambetta (New York: Basil Blackwell, 1988), 147.

14. Janet MacGaffey and Rémy Bazenguissa-Ganga, *Congo-Paris: Transnational Traders on the Margins of the Law* (Bloomington: Indiana University Press, 2000), 121.

15. Mark Chingono, *The State, Violence, and Development: The Political Economy of War in Mozambique, 1975–1992* (Aldershot, U.K.: Avebury, 1996), 114.

16. David Hecht and Maliqalim Simone, *Invisible Governance: The Art of African Micropolitics* (Brooklyn, N.Y.: Autonomedia 1994), 52–53.

17. Gastrow also offered an example of the fluidity of a different kind of "expertise": "You can see this in the extensive use of 'free-lance' expertise. An expert forger, for example, is in high demand by any number of networks. He'll be hired to forge car registration and papers to smuggle stolen vehicles; another group profiting on refugee status will hire him to provide refugee certificates. . . . As different groups hear of his work, his reliability, his success, his reputation increases, and so do the jobs he does — bills of lading, false identity papers, international transfer papers. He links across what may be seen as different criminal organizations, but this fluidity, this interchange, is core to organized crime today."

18. MacGaffey and Bazenguissa-Ganga, *Congo-Paris.*

19. Ibid., 3.

20. Ibid., 5.

10. THE INSTITUTIONALIZATION OF THE SHADOWS

1. David Hesketh, International Assistance, Her Majesty's Custom and Excise, U.K., personal communication, London, 2002.

2. The materials I cover here are all gleaned from my own attendance at meetings and from being immersed in the South Africa focus on the hearings, reported continually in the broadcast and print media, in conversations, and in virtually all gatherings.

3. Richard Goldstone, "The Role of Justice in Conflict Prevention," *Conflict Prevention* (August 1996): 83–92; and personal interview, 8 May 1997, Johannesburg.

4. Headed by Archbishop Desmond Tutu, the commission (1996–97) had three committees: one looking into violence and human rights violations; one concerned with reparations; and one considering indemnities, or amnesty.

5. Carolyn Nordstrom and Jo-Ann Martin, *The Paths to Domination, Resistance, and Terror* (Berkeley and Los Angeles: University of California Press, 1992).

6. These examples are not unusual, but common. They are all taken from public records, all thoroughly discussed in broadcast and print media during the time of the hearings. These stories were the gist of daily life for several years in the immediate post-apartheid era.

7. Derek Rodney, "Warning That Apartheid-Era 'Spooks' Have Hand in Crime," *The Star* (Johannesburg), 13 May 1997, 6.

8. June Bearzi, "Wild West Traffickers Strip Zaire of Mineral Wealth," *The Star* (Johannesburg), 13 May 1997, 13.

9. Smit, "Corrupt Police in League with Hijackers," *Rosebank Killarney* (South Africa) *Gazette*, 2 May 1997, 3.

10. Justine Arenstein, *Sunday Times* (Johannesburg), 3 June 1997, 1.

11. Rodney, "Warning," 6.

12. Peter Gastrow, *Bargaining for Peace: South Africa and the National Peace Accord* (Washington, D.C.: U.S. Institute for Peace Press, 2001), 60.

13. Ibid., 58–59.

14. Mark Shaw, "Crime and Policing in Post–Apartheid South Africa," in *War and Peace in Southern Africa,* ed. Robert Rotberg and Greg Mills (Washington, D.C.: Brookings Institution Press, 1998), 24–44; 24.

15. Jacklyn Cock, "The Legacy of War: The Proliferation of Light Weapons in Southern Africa," in *War and Peace in Southern Africa,* ed. Robert Rotberg and Greg Mills (Washington, D.C.: Brookings Institution Press, 1998), 89–121; 89.

16. Brandon Hamber, "Living with the Legacy of Impunity: Lessons for South Africa about Truth, Justice, and Crime in Brazil," paper presented at the Centre for Latin American Studies, University of South Africa, Pretoria, 24 April 1997, 14.

17. Ibid., 14. Hamber supports the conclusions of authors like Adorno, and Pinheiro that the state's ability to carry out anti–human rights actions today is linked to past immunity and "socially rooted authoritarianism." See Sérgio Adorno, "Criminal Violence in Modern Brazil: The Case of the State of São Paulo," in *Social Changes, Crime, and the Police: International Conference, June 1–4, 1992*, ed. Louise Shelley and József Vigh (Amsterdam: Harwood Academic Publishers, 1995); Paulo Pinheiro, "The Legacy of Authoritarianism in Democratic Brazil," in *Latin American Development and Public Policy*, ed. S. Nagel (New York: St. Martin's Press, 1994), 237–53.

18. Cecilia Coimbra, "Torture in Brazil," *Torture* 6 (1996), 4.

19. Pinheiro, "The Legacy of Authoritarianism in Democratic Brazil."

20. Hamber, "Living with the Legacy of Impunity," 15. See also Coimbra, "Torture in Brazil"; Pinheiro, "The Legacy of Authoritarianism in Democratic Brazil"; and Malak Poppovic and Paolo Pinheiro, "How to Consolidate Democracy: A Human Rights Approach," *International Social Science Journal: Measuring and Evaluating Development* 143 (1995): 75–89.

21. Hamber, "Living with the Legacy of Impunity," 17.

22. Carolyn Nordstrom, *A Different Kind of War Story* (Philadelphia: University of Pennsylvania Press, 1997).

23. Compiled by the Catholic Archdiocese, this book includes analyses of over seven hundred formal cases of torture tried in military courts.

24. Elaine Scarry, *The Body in Pain: The Making and Unmaking of the World* (New York: Oxford University Press, 1985); Michel de Certeau, *Heterologies: Discourse on the Other* (Minneapolis: University of Minnesota Press, 1986); Jacobo Timmerman, *Prisoner without a Name, Cell without a Number,* trans. Toby Talbot (New York: Knopf, 1981); Michael Taussig, *Colonialism, Shamanism, and the Wild Man* (Chicago: University of Chicago Press, 1987).

25. Marcelo Suarez-Orozco, "The Treatment of Children in the 'Dirty War': Ideology, State Terrorism, and the Abuse of Children in Argentina," in *Child Survival,* ed. Nancy Scheper-Hughes (Boston: D. Reidel, 1987), 227–46; Marcelo Suarez-Orozco, "A Grammar of Terror: Psychocultural Responses to State Terrorism in Dirty War and Post–Dirty War Argentina," in *The Paths to Domination, Resistance, and Terror,* ed. Carolyn Nordstrom and Jo-Ann Martin (Berkeley and Los Angeles: University of California Press, 1992), 219–59.

11. THE AUTOBIOGRAPHY OF A MAN CALLED PEACE

1. I thank Melissa Moreman for her help in translating Peace's autobiography. I have changed or omitted formal names of people and places.

12. THE TIME OF NOT-WAR-NOT-PEACE

1. For material on Angola's civil war and the peace processes, see Victoria Brittain, *Death of Dignity: Angola's Civil War* (London: Pluto Press, 1998); Paul Hare, *Angola's Last Best Chance for Peace: An Insider's Account of the Peace Process* (Washington, D.C.: United States Institute for Peace, 1998); Tony Hodges, *Angola: From Afro-Stalinism to Petro-Diamond Capitalism* (Oxford: James Currey, 2001); Human Rights Watch, *Angola Unravels: The Rise and Fall of the Lusaka Peace Process* (London: Human Rights Watch, 1999); Karl Maier, *Angola: Promises and Lies* (Rivonia, U.K.: William Waterman, 1996); William Minter, *Apartheid's Contras: An Inquiry into the Roots of War in Angola and Mozambique* (London: Zed Books, 1994).

2. Michael Taussig, *Colonialism, Shamanism, and the Wild Man* (Chicago: University of Chicago Press), 1987.

3. When the war was formally recognized at the end of 1998, Malange was hit hard; and when I tried to return in 1999, I was unable to; the city was closed off by war.

4. How, indeed, do you even see it is not working, Pierre Bourdieu would have us ask — *habitus,* in the best Bourdieu-ian tradition: Pierre Bourdieu, *Outline of a Theory of Practice* (Cambridge: Cambridge University Press, 1977).

5. One reason why UNITA failed to fully demobilize lies at the heart of the dilemmas of conflict resolution. By 1998, with the Cold War long gone and global power politics undergoing major realignments, UNITA was the bad boy of rebel forces. Most diplomatic missions and the major international organizations like the United Nations and the World Bank pushed strongly for UNITA

to abide by the Lusaka peace accord and join the newly reconstituted government, which offered seats to UNITA representatives. Clearly, UNITA didn't lay down its arms. But the government was not the hapless victim. When UNITA fought, it was called an act of war. But armed aggressions by the government against UNITA were cast, by the government at least, as "actions against criminal forces," as "the fight against banditry," and "the control of refugees." For it was a peacetime government. The result has been that in the vast majority of the political regions of the country controlled by the government, the UNITA representative(s) in the "government of unity" are gone. Either they were killed in "actions against criminals," or they fled for their lives. For these UNITA members, demobilization was not an option. Donald Steinberg, the United States Ambassador in Angola in 1998, pointed out that no matter what you call it, the government killing UNITA representatives and UNITA's counteractions is still low-intensity war. Everyone quoted Steinberg's statement because he said the taboo word: he said that war existed in Angola in the mid-1990s "peace."

6. At the turn of the twenty-first century in South Africa, Afrikaner vigilante and political groups still employ racist violence; see Jacklyn Cock, "The Legacy of War: The Proliferation of Light Weapons in Southern Africa," in *War and Peace in Southern Africa,* ed. Robert Rotberg and Greg Mills (Washington, D.C.: Brookings Institution Press, 1998), 89–121. In another vein, the Khmer Rouge continued to operate in Cambodia long after democracy was restored to the nation. In the 1980s when I traveled through Malaysia and Sarawak, I noted how often I heard Chinese speak of oppression against them, including violent government actions in a country heralded as a bastion of peace in the world press. Chinese have been targeted in political upheavals that ostensibly have nothing to do with ethnicity, and thus tend not to be reported as political or ethnic conflict. In 1965, in the wake of a failed coup blamed on communists, a countrywide purge of communists took place — taking the lives of hundreds of Chinese. More than thirty years later, when riots broke out in Indonesia protesting then president Suharto in May 1998, the Chinese again found themselves targets in a war they themselves felt had been in place for decades. After the May riots, political violence was being enacted in the widespread rape of young Chinese girls. One was killed by attackers who left her vagina filled with broken glass and nails, as John Aglionby reported in "Raped for the 'Crime' of Being Chinese," *Mail and Guardian* (Johannesburg), 17–23 July 1998, 18. The list continues around the world's hotspots.

7. Ken Menkhaus, "Stateless Stability," *New Routes* 3(2) (1998): 21.

13. PEACE

1. After leaving Angola in 1998, I traveled to Mozambique, where I spent time talking with children living on the streets, asking them about the similarities and differences between their lives and those of the children in Angola. One youth

seemed to embody the jolting intersections of violence and peace-building. This teenage boy was one of the toughest I had met. He had a hard edge; yet he had fashioned a necklace out of an empty plastic container for sugar tablets. He was willing to take me to every corner of his life, but resisted showing me where he slept. Finally, expressing what for him was probably the ultimate trust, he took me to see his sleeping quarters with a shyness I had never seen. It was an old broom closet in an abandoned, broken-down home. He had only a tattered straw mat and a very old and worn blanket; but above his head on the wall he had put pictures of the most gentle scenes common to magazines: people holding hands, holding babies, smiling in idyllic locales. Directly above his head was a picture of a ballerina, flying through the air in an embracing leap. He went over to place his hand on this picture, looked at me sheepishly, and then, having shown his vulnerability, took my hand to pull me back down the hallway. He had no problem showing me his toughness, his pain, the violence of his life; his vulnerability lay in showing his ballerina.

2. Layers of meaning, of course, abound. As I was reading this poem on the wall, a young woman who said she worked in a cafeteria stopped to read the poem, and then said to me: "Peace, yea, right. It's a tough bird and a good story, but the King is still a man and he is making all the governing decisions for the people."

3. J. M. Frost, "Strange and Extraordinary Feats of Indian Magic," in *The Magician's Tale,* ed. David Hunt (London: Hodder and Stoughton, 1997), 1.

4. Friedrich Nietzsche, "The Genealogy of Morals," in *The Birth of Tragedy/The Genealogy of Morals* (New York: Doubleday, 1956), 179.

5. I suggest we can read these processes to understand when war is entrenched and when peace is imminent in the same way we can predict the outbreak of war. In 1993 I published an article predicting that Mozambique would be able to sustain a peace accord while Sri Lanka would suffer continuing rounds of political violence. In 1996 I wrote that unlike Mozambique, Angola would continue to undergo military aggressions (published 1997). These sets of predictions can expand to include related forms of violence, such as institutions of criminal violence that plague cities. I wrote in 1996 in a United States Institute for Peace grant report that South Africa would continue to experience high levels of criminal and street violence while Mozambique would demonstrate declining rates of such violence. In each case, these predictions proved accurate. This isn't crystal ball gazing or Las Vegas luck; it's a simple reading of the sociopolitical processes that fuel war and peace. In training people to see war starting with the firing of the first bullet and the formal declarations of war, and in seeing peace launched with the signing of peace accords, we have not taught people to read the processes that actually start long before these acts. And this in part explains the poor predictive capacity that marks current scholarly and policy theories. To reconceptualize war and peace — not as set points on a unilinear continuum, but as processes constructed over time and culture — helps lay to rest our poor track records in understanding when political violence will erupt and how to deal with it when it does. If political violence is as destructive to the fabric of societal viability as I suggest here, these concerns are pressing.

14. THE PROBLEMS WITH PEACE

1. These five quotes are culled from my fieldnotes: they are a small sample of hundreds of such quotes I have gathered in the course of my field research on the profits that are made during war.

2. Peter Strandberg , "No One Is Afraid of the Nigerians in the Dark . . . ," *New African* (London) July/August 1998, 14–15. Strandberg describes how the RUF runs hospitals, schools, and well-organized communities; Elizabeth Ohene describes a different set of impressions in "Barbarity beyond Belief," *BBC Focus on Africa* (July/September 1998), 29. Ohene visited a hospital packed with civilian casualties of an RUF attack and sadly noted that the image of an abattoir kept occurring to her: The hospital was awash in the blood of people whose ears, hands, limbs, and sometimes heads had been cut off. "Cut" is perhaps not the right word; Ohene writes of the horror of tired soldiers trying to hack off limbs with dull machetes.

3. Strandberg, "No One Is Afraid," 14–15.

4. Baffour Ankomah, "Sierra Leone: How the 'Good Guys' Won," *New African* (London), July/August 1998, 8.

5. Patrick Chabal and Jean-Pascal Daloz, *Africa Works: Disorder as Political Instrument* (Oxford: James Currey, 1999), 89.

6. In the curious ironies of war, these NGOs were among the handful that were actually out risking life and limb getting food and necessities to war-devastated people. They were profiteering, but they did leave much-needed supplies in their wake.

7. Paul Collier, *Economic Causes of Civil Conflict and Their Implications for Policy* (Washington, D.C.: World Bank, 15 June 2000), 3.

8. Tony Hodges, *Angola: From Afro-Stalinism to Petro-Diamond Capitalism* (Oxford: James Currey, 2001).

9. Global Witness, *A Crude Awakening* (London: Global Witness, December 1999); Global Witness, *All the President's Men* (London: Global Witness, March 2002); Jakkie Cilliers and Christian Dietrich, eds., *Angola's War Economy* (Pretoria, South Africa: Institute for Security Studies, 2000).

10. William Reno, *Corruption and State Politics in Sierra Leone* (Cambridge: Cambridge University Press, 1995); William Reno, *Warlord Politics and African States* (Boulder, CO: Lynne Rienner, 1998).

11. Stephen O'Connell, "Macroeconomic Harmonization, Trade Reform, and Regional Trade in Sub-Saharan Africa," in *Regional Integration and Trade Liberalization in Sub-Saharan Africa*, vol. 1, ed. Ademola Oyejide, Ibrahim Elbadowi, and Paul Collier (London: Macmillan Press, 1997), 136.

12. Chabal and Daloz, *Africa Works*, xx.

13. David Hecht and Maliqalim Simone, *Invisible Governance: The Art of African Micropolitics* (Brooklyn, N.Y.: Autonomedia,1994), 21.

14. Mark Chingono, *The State, Violence, and Development: The Political Economy of War in Mozambique, 1975–1992* (Aldershot, U.K.: Avebury, 1996), 106.

15. Linda Green, *Fear as a Way of Life: Mayan Widows in Rural Guatemala*

(New York: Columbia University Press, 2000); Paul Richards, *Fighting for the Rainforest: War, Youth, and Resources in Sierra Leone* (Portsmouth, N.H.: Heinemann, 1996); Carolyn Nordstrom, "Public Bad, Public Good(s), and Private Realities," in *Cultures of Political Transition,* ed. Paul Gready (London: Pluto Press, 2003), 212–24; Krishna Kumar, ed., *Rebuilding Societies after Civil War* (London: Lynne Rienner, 1997); Nat Colletta, Markus Kostner, and Ingo Wiederhofer, *The Transition from War to Peace in Sub-Saharan Africa* (Washington, D.C.: World Bank, May 1996).

16. Chingono, *The State, Violence, and Development,* 110.

17. In 1996 in Angola, I exchanged the US dollar variously for 120,000, 200,000, and 270,000 kwanza in the space of a week: a roller coaster of currency valuations.

15. IRONIES IN THE SHADOWS

1. Janine Wedel's most recent work follows these kinds of questions across Eastern Europe and the imbroglios of western aid: *Collision and Collusion: The Strange Case of Western Aid to Eastern Europe* (New York: St. Martin's Press, 2001).

2. See A. B. Fetherston and Carolyn Nordstrom, "Overcoming Conceptual Habitus in Conflict Management: UN Peacekeeping and Warzone Ethnography," *Peace and Change* 20(1) (1995): 94–119.

3. I have elected not to give the speaker's name or work affiliation in quotes such as this, in which the speaker discusses sensitive extra-legal issues that might affect the person's ability to work in-country in the future.

4. Maria Faria, Programa Alimentar Mundial (World Food Program)/Angola, personal communication, November 2001.

5. Janet MacGaffey, ed., *The Real Economy of Zaire: The Contribution of Smuggling and Other Unofficial Activities to National Wealth* (London: James Currey, 1991); Karen Tranberg Hansen, *Salaula: The World of Secondhand Clothing in Zambia* (Chicago: University of Chicago Press, 2000); William Reno, *Corruption and State Politics in Sierra Leone* (Cambridge: Cambridge University Press, 1995).

6. Gianluca Fiorentini and Sam Peltzman, eds., *The Economics of Organised Crime* (Cambridge: Cambridge University Press, 1995); Mark Findlay, *The Globalisation of Crime* (Cambridge: Cambridge University Press, 1999); Gary Slapper and Steve Tombs, *Corporate Crime* (Essex: Addison Wesley Longman, 1999); Manuel Castells, *End of Millennium,* vol. 3 of *The Information Age: Economy, Society, and Culture* (Malden: Blackwell Publishers, 1998); Jacklyn Cock, "The Legacy of War: The Proliferation of Light Weapons in Southern Africa," in *War and Peace in Southern Africa,* ed. Robert Rotberg and Greg Mills (Washington, D.C.: Brookings Institution Press, 1998), 89–121; William Reno, *Warlord Politics and African States* (Boulder, CO: Lynne Rienner, 1998).

7. Susan Strange, *The Retreat of the State: The Diffusions of Power in the World Economy* (Cambridge: Cambridge University Press, 1996), 117.

8. Linda Gustitus, Elise Bean, and Robert Roach, "Correspondent Banking: A Gateway for Money Laundering," *Economic Perspectives* 6(2): 23–26.

9. John McDowell and Gary Novis, "The Consequences of Money Laundering and Financial Crime," *Economic Perspectives* 6(2): 4.

10. Ibid., 5.

11. Castells, *End of Millennium,* 167.

12. Mark Chingono, *The State, Violence, and Development: The Political Economy of War in Mozambique, 1975–1992* (Aldershot, U.K.: Avebury, 1996), 115.

16. WHY DON'T WE STUDY THE SHADOWS?

1. John Kenneth Galbraith and Nicole Salinger, *Almost Everyone's Guide to Economics* (New York: Penguin Books, 1978), 66–67.

2. Quoted in Dirk Hansohm, "Renewal in Africa? The Informal Sector and Its Promotion in Namibia," NEPRU Working Paper No. 55 (Windhoek, Namibia: NEPRU, 1997).

3. Ibid.

4. Pierre Bourdieu, *Outline of a Theory of Practice* (Cambridge: Cambridge University Press, 1977).

5. Charles Tilly, "War Making and State Making as Organized Crime," in *Bringing the State Back In,* ed. Peter B. Evans et al. (Cambridge: Cambridge University Press, 1985), 170. Tilly's core point in this regard is that "banditry, piracy, gangland rivalry, policing, and war making all belong on the same continuum" in the state-making process.

6. Reading Henrietta Moore's work on the anthropology of governance, *The Future of Anthropological Knowledge* (London: Routledge, 1996), 10–14, raised a new set of considerations for me, ones not directly addressed by Moore, but implicit in her ideas. She explores the place a "neo-Foucaultian" approach would have in contemporary anthropology, placing at its center the ways — the arts — by which practices of government control populations. Crucially, while this is a means to analyze the state, it is not state centered. This notion of "governmentality," says Moore, indicates "a certain mentality, a particular way of thinking about the sort of problems which can and should be addressed by particular authorities and through particular strategies" (12). The critical analysis of these forms of rationality, concludes Moore, would certainly be central to a modern anthropology. My explorations of the ways in which state and non-state actors alike benefit from the created invisibilities of extra-state networks touch on these issues of governmentality, and the systems of knowledge *as* power that undergird these.

7. Cynthia Enloe, *Maneuvers: The International Politics of Militarizing Women's Lives* (Berkeley and Los Angeles: University of California Press, 2000).

8. Carolyn Nordstrom, "Shadows and Sovereigns," *Theory, Culture, & Society* 17(4) (August 2000): 36–54.

9. If we look at the broad sweep of history — at the succession of regimes rising and falling across the millennia and the world's populations — it would be surprising if the state were to remain in force across the upcoming eras. Whether the power systems that come to replace the Enlightenment state are "good" or

"bad" of course depends on who is doing the defining. For those in positions of defining the power, it will be good, for those out-defined, it will not.

10. Ngũgĩ wa Thiong'o, *Moving the Centre: The Struggle for Cultural Freedoms* (London: James Currey, 1993).

11. Jean-François Bayart, *The State in Africa: The Politics of the Belly* (London: Longman, 1993), 209. The sentences preceding this quote read: "We should not attempt in an academic and artificial balancing act, to oppose the statist 'totalising' work with the divergent tactics of 'detotalising,' even if the latter more than any others do lead directly to the erosion or dilution of the State. In reality, the logic of deconstruction in the statist arena is not so easily separated from the loci of its construction."

12. See, for example, the now-classic example of Thomas Friedman's work, *The Lexus and the Olive Tree: Understanding Globalization* (New York: Farrar, Straus, Giroux, 1999).

13. Such theories are strongly linear and little match the current epistemological innovations demonstrating that relationships are far more interrelated. As Mark Chingono writes: "The unintended consequences of violence have been to completely discredit economic nationalism and to demystify national boundaries, both of which are the bedrock of imperialism in Southern Africa, and core principles of Western civilization." *The State, Violence, and Development: The Political Economy of War in Mozambique, 1975–1992* (Aldershot, U.K.: Avebury, 1996), 110.

14. On the basis of this analysis, if I were to predict the form of war that will most characterize the twenty-first century, it would be that of multinational and transnational businesses, however set in national sovereign law, that profit from political instability in resource-rich locales where political instability inhibits cosmopolitan development. The promise of immense profit lies in the weak political controls of warzones; in the critical call for weapons, supplies, and survival necessities from warzones; in the flux of unregulated power in warzones. Wars are infrequent in resource-poor regions. In addition, the political instability in resource-rich countries reduces these countries' own potential for developing their resources and in forming their own centers of politico-economic power capable of competing equally in the global arena.

17. EPILOGUE

1. Zezo Baptista, *A Contagem Regressiva* (Luanda, Angola: Ponto Um, 2000). Translation by the author.

2. Maria Faria, Programa Alimentar Mundial (World Food Program), Angola, personal communication, Luanda, November 2001.

3. Mattijs Van de Port, *Gypsies, Wars, and Other Instances of the Wild: Civilization and Its Discontents in a Serbian Town* (Amsterdam: Amsterdam University Press, 1998), 28.

POSTSCRIPT

1. According to the national media in the USA, it seems as if the war really did take place within the space of time it took me to finish the last chapter of this book. But that is the illusion of war. In truth, the war in Iraq started long before the first body fell, and will last long after the troops have packed up and gone home. In my work, I was introduced to the possibility of this war before the century's end. Throughout the 1990s, students in every class I taught on war predicted that while the government supported a multi-billion-dollar missile defense system, the most probable attack would be terrorist on USA ground with small-scale weaponry. Four years before the 2003 Iraqi war my classes mapped the changing extra-state warzone/commodity/resource circuits linking EurAsia and the Americas, the Middle East and Africa, pointing out how such networks showed unfolding configurations of power and new forms of political contest. Several years before the war — when western oil companies paid some of the highest prices in the industry for signature bonuses on oil blocks in Angola — people in Africa speculated that the political tensions surrounding the USA and the oil-rich countries of the Middle East could turn violent. Angolagate, the pre–September 11 scandal that linked oil rights and weapons transfers through Angola with France, the Middle East, and the political pardons President Clinton made at the end of his presidency, was a clear demonstration of emerging extra-legal power politics and economics that charted new hot spots and alliances. François Misser, "The Angolagate Scandal," *African Business* 265 (May 2001): 8–11.

BIBLIOGRAPHY

Adorno, Sérgio. "The State of Knowledge in Brazil." In *Crime and Prevention Policy*, ed. Philippe Robert. Freiburg: Krimologische Forschungsberichte aus dem Max-Planck-Institut für ausländisches und internationales Stratrecht, 1993.

———. "Criminal Violence in Modern Brazil: The Case of the State of São Paulo." In *Social Changes, Crime, and the Police: International Conference, June 1–4, 1992*, ed. Louise Shelley and József Vigh. Amsterdam: Harwood Academic Publishers, 1995.

Aglionby, John. "Raped for the 'Crime' of Being Chinese." *Mail and Guardian* (Johannesburg), 17–23 July 1998, 18.

Alves, P. Gasparini, and D. Cipollone. *Curbing Illicit Trafficking in Small Arms and Sensitive Technologies: An Action-Oriented Agenda*. Geneva: United Nations, 1998.

Ankomah, Baffour. "Sierra Leone: How the 'Good Guys' Won." *New African* (London), July/August 1998, 8–11.

Appadurai, Arjun. *Modernity at Large: Cultural Dimensions of Globalization*. St. Paul: University of Minnesota Press, 1996.

Arenstein, Justine. *Sunday Times* (Johannesburg), 3 June 1997, 1.

Ashworth, Georgina. *Of Violence and Violation: Women and Human Rights*. London: Change, 1985.

Augé, Marc. *Non-Places: Introduction to an Anthropology of Supermodernity*. Trans. John Howe. London: Verso, 1995.

Ayers, Ed. "The Expanding Shadow Economy." *World Watch* 9(4) (1996): 11–23.

Bacon, Francis. *The New Organon and Related Writings*. New York: Liberal Arts Press, 1960.

Bao Ninh. *The Sorrow of War*. New York: Riverhead Books, 1996.

Baptista, Zezo. *A Contagem Regressiva*. Luanda, Angola: Ponto Um, 2000.

Bayart, Jean-François. *The State in Africa: The Politics of the Belly*. London: Longman, 1993.

Bearzi, June. "Wild West Traffickers Strip Zaire of Mineral Wealth." *The Star* (Johannesburg), 13 May 1997, 13.

Bhabha, Homi. *The Location of Culture*. New York: Routledge, 1994.

Bourdieu, Pierre. *Outline of a Theory of Practice*. Cambridge: Cambridge University Press, 1977.

———. *Pascalian Meditations*. Trans. Richard Nice. Cambridge: Polity Press, 2000.

Brittain, Victoria. *Death of Dignity: Angola's Civil War*. London: Pluto Press, 1998.

Bureau for International Narcotics and Law Enforcement Affairs. *International Narcotics Control Strategy Report 1996*. Washington, D.C.: U.S. Department of State, March 1997.

Butler, Judith, Ernesto Laclau, and Slavoj Žižek. *Contingency, Hegemony, Universality*. London: Verso, 2000.

Castells, Manuel. *End of Millennium*. Vol. 3 of *The Information Age: Economy, Society, and Culture*. Malden: Blackwell Publishers, 1998.

Chabal, Patrick, and Jean-Pascal Daloz. *Africa Works: Disorder as Political Instrument*. Oxford: James Currey, 1999.

Chifunyise, Stephen. "Culture in the Age of Rapid Technological and Social Change." In *Culture and Conflict in Africa*, ed. Ansu Datta. Gaborone: University of Botswana, National Institute of Development Research and Documentation, 1995.

Chingono, Mark. *The State, Violence, and Development: The Political Economy of War in Mozambique, 1975–1992*. Aldershot, U.K.: Avebury, 1996.

Cilliers, Jakkie, and Christian Dietrich, eds. *Angola's War Economy*. Pretoria, South Africa: Institute for Security Studies, 2000.

Cock, Jacklyn. "The Legacy of War: The Proliferation of Light Weapons in Southern Africa." In *War and Peace in Southern Africa*, ed. Robert Rotberg and Greg Mills, 89–121. Washington, D.C.: Brookings Institution Press, 1998.

Cohen, Stanley. *States of Denial: Knowing about Atrocities and Suffering*. Cambridge: Polity, 2001.

Coimbra, Cecilia. "Torture in Brazil." *Torture* 6 (1996): 4.

Colletta, Nat, Markus Kostner, and Ingo Wiederhofer. *The Transition from War to Peace in Sub-Saharan Africa*. Washington, D.C.: World Bank, May 1996.

———. *Case Studies in War-to-Peace Transition*. World Bank Discussion Paper 331. Washington, D.C.: World Bank, June 1996.

Collier, Paul. *Economic Causes of Civil Conflict and Their Implications for Policy*. Washington, D.C.: World Bank, 15 June 2000.

Comaroff, Jean, and John Comaroff. *Of Revelation and Revolution*. Vol. 1. Chicago: University of Chicago Press, 1991.

Comaroff, John, and Jean Comaroff, eds. *Civil Society and the Political Imagination in Africa: Critical Perspectives*. Chicago: University of Chicago Press, 1999.

Daniel, Valentine. *Charred Lullabies: Chapters in an Anthropography of Violence*. Princeton: Princeton University Press, 1996.

Das, Veena. "Our Work to Cry: Your Work to Listen." In *Mirrors of Violence: Communities, Riots, and Survivors in South Asia*, ed. Veena Das, 345–98. Oxford: Oxford University Press, 1991.

———. *Critical Events: An Anthropological Perspective on Contemporary India*. Delhi: Oxford University Press, 1995.

De Boeck, Filip. "Domesticating Diamonds and Dollars: Identity, Expenditure, and Sharing in Southwestern Zaire (1984–1997)." In *Globalization and Identity: Dialectics of Flow and Closure,* ed. B. Meyers and P. Geschiere, 177–201. Oxford: Blackwell, 1999.

———. "Dogs Breaking Their Leash: Globalization and Shifting Gender Categories in the Diamond Traffic between Angola and DRCongo (1984–1997)." In *Changements au Femenin en Afrique Noire,* ed. Danielle deLame and Chantal Zabus, 87–114. Paris: L'Harmattan, 2000.

de Certeau, Michel. *Heterologies: Discourse on the Other.* Minneapolis: University of Minnesota Press, 1986.

Dyer, Gwynne. *War.* London: Guild Publishing, 1985.

Ehrenreich, Barbara. *Blood Rites.* London: Virago, 1997.

Enloe, Cynthia. *The Morning After: Sexual Politics at the End of the Cold War.* Berkeley and Los Angeles: University of California Press, 1993.

———. *Maneuvers: The International Politics of Militarizing Women's Lives.* Berkeley and Los Angeles: University of California Press, 2000.

Fabian, Johannes. *Power and Performance: Ethnographic Explorations through Proverbial Wisdom and Theater in Shaba, Zaire.* Madison: University of Wisconsin Press, 1990.

Feldman, Allen. *Formations of Violence: The Narrative of the Body and Political Terror in Northern Ireland.* Chicago: University of Chicago Press, 1991.

Ferguson, James. *The Anti-Politics Machine: "Development," Depoliticization, and Bureaucratic Power in Lesotho.* Cambridge: Cambridge University Press, 1990.

Fetherston, A. B., and Carolyn Nordstrom. "Overcoming Conceptual Habitus in Conflict Management: UN Peacekeeping and Warzone Ethnography." *Peace and Change* 20(1) (1995): 94–119.

Findlay, Mark. *The Globalisation of Crime.* Cambridge: Cambridge University Press, 1999.

Fiorentini, Gianluca, and Sam Peltzman, eds. *The Economics of Organised Crime.* Cambridge: Cambridge University Press, 1995.

Foucault, Michel. *Archaeology of Knowledge*, trans. A. M. Sheridan-Smith. New York: Pantheon Publishers, 1972.

———. *Power/Knowledge,* trans. Colin Gordon et al. New York: Pantheon Books, 1972.

———. *Discipline and Punish: The Birth of the Prison,* trans. Alan Sheridan. New York: Vintage Books, 1979.

———. *The History of Sexuality, Volume 1: An Introduction,* trans. Robert Hurley. New York: Vintage Books, 1980.

———. "The Subject of Power," in *Michel Foucault: Beyond Structuralism and Hermeneutics*, ed. H. Dreyfus and P. Rabinow, 208–26. Chicago: University of Chicago Press, 1982.

Fox, Robin. "Fatal Attraction: War and Human Nature." *National Interest* 30 (November 1992): 11–20.

Friedman, Thomas. *The Lexus and the Olive Tree: Understanding Globalization.* New York: Farrar, Straus, Giroux, 1999.

Frost, J. M. "Strange and Extraordinary Feats of Indian Magic." In *The Magician's Tale,* ed. David Hunt. London: Hodder & Stoughton, 1997.
Fry, Douglas, and Kaj Bjorkqvist, eds. *Cultural Variation in Conflict Resolution: Alternatives to Violence*. Mahwah, N.J.: Lawrence Erlbaum, 1997.
Galbraith, John Kenneth, and Nicole Salinger. *Almost Everyone's Guide to Economics*. New York: Penguin Books, 1978.
Gallant, Thomas. "Brigandage, Piracy, Capitalism, and State-Formation: Transnational Crime from a Historical World-Systems Perspective." In *States and Illegal Practices*, ed. Josiah Heyman, 25–61. Oxford: Berg, 1999.
Gambetta, Diego. "Comment on 'Corruption and Development' by Susan Rose-Ackerman." In *Annual World Bank Conference on Development Economics 1997*, ed. Boris Pleskovic and Joseph Stiglitz, 58–61. Washington, D.C.: World Bank, 1997.
———. "Can We Trust?" In *Trust: Making and Breaking Cooperative Relations,* ed. Diego Gambetta, 213–37 (New York: Basil Blackwell, 1988), 59.
———, ed. *Trust: Making and Breaking Cooperative Relations*. New York: Basil Blackwell, 1988.
Ganguly, Meenakshi. "A Banking System Built for Terrorism." *Time World,* 5 October 2001, 21.
Gastrow, Peter. *Bargaining for Peace: South Africa and the National Peace Accord*. Washington, D.C.: U.S. Institute for Peace Press, 2001.
Gellner, Ernest. "Trust, Cohesion, and Social Order." In *Trust: Making and Breaking Cooperative Relations,* ed. Diego Gambetta, 142–57. New York: Basil Blackwell, 1988.
Gibson, Janice, and Mika Haritos-Fatouros. "The Education of a Torturer." *Psychology Today* 20, November 1986, 50–58.
Glantz, L. "Patterns of Crime: Deciphering the Statistics." *Indicator South Africa: Crime and Conflict* 1 (Autumn 1995): 11–15.
Global Witness. *A Rough Trade: The Role of Companies and Governments in the Angolan Conflict*. London: Global Witness, December 1998.
———. *A Crude Awakening*. London: Global Witness, December 1999.
———. *All the President's Men*. London: Global Witness, March 2002.
Goldstock, Ronald, Martin Marcus, Thomas Thacher, and James Jacobs. *Corruption and Racketeering in the New York City Construction Industry: The Final Report of the N.Y. State Organized Crime Task Force*. New York: New York University Press, 1990.
Goldstone, Richard. "The Role of Justice in Conflict Prevention." *Conflict Prevention* (August 1996): 83–92.
Gramsci, Antonio. *The Modern Prince and Other Writings*. New York: International Publishers, 1968.
———. *Selections from the Prison Notebooks*. London: Lawrence and Wishart, 1971.
Green, Linda. *Fear as a Way of Life: Mayan Widows in Rural Guatemala*. New York: Columbia University Press, 2000.
Greif, Avner. "Contracting, Enforcement, and Efficiency: Economics beyond the Law." In *Annual World Bank Conference on Development Economics 1996*, ed.

Michael Bruno and Boris Pleskovic, 239–65. Washington, D.C.: World Bank, 1996.

Grossman, David. *On Killing: The Psychological Cost of Learning to Kill in War and Society*. Boston: Little, Brown, 1995.

Gupta, Suraj. *Black Income in India*. New Delhi: Sage, 1992.

Gustitus, Linda, Elise Bean, and Robert Roach. "Correspondent Banking: A Gateway for Money Laundering." *Economic Perspectives* 6(2): 23–26.

Hamber, Brandon. "Living with the Legacy of Impunity: Lessons for South Africa about Truth, Justice, and Crime in Brazil." Paper presented at the Centre for Latin American Studies, University of South Africa, Pretoria, 24 April 1997.

Hanley, Lynne. *Writing War: Fiction, Gender, and Memory*. Amherst: University of Massachusetts Press, 1991.

Hansen, Karen Tranberg. *Salaula: The World of Secondhand Clothing in Zambia*. Chicago: University of Chicago Press, 2000.

Hansohm, Dirk. "Renewal in Africa? The Informal Sector and Its Promotion in Namibia." Namibian Economic Policy Research Unit Working Paper No. 55. Windhoek, Namibia: NEPRU, 1997.

Hardt, Michael, and Antonio Negri. *Empire*. Cambridge: Harvard University Press, 2000.

Hare, Paul. *Angola's Last Best Chance for Peace: An Insider's Account of the Peace Process*. Washington, D.C.: United States Institute for Peace, 1998.

Hecht, David, and Maliqalim Simone. *Invisible Governance: The Art of African Micropolitics*. Brooklyn, N.Y.: Autonomedia,1994.

Heyman, Josiah, ed. *States and Illegal Practices*. Oxford: Berg, 1999.

Hibou, Béatrice. "The 'Social Capital' of the State as an Agent of Deception." In *The Criminalization of the State in Africa*. Trans. Stephen Ellis, 69–113. Oxford: James Currey, 1999.

Hodges, Tony. *Angola: From Afro-Stalinism to Petro-Diamond Capitalism*. Oxford: James Currey, 2001.

Howell, Signe, and Roy Willis. *Societies at Peace*. New York: Routledge, 1989.

Human Rights Watch. *Arms Project and Human Rights Watch/Africa, Angola: Arms Trade and Violations of the Laws of War since the 1992 Elections*. New York: Human Rights Watch, 1994.

———. *Angola Unravels: The Rise and Fall of the Lusaka Peace Process*. London: Human Rights Watch, 1999.

Institute Diethone Scheseone. *The Gangsterization of Turkish Politics*. Athens: Panteiro Panepistimio Kiononikon and Politicon Epistimon, 1998.

International Labour Organization. *Employment, Incomes and Equity: A Strategy of Increasing Productive Employment in Kenya*. Geneva: ILO, 1972.

———. *Employment in Africa: Some Critical Issues*. Geneva: ILO, 1973.

Jost, Patrick, and Harjit Singh Sandhu. "The Hawala Alternative Remittance System and Its Role in Money Laundering." Lyon: Interpol General Secretariat, January 2000. http://www.interpol.int/Public/FinanceCrime/Money Laundering/hawala/default.asp [10 November 2002].

Keane, John. *Reflections on Violence*. London: Verso, 1996.

Kumar, Krishna, ed. *Rebuilding Societies after Civil War*. London: Lynne Rienner, 1997.

Lippert, Owen, and Michael Walker, eds. *The Underground Economy: Global Evidence of Its Size and Impact*. Vancouver, B.C.: Fraser Institute, 1997.

Lopez, George, and David Cortright. "Making Targets 'Smart' from Sanctions." Paper delivered at the International Studies Association meetings, Minneapolis, 18–22 March 1998.

Lukes, Steven. *Power: A Radical View*. London: Macmillan Press, 1974.

MacGaffey, Janet, ed. *The Real Economy of Zaire: The Contribution of Smuggling and Other Unofficial Activities to National Wealth*. London: James Currey, 1991.

MacGaffey, Janet, and Rémy Bazenguissa-Ganga. *Congo-Paris: Transnational Traders on the Margins of the Law*. Bloomington: Indiana University Press, 2000.

Macieira, Antonio Carlos. "Os Falsos Profetas de Paz." *Jornal de Angola* (16 November 2001): 5.

Maier, Karl. *Angola: Promises and Lies*. Rivonia, U.K.: William Waterman, 1996.

Marcus, George. *Ethnography through Thick and Thin*. Princeton: Princeton University Press, 1998.

Marshall, S. L. A. *Men against Fire*. Gloucester, MA: Peter Smith, 1978.

McDowell, John, and Gary Novis. "The Consequences of Money Laundering and Financial Crime." *Economic Perspectives*, 6(2) (May 2001): 4–6.

Mearscheimer, John. "German Security Policy in Post–Cold War Europe." Talk delivered at the Institute for International Studies, University of California, Berkeley, 5 March 1997.

Menkhaus, Ken. "Stateless Stability." *New Routes* 3(2) (1998): 21–24.

Minter, William. *Apartheid's Contras: An Inquiry into the Roots of War in Angola and Mozambique*. London: Zed Books, 1994.

Misser, François. "The Angolagate Scandal." *African Business* 265 (May 2001): 8–11.

Mollica, Richard. "Invisible Wounds." *Scientific American*, June 2000, 54–57.

Mollica, Richard, et al. "Disability Associated with Psychiatric Comorbidity and Health Status in Bosnian Refugees Living in Croatia." *Journal of the American Medical Association* 282(5) (4 August 1999): 433–39.

Moore, Henrietta. *The Future of Anthropological Knowledge*. London: Routledge, 1996.

Naylor, R. T. *Wages of Crime: Black Markets, Illegal Finance, and the Underworld Economy*. Ithaca: Cornell University Press, 2002.

Neto, Hendrik. *O Roque: Romance de um mercado*. Luanda, Angola: Fundação Eshivo, 2001.

Ngũgĩ wa Thiong'o. *Moving the Centre: The Struggle for Cultural Freedoms*. London: James Currey, 1993.

Nietzsche, Friedrich. "The Genealogy of Morals." In *The Birth of Tragedy/The Genealogy of Morals*. New York: Doubleday, 1956.

———. *The Will to Power*. Garden City: Doubleday, 1968.

Nordstrom, Carolyn. "Rape: Politics and Theory in War and Peace." *Australian Feminist Studies* 23 (1996): 147–62.

———. *A Different Kind of War Story*. Philadelphia: University of Pennsylvania Press, 1997.

———. *Girls and Warzones — Troubling Questions*. Uppsala, Sweden: Life and Peace Institute Press, 1997.

———. "Terror-Warfare and the Medicine of Peace." *Medical Anthropology Quarterly* 11(2) (1998): 1–19.

———. "A War Dossier." *Public Culture* 10(2) (Winter 1998).

———. "Deadly Myths of Aggression." *Journal of Aggressive Behavior* 24(2) (1998): 147–59.

———. "Requiem for the Rational War." In *Deadly Developments: Capitalism, States, and War,* ed. S. Reyna, 153–76. Amsterdam: Gordon and Breach, 1999.

———. "Visible Wars and Invisible Girls: Shadow Industries and the Politics of Not-Knowing." *International Feminist Journal of Politics* 1(1) (1999): 14–33.

———. "Shadows and Sovereigns." *Theory, Culture, and Society* 17(4) (August 2000): 36–54.

———. "Out of the Shadows." In *International Intervention and Local Governance in Africa*, ed. Thomas Callaghy, Ronald Kassimir, and Robert Latham, 216–39. Oxford: Cambridge University Press, 2002.

———. "Public Bad, Public Good(s), and Private Realities." In *Cultures of Political Transition,* ed. Paul Gready, 212–24. London: Pluto Press, 2003.

Nordstrom, Carolyn, and Jo-Ann Martin, eds. *The Paths to Domination, Resistance, and Terror*. Berkeley and Los Angeles: University of California Press, 1992.

Nordstrom, Carolyn, and Antonius C. G. M. Robben, eds. *Fieldwork under Fire: Contemporary Studies of Violence and Survival*. Berkeley and Los Angeles: University of California Press, 1995.

Norton-Taylor, Richard. "Trade in Torture Weapons Rises." *Guardian* (Manchester, U.K.), 27 February 2001, 17.

O'Brien, Tim. *The Things They Carried*. Boston: Houghton Mifflin/Seymour Lawrence, 1990.

O'Connell, Stephen. "Macroeconomic Harmonization, Trade Reform, and Regional Trade in Sub-Saharan Africa." In *Regional Integration and Trade Liberalization in Sub-Saharan Africa*. Vol. 1, ed. Ademola Oyejide, Ibrahim Elbadowi, and Paul Collier, 89–158. London: Macmillan Press, 1997.

Ohene, Elizabeth. "Barbarity beyond Belief." *BBC Focus on Africa* (July/September 1998): 29.

Okely, Judith. "Presentation." In *Social Anthropology Is a Generalizing Science or It Is Nothing*, ed. Tim Ingold. Manchester, U.K.: Group for Debates in Anthropology, 1989.

O'Kane, Maggie. "The Soldiers Are out of Control: They Are Feasting on a Dying City." *Guardian Weekly* (London), 5 September 1993, 1.

Pinheiro, Paolo. "The Legacy of Authoritarianism in Democratic Brazil." In *Latin*

American Development and Public Policy, ed. S. Nagel, 237–53. New York: St. Martin's Press, 1994.
Pinnock, Patricia. *Skyline*. Johannesburg: David Philip Publishers, 2000.
Poppovic, Malak, and Paolo Pinheiro. "How to Consolidate Democracy: A Human Rights Approach." *International Social Science Journal: Measuring and Evaluating Development* 143 (1995).
Pozo, Susan. *Price Behavior in Illegal Markets*. Aldershot, U.K.: Avebury, 1996.
Redding, Arthur. *Raids on Human Consciousness: Writing, Anarchism, and Violence*. Columbia: University of South Carolina Press, 1998.
Reno, William. *Corruption and State Politics in Sierra Leone*. Cambridge: Cambridge University Press, 1995.
———. *Warlord Politics and African States*. Boulder, CO: Lynne Rienner, 1998.
Richards, Paul. *Fighting for the Rainforest: War, Youth, and Resources in Sierra Leone*. Portsmouth, N.H.: Heinemann, 1996.
Rodney, Derek. "Warning That Apartheid-Era 'Spooks' Have Hand in Crime." *The Star* (Johannesburg), 13 May 1997, 6.
———. "Torrent of Tax Revenue Slipping across Borders." *The Star* (Johannesburg), 13 May 1997, 6.
Roitman, Janet. "The Garrison-Entrepôt." *Cahiers d'Etudes Africaines* 140 (1998).
Rupesinghe, Kumar, ed. *Conflict Transformation*. London: Macmillan, 1995.
Rupesinghe, Kumar, and Marcial Rubio, eds. *The Culture of Violence*. Toyko: United Nations University Press, 1994.
Rutherford, Donald. *Dictionary of Economies*. New York: Routledge, 1992.
Sainsbury, R. M. *Paradoxes*. 2nd ed. Cambridge: Cambridge University Press, 2000.
Scarry, Elaine. *The Body in Pain: The Making and Unmaking of the World*. New York: Oxford University Press, 1985.
Sevigny, John. "Mexican, U.S. Officials Discuss Measures to Combat Freon Smuggling." Environmental News Network. http://www.enn.com/News/2003-02-07/S_2548.asp [7 February 2003].
Shaw, Mark. "Exploring a Decade of Crime." *Indicator South Africa: Crime and Conflict* 1 (Autumn 1995): 12–15.
———. "Crime and Policing in Post–Apartheid South Africa." In *War and Peace in Southern Africa*, ed. Robert Rotberg and Greg Mills, 24–44. Washington, D.C.: Brookings Institution Press, 1998.
Shawcross, William. *The Quality of Mercy: Cambodia, Holocaust, and Modern Conscience*. New York: Simon and Schuster, 1984.
Simmel, Georg. *The Sociology of Georg Simmel*. Trans. and ed. Kurt Wolff. Cambridge: Cambridge University Press, 1950.
Sivard, Ruth Leger. *World Military and Social Expenditures 1996*. Washington, D.C.: World Priorities, 1996.
Slapper, Gary, and Steve Tombs. *Corporate Crime*. Essex: Addison Wesley Longman, 1999.

Smit. "Corrupt Police in League with Hijackers." *Rosebank Killarney* (South Africa) *Gazette*, 2 May 1997, 3.

Stellman, Jeanne Mager, and S. Stellman. "Post-traumatic Stress Disorders among American Legionnaires in Relation to Combat Experience." *Environmental Research* 47 (February 1988): 175–210.

Stockholm International Peace Research Institute. *SIPRI Yearbook of World Armaments and Disarmament*. New York: Humanities Press, 2002.

Strandberg, Peter. "No One Is Afraid of the Nigerians in the Dark . . ." *New African* (London), July/August 1998, 14–15.

Strange, Susan. *The Retreat of the State: The Diffusions of Power in the World Economy*. Cambridge: Cambridge University Press, 1996.

Suarez-Orozco, Marcelo. "The Treatment of Children in the 'Dirty War': Ideology, State Terrorism, and the Abuse of Children in Argentina." In *Child Survival*, ed. Nancy Scheper-Hughes, 227–46. Boston: D. Reidel, 1987.

———. "A Grammar of Terror: Psychocultural Responses to State Terrorism in Dirty War and Post–Dirty War Argentina." In *The Paths to Domination, Resistance, and Terror*, ed. Carolyn Nordstrom and Jo-Ann Martin, 219–59. Berkeley and Los Angeles: University of California Press, 1992.

Swank, Roy L., and W. E. Marchand. "Combat Neuroses: Development of Combat Exhaustion." *Archives of Neurology and Psychology* 55 (1946): 236–47.

Tambiah, Stanley. *Leveling Crowds*. Berkeley and Los Angeles: University of California Press, 1996.

Taussig, Michael. *Colonialism, Shamanism, and the Wild Man*. Chicago: University of Chicago Press, 1987.

Tilly, Charles. "War Making and State Making as Organized Crime." In *Bringing the State Back In*, ed. Peter B. Evans et al., 169–91. Cambridge: Cambridge University Press, 1985.

Timmerman, Jacobo. *Prisoner without a Name, Cell without a Number*. Trans. Toby Talbot. New York: Knopf, 1981.

Turpin, Jennifer, and Lester Kurtz, eds. *The Web of Violence: From Interpersonal to Global*. Urbana: University of Illinois Press, 1997.

UNICEF. *Annual Report*. Geneva: United Nations Press, 1996.

———. *The State of the World's Children*. Oxford: Oxford University Press, 1996.

———. *The State of the World's Children*. Oxford: Oxford University Press, 1997.

———. *Adult Wars, Child Soldiers*. Geneva: UNICEF, 2002.

———. *The State of the World's Children 2003*. Oxford: Oxford University Press, 2003.

United Nations Research Institute. *States of Disarray: The Social Effects of Globalization*. London: UNRISD, 1995.

United Nations Security Council. *Compendium of Presidential Statements and Resolutions, Security Council*. Geneva: UN Publications, 2000.

United States Agency for International Development. *After the War Is over, What Comes Next? Promoting Democracy, Human Rights, and Reintegration in Post-*

Conflict Societies. Washington, D.C.: USAID, Center for Development Information and Evaluation, 1997.

Vagts, Alfred. *A History of Militarism*. New York: Meridian Books, 1959.

Van de Port, Mattijs. *Gypsies, Wars, and Other Instances of the Wild: Civilization and Its Discontents in a Serbian Town*. Amsterdam: Amsterdam University Press, 1998.

Vincent, Joan, ed. *The Anthropology of Politics*. Oxford: Blackwell, 2002.

Warren, Kay, ed. *The Violence Within: Cultural and Political Opposition in Divided Nations*. Boulder, CO: Westview Press, 1993.

Wedel, Janine. *Collision and Collusion: The Strange Case of Western Aid to Eastern Europe*. New York: St. Martin's Press, 2001.

Wright, A. "Argentina's Bad Guys Are back in Business." *Sunday Times* (Johannesburg), 2 February 1997.

Xinhua News Agency. "The Story behind China's Biggest Smuggling Case." http://www.China.org.CN/English/2001/Jul/16632.htm [26 July 2001].

INDEX

Compositor:	BookMatters, Berkeley
Indexer:	Kevin Millham
Text:	Galliard and Akzidenz Grotesk Light
Display:	Akzidenze Grotesk Condensed
Printer and binder:	Edwards Brothers